WOMEN OF THE SEA

Women of the Sea

EDWARD ROWE SNOW

Updated by Jeremy D'Entremont

———————— ❧ ————————

*Issued to commemorate the
centennial of the birth of Edward Rowe Snow*

———————— ❧ ————————

Commonwealth Editions
Beverly, Massachusetts

Library of Congress Cataloging-in-Publication Data
Snow, Edward Rowe.
    Women of the sea / Edward Rowe Snow; updated by Jeremy D'Entremont; foreword
by Dorothy Snow Bicknell.
        p. cm.
    "Issued to commemorate the centennial of the birth of Edward Rowe Snow."
    Includes index.
    ISBN 978-1-933212-86-9
    1. Naval biography. 2. Women—Biography. I. Title.
    VK139.S637 2004
    387.5′092′2—dc22   2004016196

Previously published by the Yankee Publishing Company, Boston.

Unless noted otherwise, all illustrations are from the 1962 edition of *Women of the Sea*.

Jacket and interior design by Judy Barolak.

Printed in the United States.

Commonwealth Editions
an imprint of Memoirs Unlimited, Inc.
266 Cabot Street, Beverly, Massachusetts 01915
www.commonwealtheditions.com

Contents

"Twelve feet of Snow on Winthrop Beach." Alice Rowe Snow stands with her sons (left to right) Donald, Nick, Edward, and Win, and her husband, Edward S. Snow. (Photo courtesy of Dorothy Snow Bicknell)

Foreword

Ever since the beginning of time, women have played a far greater part in the lives of men, both ashore and at sea, than the average man cares to admit.

So began the introduction to the 1962 edition of Women of the Sea. My father, Edward Rowe Snow, continued:

I have on hand a list of more than 600 items which show women out on the ocean at their best and their worst. Included are several hundred women who have performed outstanding feats of daring while living at lighthouses, on islands, and ashore at the edge of the ocean from which I've drawn a number of stories for this book.

Written on a subject which combines two great unknowns—women and the sea—this book has been the most exacting effort of all the volumes I've published concerning the ocean and the shore.

Several of the chapters took research far beyond my original plans. But I believe that the reader will enjoy the stories to a greater degree because of my extra effort. . . .

Two women in particular had a profound effect on my father. They were his mother, Alice Rowe Snow, and his wife, Anna-Myrle Snow. His mother's stories of her exploits on the sea as the child of a ship captain fascinated him in his youth. Indeed, to quote him, "The earliest stories I can recall are of Mother's adventures at sea and ashore in foreign lands."

It was at his suggestion in 1944 that she published her own small book of her adventures, *Log of a Sea Captain's Daughter*. His love, respect, and admiration for his mother was obvious. *Women of the Sea* has an entire chapter about her—"Alice on the Bark Russell." Although Alice was a tiny woman—barely five feet tall, she raised four sons, each over six feet in height.

My mother, Anna-Myrle Haegg, was born in Illinois and grew up in Montana, so it wasn't until she married my father and moved to the coastal town of Winthrop, Massachusetts, that she became a "woman of the sea." Before they were married, she actually took canoeing lessons so that she could accompany him on his adventures. Together they canoed to all the islands in Boston Harbor and to many of the islands of Casco Bay, Maine. She flew with him for the forty-four years that he was Flying Santa of the Lighthouses. They collaborated. After they researched his subjects together, my father would write the text for books, newspaper columns, or other publications. My mother would then proofread his works and index his books (an enormous task). He respected her work greatly. As he thanked her in *Women of the Sea*'s introduction, "My wife, Anna-Myrle, ever at my side with her keen literary mind, made my task lighter when the path seemed especially hard to follow." I believe that this book was originally begun at her urging.

At the time that *Women of the Sea* was first published in 1962, women still were very limited in many of their roles on the sea and opportunities were few. This may have been due in part to an old superstition that it was unlucky to have a woman on board any vessel. So it is important that today's readers attempt to put themselves in the mindset of long ago, to appreciate fully the heroics of the women in the stories of this book. I hope you enjoy Commonwealth Editions' sixth republished book by my father: Edward Rowe Snow's *Women of the Sea*.

Dorothy Snow Bicknell
June 2004

Introduction to the Snow Centennial Edition

A unique confluence of circumstances and genes produced the man called "Mr. New England," Edward Rowe Snow. His childhood home of Winthrop, Massachusetts, is a peninsula jutting into romantic Boston Harbor, and he canoed his way to every rocky ledge and sandy isle in the harbor as a teenager. But he may never have taken more than a passing interest in the treasure trove of history and legends at his doorstep if not for the powerful influence of his mother, Alice Rowe Snow.

From all accounts, Alice Rowe Snow was a tiny woman with an expansive, cheerful personality. Edward's imposing physical frame apparently came from elsewhere in the family tree, but a larger-than-life personality and love of storytelling seem to have been passed directly from mother to son.

Snow began his introduction to the first edition of this book with the playful words, "Ever since the beginning of time, women have played a far greater part in the lives of men, both ashore and at sea, than the average man cares to admit." In a sense this idea seems chauvanistic, as if women should be recognized simply for their roles in men's lives rather than for their own merits. But Snow was undoubtedly thinking of himself when he wrote that sentence.

Young Edward was weaned on his mother's colorful tales of her travels at sea, some of which are recounted on these pages. As a boy, Snow may not have been able to visit Robinson Crusoe's island as his mother did, but the dozens of Boston Harbor Islands were a worthy substitute.

Arguably the three most important people in Snow's life were strong women: his mother; his wife and life-partner, Anna-Myrle; and his only child, Dorothy ("Dolly"), already a formidable tennis foe as a preteen. And dating back to the 1940s, his earlier books had included substantial chapters on woman pirates and lighthouse heroines. Apparently at the urging of his wife, Snow embarked on writing *Women of the Sea*—but he was also simply following one of his great longstanding fascinations.

Edward Rowe Snow wrote about things for which he felt great passion. The subjects commonly associated with him—such as shipwrecks, pirates, and lighthouses—were consuming interests that took him far and wide in the course of his research. But Snow's writing and storytelling were most compelling when they dealt with subjects he knew first-hand. This volume includes tales of far-off lands, but it also

Anna-Myrle Haegg Snow in 1932, just after her marriage to Edward Rowe Snow (photo courtesy of Dorothy Snow Bicknell)

has a lengthy chapter on a subject very near and dear to the author, his own mother. He knew some of the other subjects personally as well, such as Madaket Millie, Joanna Carver Colcord, and Commodore Ann White.

Although this is the only one of Snow's books completely devoted to the subject, maritime women were present in much of his work—most conspicuously lighthouse heroines and female pirates. Most earlier books on maritime history, written almost exclusively by men, included little or nothing about women of the sea. Snow was one of the first authors to write a volume devoted to the subject of maritime women, although such books have become fairly commonplace in recent years. Snow, although probably not consciously a feminist, seems to have simply believed that it was high time that these fascinating women got their due. In his introduction, he wrote that he could have included an additional "two score women"; it's a shame he never wrote a sequel.

As with the books earlier republished in this series of Snow Centennial Editions, the text presented here is almost entirely as it was written by Snow, with my notes at the ends of the chapters adding pertinent bits of information. There have been some minor corrections to punctuation and spelling, and in some places I've pointed out factual errors. Most of the illustrations from the 1962 edition have been included, along with a few additional illustrations. Another feature of this edition is a new comprehensive index.

Besides the authors cited and the various people and organizations mentioned in my notes, I want to thank those most responsible for this new edition. Webster Bull of Commonwealth Editions has kept this ship on course through six new editions of E. R. Snow's books, with a clear understanding and conviction about Snow's place in our region's history. Managing Editor Penny Stratton continues to see the forest through the trees, navigating each new volume to safe harbor. Bob Jannoni has been a catalyst and vital supporter of the effort to return Snow to print. And Dolly Snow Bicknell, daughter of Edward Rowe Snow, has been unfailingly good natured and supportive since I first met her more than fifteen years ago. She's a beacon as steadfast as any lighthouse, and I'm thankful for her friendship.

Jeremy D'Entremont
June 2004

CHAPTER 1

Susanna

The little girl was terrified. The brig on which four-year-old Susanna and her father were sailing was in serious trouble, and the pitching and tossing of their ocean home was almost unbelievable. The craft had encountered stormy weather soon after leaving Deal, England, early in October when they had started their long journey across the Atlantic. Week after week the gales continued, and the battered vessel fell more than a month behind her schedule. In spite of extreme rationing, supplies were almost exhausted. Before long the daily fare became a single biscuit and half a pint of water.

Susanna, whose mother had died bringing the girl into the world, was on her way to Massachusetts with her father, Lieutenant Haswell, who had married again. He was taking his daughter across the ocean to live with him in his new home at Nantasket.

At noon on January 28, 1767, with land almost in sight, the winds continued to harass the brig with renewed force, and heavy, freezing rain lashed the deck of the Boston-bound craft. Two hours later hopes rose high when the lighthouse at the entrance to Boston Harbor was sighted far in the distance. Almost immediately, however, the rain changed to snow, and Boston Light faded from view in a blur of tiny flakes.

As the hours passed and the heavy snow persisted in shutting out any view of land, all on board the ship realized that only a miracle could save them. Great freezing billows continually smashed into the stern of the brig until the officers, sailors, and passengers were filled with despair, which Susanna soon shared. Her father tried to comfort her as best he could but failed.

Then darkness began to fall, and the short dusk ended with the blackness of night shrouding the ship. To add to the peril, the weather grew much colder as the storm continued unabated. Heavy, drifting snowflakes came pelting down, and the craft continued to be buffeted incessantly by giant seas, the spray from which froze on the ropes and shrouds.

By midnight the vessel was entirely encased in ice. The ropes became unmanageable, and the sailors slid about on the ice-coated decks, unable to work the lines. Then the wheel froze and could not be turned. The brig was now a helpless hulk.

Realizing there was no hope, the captain told his shipmates that the islands of Boston Harbor were about to claim another victim. Neither the gleam of Boston Light nor the warm glow from an islander's cottage could be seen. About ten o'clock that fateful night, enormous, breaking waves were encountered, and the captain saw that his vessel was entering an area of extreme danger. Suddenly she struck heavily on a great boulder, drove across, and came to rest in a cradle of rocks which held her at a slight angle. The passengers and crew huddled together in the cabin, expecting death at any moment.

Luckily, the brig was made of sturdy English oak and failed to break apart. All the remainder of the night, especially after the tide turned and started to come in, the waves broke completely over the stranded craft, but she managed to hold together until dawn. The snow then stopped, the sun came out, and later the tide began to recede.

With the coming of daylight the captain was able to recognize the place where they had been tossed as Ram's Head, the northern tip of Lovell's Island, one of the central isles which divide inner from outer Boston Harbor. Off to their larboard quarter stood Boston Light, the beacon they had tried so desperately to sight in the storm.

The survivors could see a house ashore, from which several residents had emerged, who were walking along the beach near Ram's Head. Evidently they had sighted the wreck. Those on the brig watched hopefully as two islanders, carrying a ladder, made their way through the snowdrifts and down onto the ice-covered beach. Proceeding slowly, for it was dangerously slippery, they were soon a hundred yards offshore in waist-deep water. Several waves, continuing to roar in, broke dangerously near them, and by the time they reached the lee of the brig, the ladder was solidly encased in ice.

A line lowered from the wreck was tied to the top rung, and the icy ladder was secured against the cathead.* The sailors then busily chopped away the ice. As it was now dead-low tide, the bow of the brig was relatively free from surf, except for an occasional great billow sweeping in toward shore. One by one the passengers inched their way down the ladder and were carried to shallow water.

Susanna was considered too small and inexperienced to negotiate the ladder, whose lower rungs were still inches thick with ice. Finally an old sailor shouted up to Lieutenant Haswell that if the lieutenant could fasten a cord around his daughter's waist and let her down, he would carry her ashore. The father agreed, and carefully lowered the child into the arms of the man standing right below the cathead in knee-deep water. He grabbed for the little girl as she dangled on the rope, and then she was in his arms. Slowly he trudged toward the island with his human burden, and a short time later Susanna was safe on shore.

After a few hours in the home of an island resident, the girl recovered enough from her experience to become interested in the world again. Looking out of the window, she saw snowdrifts everywhere and noticed that the harbor was filled with heavy ice.

The next morning a boat was made ready, and the rescued survivors were put aboard for a trip to Hull. Two men in the bow broke the ice with heavy oars as the others rowed through what is still known as the Narrows. Reaching the lee of Georges Island, where the waves were not as high, they then started toward Hull Gut, finally pulling around to what is now Pemberton Pier. Going ashore, Lieutenant Haswell took Susanna to her new home at Nantasket,† where they arrived at two o'clock on the afternoon of January 30, 1767.

On reaching her father's house, Susanna was brought before a large crackling blaze in the fireplace and covered with warm, heavy blankets.

---

*A cathead is a beam projection near the bow for raising the anchor.

†The building, probably built by Reverend Marmaduke Matthews in 1644, was torn down many years ago, and the Hull Public Library now stands on the same location. Poet John Boyle O'Reilly removed the old dilapidated house in 1880 to erect the present edifice in which he made his home. His memorial stands on the lawn today.

After a hot meal, she was put to bed upstairs. It had been quite an adventure for a four-year-old girl.

When Susanna was allowed to go out of doors, she soon became fascinated by what she saw of Boston Harbor with all its islands and ledges. She wrote her memories of it years later and described Nantasket as indeed a beautiful place. At the time it consisted of two gradually rising hills, abundant with orchards, cornfields, and pasture lands. The little village in the valley had about fifty houses, the inhabitants of which could "just make shift to decently support a minister who on Sunday was sent to a pulpit in the rustic temple." There, according to Susanna, the minister taught to the best of his ability the true principles of Christianity.

The neck of land connecting Nantasket to the South Shore was extremely narrow and at times was inundated by tides, Susanna explained. In other words, Nantasket and Hull in those days often became delightful little islands, washed during occasional high tides by the ocean on one side and the calm waters of the bay on the other.

Susanna lived at Nantasket for the next six years without interruption. Then, when the war between the colonies and England became almost certain, with the Boston Tea Party following the Boston Massacre, one by one the terrified inhabitants moved away, until only the Haswells remained. Finally came the battles of Lexington, Concord, and Bunker Hill.

On July 20, 1775, the sound of musket fire was heard coming from Boston Light. That morning Major Vose had led a group of Yankee soldiers in whaleboats to Little Brewster Island, where they attacked the British party and burned the upper works of the lighthouse. On their way back they were met by an armed British schooner, which they outmaneuvered to reach the mainland. An eyewitness says that he saw "the flames of the lighthouse ascending up to heaven like grateful incense and the ships wasting their powder." The Americans had already cut a thousand bushels of grain in Hull and eventually returned in safety with all their spoils.

Almost at once the British began to repair the lighthouse on Little Brewster Island, with marines guarding the workmen against further "rebel" depredations. But the Americans had not finished.

On July 31, armed men appeared at Nantasket and surrounded the Haswell residence. Two soldiers entered the home and made Susanna's father a prisoner.

The other members of the family asked the soldiers what they intended to do, for they were afraid that Lieutenant Haswell would be killed. That was not the plan at all, explained the Yankee soldiers, but the Americans were going out to attack Boston Light and they did not want Tory Haswell to sound a warning. They then left for Hull, where they put their prisoner under house arrest.

George Washington himself had placed Major Tupper in charge of 300 men to storm and destroy the lighthouse. As soon as the major arrived off Boston Light the battle began, and Susanna could plainly hear the shooting. The guards at the light were defeated. Tupper and his men tore down the new repair work and prepared to leave, but before they could do so, the tide stranded the whaleboats. Meanwhile, the British ships in Nantasket Road sent their own small boats to the island, and Major Tupper had another battle on his hands.

Across on Nantasket Head Major Crane set up a cannon. When the situation looked threatening for the Yankees, a direct shot from the American gun crashed into one of the British boats and turned the trend of the conflict. Only one American had lost his life, but eighteen to twenty British marines were killed.

Major Tupper was then informed that the British warship *Lively* was sailing down the bay. He quickly gave orders for the American whaleboats to row back to Hull with the wounded and dying British soldiers. On reaching Hull, Tupper ordered two of his men to carry a British marine who had been badly wounded into the Haswell residence.

Susanna was at the open window when they landed, and they told her how lucky they had been to get back before the British frigate caught them. Susanna was upset when she saw the wounded marine, and tears streamed down her face.

The Americans entered the house, carrying their prisoner between them. They laid him on the floor on a mattress and were preparing to depart when Susanna's mother rushed out.

"What are you doing? You are not going to leave him here!"

One of the men replied, "Damn him, he is a wretch, and had best die quickly. We will kill him."

"Don't kill me," pleaded the dying soldier.

At this moment Major Tupper entered.

"We can't help that man," said Mrs. Haswell.

"What can *we* do?" countered the major. "We can't take him with us. He'll probably die, anyway. If I can, I'll send for him tomorrow."

Lieutenant Haswell, who had been freed from custody, entered and turned to the soldier, who had fainted but now awakened.

"Please don't kill me," the man whispered.

"You are among friends," said Haswell. "I am an Englishman."

Soon the Americans left the area, went aboard their whaleboats, and began the long journey back to Squantum and Dorchester.

Of this historic Battle of Boston Light, which Susanna witnessed, a writer of the period, Reverend Elisha Rich, tells us that:

> *When Tupper and his men had landed there*
> *Their enemies to fight them did prepair*
> *But all in vain; they could not them withstand*
> *But fell as victims to our valient band.*

George Washington, in his General Order for August 1, 1775, was to commend Major Tupper and his men for their "gallant and soldierlike behavior in possessing themselves of the enemies' post at the lighthouse."

Back at the Haswell residence the family did what they could to ease the pain of the dying soldier, who had become unconscious. Half an hour later he awakened suddenly, and told the others that he had a strange story which he wished to relate.

"'Tis awful to die with the weight of murder on my conscience. Please pray for me." Then he fainted, but after a drink of wine, revived.

"I am a most unhappy man, the victim of my own folly. My father was a clergyman and I his only child. Living in the north of England I received from him good public education, and he meant to place me in the church, but, alas, I despised his plans and joined the most dissolute set. He complained of my way of life, but I was too attached to my vices to quit it."

The man lapsed again into unconsciousness, but recovered almost at once, eagerly sipping at the water which Susanna brought him.

"I must tell my story before I die. I enlisted in a regiment bound for this place. I am sorry that I have to say this, but my conduct shortened my mother's life, and I have embittered the last moments of my father as well."

"What is your name?" asked Mrs. Haswell, kindly.

"Daniel Carnagon. I am twenty-six years of age." He looked around the group, and his eyes fastened on Susanna.

"Poor girl," he said, "take the advice of a dying sinner and treasure it in your heart. Obey your parents."

Susanna was dismayed and hid her face deep in her handkerchief.

"Good-by. I am going to die now," muttered Carnagon. "Oh, may he whose fatal aim took my life have it not remembered against him. May the Father of Mercy forgive him as freely as I do."

Daniel then began to repeat the Lord's Prayer. "Our Father, who art in heaven, Hallowed by Thy—" but he passed on to the other world before he could complete the sentence.

"Peace to his repentant spirit," said Lieutenant Haswell as he raised his weeping daughter from her knees.

Now came the problem of a funeral service and burial. The heat of the season made it imperative that the body be interred that same day. Susanna's father chose a spot at the side of his garden, and together with the other members of the family he dug a shallow grave, which was completed just as the faint rays of the setting sun tinted the summit of the distant Blue Hills.

Then, sighting a small fishing boat drawing near the shore, Lieutenant Haswell ran down and asked the fisherman aboard to help him. The two came up to the house where Susanna had provided a sheet. The body was carefully wrapped in this shroud, and the two men carried it to the grave. Susanna's father gave the prayer book to his daughter and she opened it. With her mother and the others standing by, the young girl began the service, but soon her voice faltered and the tears burst forth. She sobbed and could no longer speak. Her father took the prayer book from her, and his tremulous voice completed the reading of the burial service.

An hour later the family was back in the house ready to partake of the evening meal, and Lieutenant Haswell gave the blessing. Twenty minutes later, with supper finished, Susanna stood up.

"What a day this has become," she said.

"Indeed it has been a heavy day," said her mother, "but how much heavier would it have been had the poor departed been related to us. A father, husband, or a brother, perhaps." The family retired shortly afterward, each member exhausted by the events which Susanna would never forget.

A short time following this battle, American officers visited the Haswell residence and conferred with the lieutenant. They asked him if he would like to become an American officer. After briefly considering this proposition, he decided to refuse, and his wife supported him in this decision. The officers departed, determined to see that Haswell and his family were taken to a location where they would be less of a threat to the American plans of war.

Soon the lieutenant was informed that he would be moved to the neighboring town of Hingham. After several months there, he was told that the family would have to be transported a greater distance inland.

Susanna Rowson, who was wrecked in Boston Harbor at the age of four when the brig carrying her from England to the New World struck the northern tip of Lovell's Island in 1767

Boston had already been evacuated, and Lieutenant Haswell was miserable. Many people in Hingham treated him as a spy, and he did not know what to do.

In the autumn of 1777 the threat to move him materialized. He was informed by two Hingham residents, General John Barker and Captain Peter Lane, that they had obtained a "ramshackle" house nine miles away in Abington where the Haswells would be allowed to live. A team was loaded with their furnishings, and again they began a journey from one town to another.

Driving through Weymouth, they reached Abington, stopping at an old building located about half a mile from the church, on the outskirts of a heavily wooded area. The face of the country was rocky and dreary, covered with snow and ice. There was but one habitation within two miles of them, and that was occupied by people more wretched, if possible, than themselves. In this dismal situation, with no amusement, for they had not even the consolation of books, they passed four wearisome months. During this time they often had nothing to eat but coarse Indian bread and potatoes. There was no warmth except from wood that members of the family brought in from the adjacent forest.

To make matters worse Lieutenant Haswell became ill and was soon confined to bed. In their daily trips to get fuel, the family wore out their shoes on the rugged path over which they were obliged to pass, and often returned to the house with their bare feet bleeding.

Then came the day when they were allowed to go to Boston to sail away for Halifax and eventually from there to England. The war ended with the Americans victorious, and Susanna feared she would never return to her childhood home.

She first became a governess but soon decided upon a writing career. While in London in the year 1786, William Rowson, a friend of Lieutenant Haswell, proposed marriage to Susanna and was accepted. Rowson was engaged in the hardware business, but acted also as a trumpeter in the Royal Horse Guards. Unfortunately, their married life was not altogether happy.

In the same year that she was wed, Susanna published, under the patronage of the Duchess of Devonshire, her first work entitled *Victoria: A Novel in Two Volumes*. Printed in Covent Garden, the book consists of a series of letters interspersed with poetry. The plot is weak, and not until 1790, when she published *Charlotte Temple* [originally titled *Charlotte: A Tale of Truth*], did her literary efforts succeed.

Susanna now went on to great heights in the literary world, her *Charlotte Temple* outdistancing another great favorite, Horace Walpole's *Castle of Otranto*. She had a brief, but important, career on the stage, and then she established a girls' school in Greater Boston which is still operating today.* Nevertheless, she never forgot her dramatic entrance into Boston Harbor.

In the spring of 1822 Mrs. Rowson committed her beloved school into the hands of her adopted daughter, Miss Fanny M. Mills. Without her school, Susanna declined rapidly. Her closing hours were soothed by the kind attentions of three of her friends, Miss Mattie Mills, Miss Rebecca Haswell, and Miss Susan Johnston, whom she always called her children. Mrs. Rowson died on the second day of March 1824, at the age of sixty-three, and was entombed in her family vault beneath St. Matthew's Church, South Boston.†

The next time you sail down Boston Harbor, and the tide is low, you can look across at the ugly rocks off Lovell's Island where in 1767 Susanna Haswell had her first great adventure with the sea on which she was transported to lead her useful life in the New World.

Susanna Haswell Rowson is often referred to as America's first bestselling author, even though her *Charlotte Temple* was originally published in England. The book remained popular for many years and went through at least 161 editions, 42 of them printed in seventeen different cities before 1820. By 1812 sales were estimated at more than 50,000. It was America's best seller until *Uncle Tom's Cabin* came along in 1852.

Charlotte Temple was the first novel to use the American Revolution as its background. Its target audience was young women, and it began with the words, "For the perusal of the young and thoughtless of the fair sex, this Tale

---

*The Rowsons emigrated to the United States in 1793, and Susanna joined a theatrical company in Philadelphia before returning to Boston in 1796. In Boston during the next five years, she acted in 126 different production, writing many of them herself.—*Ed.*

†This church was demolished in 1866 and the remains of bodies not claimed by relatives were transferred to Mt. Hope Cemetery "where all that is mortal of this excellent woman now reposes."

of Truth is designed; and I could wish my fair readers to consider it as not merely the effusion of Fancy, but as a reality." The heroine of the story is seduced by a man who turns his back on her, and she dies in childbirth as Rowson's own mother did. Many apparently believed the novel and its characters to be real, and the gravesite of an actual person named Charlotte Temple in New York drew crowds of weeping women.

The Young Ladies Academy founded in Boston by Rowson offered instruction in public speaking, art, and music, as well as science and math, at a time when education for girls above the elementary level was rare. Rowson even created her own textbooks for the school.

Susanna Rowson is now buried in the Forest Hills Cemetery in the Jamacia Plain section of Boston, also the final resting place of such literary luminaries as Eugene O'Neill and E. E. Cummings.

CHAPTER 2

Mary Read

On a recent visit, Mr. Norman Reed, a resident of Washington, D.C., gave me additional information concerning his illustrious British pirate ancestor, Mary Read.

Mary's mother lived in Bristol, England, and had married a sailor by the name of Thomas Read. Second Mate Read then sailed away, and was lost at sea. Nine months later a son of the union was born, and the mother moved to another village.

Thomas Read's mother gave her daughter-in-law a crown a week for the care of her baby son. Two years later another child, a girl named Mary, was born, and shortly after that the boy died. The desperate mother dressed Mary in her half-brother's clothes so that her crown a week would continue, and four years later the two returned to Bristol.

Thus Mary Read was brought up as a boy. Several years afterwards when the "grandmother" died, the allowance ended, and at thirteen years of age Mary became a page to a French lady who lived nearby. Six years later the old lady died, and Mary joined the infantry to fight with the Duke of Marlborough. Later she transferred to a horse regiment and became an expert duelist.

The fortunes of war threw her into comradeship with a young Flemish soldier. Falling in love with the lad, she told him she was a woman. They went to the regimental chaplain and were married publicly. Obtaining their release from the army, they purchased an inn in Flanders, which they called "The Three Horse Shoes." Mary was left a widow in

1717. She sold her inn, resumed trousers, went to Holland, and took services on a vessel for a trip to the West Indies. One account says: "Their ship was taken by pirates and, she being English, was asked to join the 'Brethren of the Coast.'"

'Mary Read soon became a full-fledged member of the pirate crew, and for the next few years so effectively demonstrated the manly qualities of hardihood and courage that the other pirates, it was said, never suspected that she was a woman.

When a royal pardon was announced for all pirates, Mary Read left the sea, but later when she heard that Captain Rogers was planning a pirate expedition, she signed on. Also aboard were the notorious Jack Rackam [often spelled "Rackham"], known as "Calico Jack," and Ann Bonney [usually spelled Anne Bonny], a native of Cork, Ireland. Ann also had had an adventurous career before she became a pirate. Unaware that Mary was a woman, Ann became attracted to the youthful-appearing Pirate Read, as Mary called herself, until the latter revealed that she, also, was a woman.

Finally, Rackam, Mary Read, and Ann Bonney decided to take the ship away from Captain Rogers, and one night carried out their plan with the aid of the other pirates who had decided to join them. For the next few weeks they sailed up and down the Atlantic, capturing victim after victim with almost monotonous regularity. Then came the day when a young navigator taken from a British merchantman attracted Mary's attention, and she fell violently in love with him.

When a pirate decided to fight a duel with the navigator, who was not a swordsman, Mary picked a quarrel with the assailant, challenged him, and fought and killed him.

The following week, Captain Rackam asked her about her pirate career. "Why do you follow a line of life that exposes you to so much danger, and at last to the almost certainty of being hanged?"

Her reply was typical of her unusual life.

> *As to hanging, I think it no great hardship, for were it not for that, every cowardly fellow would turn pirate, and so infest the seas that men of courage would starve. If it were my choice, I would not have the punishment less than death, the fear of which kept some dastardly rogues honest. Many of those who are now cheating widows and orphans, and oppressing their poor neighbors who have no money to obtain justice, would then rob at sea, and the ocean would be as*

Mary Read

*crowded with rogues as the land, so that no merchant would venture
out, and the trade in a little time would not be worth following.*

One day in 1720, Captain Jack found his vessel caught by a Spanish
man-of-war south of Cuba, where he had been careening her. The
Spaniards warped their great battleship into the channel that evening,
completely blocking all possibility of the ship's escape. Captain Rackam
told the two women that the game was up, and they prepared to sell
their lives dearly. Near the Spanish man-of-war, just a little farther out
to sea, was a small English sloop, which had been captured as an inter-
loper in Spanish waters. A prize crew was then aboard.

Rackam called his fellow pirates together to explain his plan. They
would launch their longboat, into which everything of value would be
placed, and row in the dead of the night far to the south of the man-of-
war, after which they would come up on the English sloop and capture
the prize crew. The program was carried out without a mishap. Captain
Jack and his crew soon were aboard the vessel, where they quickly
silenced the Spanish crew, slipped cable, and sailed triumphantly out to
sea. The following morning the Spaniards opened fire upon the pirate's
ship, but in a short time they discovered the true state of affairs and
cursed themselves for the fools they had been.

Rackam had escaped this time, but his luck was slowly running out.
In October 1720, an armed sloop, outfitted by the governor of Jamaica,
caught the pirate ship and boarded it. A bloody engagement followed,
but the soldiers and marines were too strong for the buccaneers, and
after a few quick skirmishes most of the pirate crew ran below decks.
There were three exceptions, Ann Bonney, Mary Read, and another
pirate whose name is not known. Captain Jack, to the scorn of Ann
Bonney, had fled with the others. Unquestionably, the two women
were braver than the majority of pirates aboard the ship that day, fighting on long after the other buccaneers had deserted them. Finally Mary
and Ann had to admit the hopelessness of their situation and they surrendered. All the buccaneers were brought to Port Royal, Jamaica, given
a quick trial, and sentenced to be hanged.

Mary Read and Ann Bonney announced that they were expectant
mothers. Therefore, according to the custom of the day, their execution
was put off until such time as they could be properly hanged. Poor Mary,
however, grew sick in jail and died. Her thoughts to the last were of the
handsome young navigator who ended his career at Gallows Point,

Jamaica. Ann, more fortunate, outlived her companion, and actually disappeared from the prison about a year later. All we are sure of is that she was not executed, but whether her child was born in prison or not, the records of Jamaica do not tell.

———————————— ⌁ ————————————

Much of the sketchy knowledge we have of the lives of Mary Read and Anne Bonny comes from the 1724 volume, *A General History of the Robberies and Murders of the Most Notorious Pyrates*, by Captain Charles Johnson. Scholars debate whether or not the book's true author was Daniel Defoe of *Robinson Crusoe* fame. It's hard to separate fact from pulp fiction in the biographies of many pirates, but the saga of these female buccaneers continues to fascinate.

There were other notorious women pirates who came later, like Rachel Wall and Maria Cobham. But according to Joan Druett in her book *She Captains: Heroines and Hellions of the Sea*, Read and Bonny remain the archetypal female pirates because, unlike Wall and Cobham, they never expressed any regrets for their crimes. Instead, they pled their "great bellies," affirming that they were women of great passion and that they were vulnerable to men. This added to their appeal, according to Druett.

Captain Barnett of the sloop that overtook Rackam (or Rackham) and his crew later described the fierce fighting of Bonny and Read while most of the men cowered below deck. The two woman screamed as they swung their cut-lasses and fired their pistols. Legend has it that Bonny shouted for the men to come on deck and fight. When they refused, she fired into the hold and killed one of the pirates.

Pirate historian Tamara Eastman speculates that Mary Read died in child-birth. She died a few months after the trial and was given a proper burial, indi-cating that she may have been buried with the baby. What happened to Anne Bonny after the trial remains a tantalizing mystery. According to Eastman, her wealthy father probably bought her way out of prison. Records indicate that she married a gentleman from Virginia in 1721 and apparently lived the rest of her life in relative quiet. According to David Cordingly in *Heroines and Harlots: Women at Sea in the Great Age of Sail*, a source indicates that Bonny's husband was James Burleigh, and they had eight children. The same source indicates that Bonny lived to the age of 84.

Rackham Cay near Port Royal is named for Calico Jack. It was there that his tarred body was displayed in irons after his execution, a grisly warning for other would-be buccaneers.

CHAPTER 3

Mademoiselle De Bourk

On October 25, 1719, a girl of nine was sailing aboard a Genoese tartan* on her way from Cette, France, to Barcelona. She had gone aboard the vessel with her mother, the Comtesse de Bourk [usually spelled de Bourke], wife of an officer in the service of Spain.

Madame de Bourk had embarked with her daughter, her eight-year-old son, the Abbé de Bourk, four female servants, a steward, and a footman. She had a rich service of silver plate aboard, a portrait of the King of Spain set in gold and embossed with diamonds, and much other valuable property, making in all seventeen bales or packages.

At daybreak that morning of the 25th an Algerian corsair commanded by a Dutch renegade appeared about two leagues to windward. Both craft were then in sight of the coast of Palamos. The captain of the corsair sent twenty armed Turks to take possession of the tartan. In the fighting which followed one of Madame de Bourk's servants was wounded. Going below, the Turks ransacked every part of the vessel. They found some great hams which they threw overboard, but they ate the pastries which the cook had just made and broke into the wine and brandy locker. Several of them soon became drunk.

When the tartan was brought alongside the corsair, the Turks took off all the Genoese sailors and put them in irons aboard their craft. Then the Turkish captain went aboard the tartan to visit Madame de Bourk's cabin.

---

*A one-masted vessel with a large lateen sail and a foresail.

He asked her who she was, what nation she belonged to, and where she was going. She answered that she was a Frenchwoman on her way from France to Spain. She showed him her passport, and he agreed that everything was in order, after which Madame de Bourk requested that he land her in his longboat on the coast of Spain to which they were so close.

"You owe this mark of respect to the passport of France," she told him, "and by your agreement you will spare me much fatigue and my husband much anxiety. If you render this service, I will make a suitable acknowledgment to you of your kindness."

"Madame," the corsair replied, "I am a renegade. It would imperil my life if I sent you ashore in a small boat and was then captured, but what I will do is to persuade the Dey of Algiers that because you have a French passport I will release you and your family to him, and we will land you upon Christian ground. It is absolutely necessary that you come with me to Algiers, to present your passport to the Dey who will take you to the French consul, and then you will reach Spain. I am sorry, but there is no other way out."

He also told her that she had the privilege of removing her possessions from the tartan to his vessel, but he indicated that it would not be prudent for her to go aboard the corsair among nearly two hundred Turks in the crew. Madame de Bourk accepted the proposal that she stay on the tartan. The captain sent seven Turks on board to work the vessel which he took in tow. Both craft now began the passage to Algiers. Madame de Bourk gave the captain a present of her watch and she gave another watch to the Turkish commander of the tartan.

All might have gone well but for the fact that a terrible tempest arose on the 28th of October and continued for two days during which time the cable that lashed the two craft together snapped, and the tartan drifted away from the pirate ship. The commanding officer of the tartan, being extremely ignorant of nautical maneuvers and without a compass, allowed the vessel to be buffeted by the winds, and so it was that on November 1 she was driven ashore on the Barbary coast. There they were able to anchor. The commander, unacquainted with that area, ordered two Moors to swim ashore and find out from the inhabitants their exact location.

Successful in their attempt to reach land, the Moors determined where they were. One of the sailors remained on shore, and the other two swam back to tell the captain that he was in a gulf called Colo some distance from Algiers. The commander, anxious to depart and join the corsair, cut the cable, set sail, and again was on the Mediterranean without anchor, boat, or compass.

A short time later a contrary wind arose and drove him back to the shore. He attempted to use the galley oars, but with the few hands he still had on board they could row him nowhere. Within a short time the tartan struck a rock and went to pieces. The entire stern soon was under water, and Madame de Bourk, who was in the cabin at prayer with her son and the female servants, perished.

Those who were up in the bow of the ship, among whom were the Abbé de Bourk, Mr. Archeur, an Irishman, the steward, one of the maids, and the footman, clung to that part which remained on the rocks. Mr. Archeur, perceiving someone struggling in the waves, climbed down as near as he could and found that it was the little girl, Mademoiselle de Bourk, whom he rescued from her perilous situation. After a time he climbed over to the other side of the rock. He was never seen again, and probably drowned.

The abbé climbed down on the rock and clung for some time to his knife which he stuck into a cleft of the rock so that when the sea swept

The wreck of the vessel carrying Mademoiselle de Bourk from Cette, France, to Barcelona, Spain, as a result of which she was enslaved by Moors in 1719

over him he would not be washed to his death. He had only a small distance to cross in order to reach safety, but he was reluctant to go ashore. At length, summoning his courage and grabbing an oar, he pushed himself across to the mainland. There he was seized, and all his clothes were taken by the Moors, who then beat him.

Other Moors, noticing the ship and hopeful of getting something valuable from her cargo, swam out through the waves and brought back many articles of great worth which they could use or barter.

Standing in the water, the steward, who held Mademoiselle de Bourk in his arms, made a signal to the barbarians and threw the little girl to them. They caught her, one by an arm and one by a leg, and carried her ashore, where they took away one of her shoes and one of her stockings as a token of servitude.

The maidservant and the footman then threw themselves into the water and were captured by the Moors who helped them across the rocks onto the dry land, where they then removed all their clothes.

The steward made use of a line in getting from rock to rock, and he was met by another Moor who disrobed him. In this deplorable state the prisoners were taken first to a hut on the nearest mountain. The maidservant in particular was to be pitied for the poor girl was covered with blood from the cuts she had received in scrambling over the rocks. They finally arrived half dead at the hut where they were received amid the taunts of the Moors and their children. These barbarians had a great many fierce dogs which, excited by the tumult, joined their barking to the general discord. One of them tore the footman's leg, and another took a piece out of the thigh of the maidservant.

The survivors, now five in number, were separated. A female servant and the footman were sold to a resident of the village, but Mademoiselle de Bourk remained under the same master as the abbé and the steward. He gave each of them a miserable cloak crawling with vermin, and their only food was a morsel of rye bread baked under ashes, and a little water, while their bed was the bare ground. The steward, seeing that his young mistress was chilled, started a fire with difficulty. He was given the young girl's clothes, which he dried out, and she put them on.

In this manner she passed the first night, terrified and comfortless. The village contained about fifty people all of whom, men, women and children, lived in six huts, built of branches of trees and reeds, with dogs and cats of every description. The barbarians assembled in one dwelling to determine the fate of the five prisoners. They decided to send word to the inhabitants of several neighboring villages, and hundreds of people came to the great conclave which was to be held. Many of the new arrivals pointed to the fire which had been built, giving the five unfortunates to understand they would be burned alive. Others, drawing their swords, told them by gesticulation that their heads would be cut off. One of the barbarians seized Mademoiselle de Bourk by the hair, applying the edge of his saber to her throat. Others loaded their muskets and put the muzzles against the cheeks of the captives to frighten them.

The steward indicated by sign language that he and his companions would be glad to die for the Christian religion, but the natives would get no ransom if they were killed. Realizing the truth of his remarks, the men relented a little, but the women and children renewed their abuse.

Back at the wreck, the Moors, not content with having in their possession the five survivors, swam out and raised the bales and chests as well as the dead bodies from the bottom of the sea. They dragged the corpses on shore and stripped them of their clothes. With flints they cut off Madame de Bourk's fingers to get her rings, fearing that they would profane their knives if they came in contact with the bodies of Christians. They then divided the booty. The richest bales of cloth were cut in pieces and distributed to the children to decorate their hair, while the silver plate was sold to the highest bidder. Three goblets, each of which was worth at least twenty pound sterling, were sold in a lot for less than five shillings. Because they were tarnished by seawater they were assumed to be copper and of little value.

The steward saved his writing desk, and during the weeks they remained at this village, Mademoiselle de Bourk put it to use, writing three letters to the French consul at Algiers, none of which was ever received.

Three weeks after their shipwreck the prisoners were taken to the lofty mountains of Couco where the sheik who commanded the barbarians lived. The sheik and the chief of the Moors held a consultation regarding their captives, but they could not agree. Meanwhile, the steward had noticed a pile of straw near one of the beasts and had Mademoiselle de Bourk lie on it to rest. The master of the hut was so enraged at this that he picked up an axe, made the steward put his head on a block, and was about to strike the fatal blow when a Moor who was passing by stopped him.

Several times the captors came and seized the five survivors by the throat and with their sabers in their hands threatened them with instant destruction, but they never carried out their plans.

Deciding to make a final try, Mademoiselle de Bourk wrote a fourth letter to Algiers, in which she pleaded:

> *To the French Consul:*
> *After the shipwreck of my mother, I and my suite were consigned to the most frightful and abject slavery. We are dying of hunger and subject to every kind of ill treatment that could be inflicted by the enemies of religion and humanity, and we are being devoured by vermin. I implore you instantly to take compassion on our misery and to send us some relief until you can procure our liberty of which the continual menaces of the barbarians tend to deprive us of all hope.*

This letter deeply affected all those who read it on November 24 when it arrived in Algiers, and Monsieur Desault, the Frenchman who was given the letter by the consul, was anxious to obtain aid for the five survivors as soon as possible. He wrote a letter at once, purchased clothes and provisions, and obtained from the Dey of Algiers a letter of recommendation to the Grand Marabout, or high priest, of Bougia. On the evening of the same day, a tartan set sail and arrived at Bougia. There Ibrahim Aga, the interpreter sent by Monsieur Desault, presented the communication of the Dey and Monsieur Desault to the Grand Marabout. Although sick in bed, the latter instantly rose, mounted his horse, and with the Marabout of Gigeiri, the interpreter, and seven other Moors proceeded to the mountains and finally arrived at the place where the French were imprisoned.

Knocking violently at the door where he knew the five survivors were the Grand Marabout received word that the prisoners were not there, but at the farther side of the village. However, a Moor standing nearby made a sign that the girl and her four companions were still in the hut. The company thereupon ordered the door to be opened. The Moors fled, and the Marabouts entered.

At the sight of them the captives believed that their last hour was come, but their apprehensions were soon dispelled by the Grand Marabout, who went up to Mademoiselle de Bourk, and delivered the consul's letter together with the provisions he had sent her. The Marabout and all his suite passed the night in the hut, and in the morning he sent the children of the Moors in quest of the fugitives. They came in answer to his orders and kissed his hand, for they entertained a profound veneration for their Marabouts. At once the Grand Marabout sent for the governor of the mountains, and then at a great assembly he informed them that the purpose of his visit was the release of the five French subjects who had escaped from the shipwreck, that France was at peace with the kingdom of Algiers, and that they ought not to detain their prisoners in violation of the treaty with France.

Although the Moors argued as best they could, their protests were ineffective, and the Marabout was inflexible. The interpreter finally told the survivors that the Moors agreed to set them at liberty on condition that the sheik be given the girl. He intended her for a wife for his son who was fourteen years old. This new development appeared more distressing than all the others. The sheik remained adamant until the Marabout took him aside and put into his hands a few sultans of gold with the promise of more, and then the Moorish commander agreed to release all the captives for the sum of 900 piasters to be paid immediately. The Grand Marabout left a Turk as a hostage together with several jewels belonging to his wives and then departed with the five survivors. They traveled to Bougia where they arrived on the 9th of December. They sailed the following day for Algiers, at which port they arrived on the 13th at daybreak. The consul was on the pier to meet them and took them from the port to the ambassador's house. The ambassador received the young lady at the entrance and first conducted her to his chapel where she heard Mass for their happy deliverance.

When they heard her story scarcely any of the spectators could refrain from tears, for Mademoiselle de Bourk, not quite ten years of age, still retained a certain air of dignity despite having endured the privations and humiliations of slavery. The persons in her suite declared that she had always been the first to encourage them and had frequently exhorted them rather to suffer death than betray their fidelity to their God.

On the 3rd of January, 1720, Mademoiselle de Bourk, accompanied by a female attendant, embarked in Monsieur Desault's ship and arrived in Marseilles on March 20, 1720. Her uncle, the Marquis de Varenne, came to receive her from the hands of Monsieur Desault. Mademoiselle de Bourk remained several years in the bosom of her family, and eventually achieved a happy marriage with the Marquis de Toulonne.

The incredible story of Mademoiselle de Bourke's shipwreck and survival was recounted in contemporary sources including a book called *The Mariner's*

Chronicle and a volume published in Paris in 1720 with the title *Voyage pour la redemption des captifs, aux royaumes d'Alger et de Tunis*. Excerpts of the French book were published in English under the title "Among the Moors" in *The Catholic World* in 1881, and that version appears to have been a primary source for Snow. In 1886 best-selling Victorian author Charlotte Mary Yonge (1823-1901) adapted the story into a novel called *A Modern Telemachus*.

In the introduction to *A Modern Telemachus* Yonge wrote, "Curiously enough, history mentions the very tempest which drove the tartane apart from her captor, for it also shattered the French transports and interfered with Berwick's Spanish campaign." She believed the reported details of the tale to be accurate, as they dovetailed with descriptions of a tribe inhabiting Mounts Araz and Couco. According to Yonge, "They were in the habit of murdering or enslaving all shipwrecked travellers, except subjects of Algiers, whom they released with nothing but their lives."

CHAPTER 4

Margaret Bigelow Longfellow

One of the most unusual women of the sea was Margaret Bigelow Longfellow, who was born in Colchester, Connecticut, in 1747. A descendant of hers, Lieutenant Thomas P. Curtis, has told me of her interesting life. On many occasions during the annual family reunions at Machias, Maine, Lieutenant Curtis has been fascinated by one story in particular, the account of Margaret Bigelow's adventuresome escape from British-held Nova Scotia to what is now the State of Maine.

If one were to stroll through the old iron latticework gateway that stands at the entrance to the Longfellow graveyard, centered in the "downeast" town of Machias, Maine,* one might chance upon an old gravestone of no great size, displaying on its well-worn surface a weeping willow tree and the hardly legible notice that below lay the mortal remains of "MARGARET, wife to NATHAN LONGFELLOW" of Machias. Closer examination would also reveal that this brave old soul died on January 29, 1842, at the age of ninety-four years,† and that she was a woman of firm purpose, energetic in action, and of constant Christian character.

To understand how truly these attributes apply to Margaret Longfellow, let us go back to the year 1778 when the American colonists

---

*The seat of Washington County.

†The couple had 11 children, 58 grandchildren, 299 great-grandchildren, and 444 great-great-grandchildren.

were in the middle of the Revolutionary War. At the time, the British controlled all of Canada, and the North Atlantic was said to be little more than an English lake. In that year Margaret had an adventure with the cold, gray waters of the Bay of Fundy.

The daughter of Isaac and Abigail Skinner Bigelow, Margaret was four feet, nine inches tall, of stocky frame and resolute heart. She had a small nose, a kindly mouth, and intense blue eyes set closely together in a square face beneath brown hair.

In the early summer of 1778, she was with her family in British-controlled Cornwallis, Nova Scotia, while her husband, Nathan, was in Machias building a new house. When he sent word that the house was actually ready she started out with all six of her children to join him.*

Nathan had originally set up shop as a merchant in Cornwallis. In 1776 he went to Machias to get away from the redcoats, and left his family behind comfortably settled. He had begun building a new home in the "Land of the Free" and contributed to the American cause. It was two years later that he sent word for his wife to bring the children to Machias, as he did not dare to return to accompany them for fear of being captured by the British. Margaret must somehow manage to transport her offspring, of whom the oldest, Jacob, was only twelve,† and the family cow through the wild back roads of Nova Scotia and New Brunswick, mile after mile, all the way down to Machias.

The first part of this perilous journey you must imagine for yourself. Somehow she did manage to get all her charges through to St. John, but the details have not come down to us. On arriving there, she was captured by the redcoats, who took away her cow.

Unfortunately, the name of Longfellow was not a popular one with the British in Canada. Two of them had marched up to Quebec with Arnold, there to give their all in the attempt to capture that city. In fact,

---

*The Bigelow family had moved from Colchester, Connecticut, to Cornwallis, Nova Scotia, in 1760. In the same year, one Nathan Longfellow, together with his father and mother—Mr. and Mrs. Jonathan Longfellow—and his eleven brothers and sisters, moved from Nottingham, New Hampshire, also to Cornwallis.

†The others were Samuel, born 1768; Jonathan, 1770; Isaac, 1772; Enoch, 1775; and Ratchford, 1777.

these two had, together with another Longfellow, fought the soldiers of the Crown at the Battle of Bunker Hill. Other members of the clan had contributed in lesser degrees to the Revolution, and the name was well known by the British.

It is believed that one of the younger children inadvertently revealed that the family was on its way to Machias, which was known as an assembling point for American troops intent upon attacking British forces

Margaret Bigelow Longfellow, who brought her children from Cornwallis, Nova Scotia, to Machias, Maine, on a perilous journey in a whaleboat to escape the British in 1778, as drawn by one of her descendants

in the Maritime Provinces. It is also possible that some "former acquaintance" then betrayed them to the enemy as being Longfellows. In any case, only hours after entering St. John, Margaret Longfellow and her family found themselves in the red brick jail with little hope of escape.

The prison was kept by a turnkey, whose loyalties Margaret soon discovered could be purchased for several guineas. So it was that only two weeks later they made a guided escape on a dark and windy night and were free again.

Reaching the waterfront, Margaret loaded her family and their possessions into an open whaleboat and started out in the darkness for Machias. Here began her great struggle with the sea. Four of her children were extremely young and had to be protected by a strong, heavy tarpaulin against the rigors of the ocean and the dampness of the night.

The whaleboat was designed to be rowed by at least half a dozen husky oarsmen, and the only one whom Margaret had to help her was her twelve-year-old son, Jacob. They did have a sail which could be stepped when needed, but as she explained later, the prevailing winds of the Bay of Fundy were not favorable. The tide rips, which sometimes rose to a height of ten feet, terrified the children, but they managed to ride out every one successfully.

The hours wore on, with Margaret afraid to set foot on land for fear of being recaptured. All that long night and the following day they rowed and steered the heavy longboat, until they were so tired Margaret almost gave up and turned shoreward. But each time she planned to surrender she derived added strength to continue from the thought that at the end of the journey she would again meet her husband.

That evening, when darkness began to descend, she set the sail and tacked back and forth all night. When morning came she and Jacob got out the oars and rowed as hard as they could. Late in the afternoon, with the younger children crying from fear and fatigue, she sighted Cross Island, and just as the last glimmer of daylight vanished in the western sky Margaret reached the lee of the island. From there she was able to sail the remainder of the distance to the Machias River and the wharf at Machiasport.

Two days later she located her husband, and when she reached the residence which he had built for her, she never left it for the remainder of her life. They had five more children in the next few years, and there are now hundreds of descendants of this brave woman of the sea.

According to Bigelow family genealogical material, while she and her sons were in the prison at St. John, Margaret Bigelow Longfellow refused rations, believing that this might win a faster release. She performed work for the soldiers, and her oldest son, Jacob, received a quart of milk every morning and evening in exchange for milking a cow for one of the officers. Margaret said later that the family barely escaped starvation.

CHAPTER 5

Two Women of the China Seas

Chen ke kin seaou hee,
Chuy sze chung soo meen.
Tang she shwuy fan leih,
Yew neu tuh nang tsuy;
Tseen heue ying kwang nee,
Yen keu yuen shwuy wei.
Shwuy hwan po shang hea,
*Ying lee shang pei hwuy.**

Thus did the Chinese poet Yung Lun Yuen extoll the virtues of a brave woman who had been captured by pirates early in the nineteenth century. The prisoner's name was Mei Ying, and her story is told in this chapter, along with that of a woman named Hsi Kai Ching Yih, whom many consider the world's greatest pirate.†

I first became interested in Chinese women pirates in the year 1931 when gathering information concerning pirates in general. I found a volume written by Joseph Gollomb, entitled *Pirates Old and New*, which told of the experiences of a Chinese lady who went "a-pirating."

---

*The translation appears at the end of this chapter.

†Her name is now generally given as Cheng I Sao.—*Ed.*

Since that time I have delved into the writing of various Chinese authors and discovered among other things that at one time the pirates were so plentiful around Canton that a single executioner beheaded a thousand of them in less than a year!*

I was also able to increase my knowledge concerning the female pirates of China, and during my research became so enamored of an unusual sword, or cresse, that I purchased this curved blade, formerly owned by Hsi Kai, from the collection of the late Charles Driscoll, a prominent writer on pirates and treasure.

In two of my former books I have mentioned Hsi Kai Ching Yih, but in this chapter certain aspects of her career are given in greater detail hitherto not possible. During the summer of 1961 I obtained much additional information from the writings of two Chinese historians, Ying Hing Soo and Yuen Tsze.

You may wonder what caused such a great number of Chinese to adopt piracy as a profession. Hunger was the principal reason, intense hunger which often changes the personality of the average man from relative mildness to a being possessed of ferocious, animal-like tendencies.

In the year 1799 a mighty famine raged along the southern part of the Chinese coast, with spring floods drowning the crops in entire areas. Although it has been said that births in China far outrun deaths, nevertheless because of the famine of 1799, this usual trend was reversed. An overwhelming number of people living on the edge of the sea were forced to watch their loved ones die of starvation in that terrible period. As the days went by, parents would observe sailing by their homes great ships which they were told were heavily laden with all kinds of life-giving food, including meat, vegetables, and fruit, destined for other, more fortunate people. The starving Chinese fathers and mothers would then look down at their own dying children and despair. Most of the craft which passed their shores were manned by Chinese. Often the vessels would be Portuguese, and once in a while, English.

Then came a miraculous day. A great storm had begun to batter the coast, and at the height of the gale a small ship was seen struggling to keep offshore. Heavily loaded with food, she was carried by a giant breaker to smash against a ledge of rocks.

---

*The *Canton Register*, 1829, No. 20.

Early the next morning, as soon as the gale went down, the natives made plans to visit the wreck. Rowing every sort of craft which might hold them, they started for the scene of disaster. The hopeful farmers and fishermen reached the ship, found her cargo, and then held a conference. Their decision was quick in coming, as there were only a few sailors guarding the supplies. The desperate men fell on the crew and killed every one.

Loading their craft with every ounce of life-giving food they could carry, the farmers and fishermen guided the boats back to land. Word spread rapidly, and that very night the whole countryside heard about the good fortune of the visitors to the shipwreck. But the famine did not abate. Soon farmers and fishermen up and down the coast decided to take any means at their disposal to obtain additional supplies for their loved ones from the next food ship sailing by.

At first these desperate men who committed sporadic acts of piracy had only small boats for their use, but later they were able to adapt the larger cargo ships which they captured. Gradually it was realized that they had discovered a method to get enough food to keep starving families alive indefinitely.

At first, when this unusual system of piracy was inaugurated, there were almost as many different pirate bands as there were craft on which to sail. A very successful plan for capturing food ships was ultimately set up by Ching Yih,* a strong, middle-aged man with a huge, round face and a penchant for leadership and organization.

Around the year 1800 Ching Yih was captain on a disreputable twenty-foot junk. Operating with his trusted crew of twelve fierce fighters, he was able to capture ship after ship with amazing regularity. Realizing that he had outstanding ability, the other fishermen and farmers eagerly accepted his invitation to become part of a pirate fleet. Within a year of the consolidation, his fleet had captured twenty-four sailing vessels, and then the pirate armada expanded with unbelievable rapidity. Finally his outlaw fleet made such heavy inroads on shipping that word of his depredations reached the mandarins at Peking. They decided to send a mighty aggregation of forty warships against him, but they did not realize his great strength.

In the battle which followed, twenty-eight imperial craft of the mandarins were captured outright by Ching Yih, and the other twelve either

---

* His name is now generally given as Cheng I.—*Ed.*

fled the scene or were sent to the bottom. The pirates triumphed year after year. According to the records, by 1807 Ching had 800 large craft and 1,015 smaller junks in his fleet with a total personnel of 70,000 sailors. Dividing the gigantic armada into six units, he assigned each squadron a different color—red, yellow, blue, green, black, and white.

He exhibited remarkable control over all his men. Finally he found someone who was not afraid of him, Hsi Kai, the woman who finally became his wife. She had been captured in one of his annual piratical expeditions ashore when the pirates scoured the countryside to obtain all desirable women they could find.

His men had brought back several hundred females, of whom twenty had been chosen to appear in person before Ching Yih so that he could make a choice of a mate for himself. Attracting his attention was one captive larger than the average woman of her race and "gloriously" formed. A Chinese historian said of her: "Before the beauty of her face and figure the eyes of men grew confused." We are told that "her skin was of the tint of rich cream but at the cheek became a deep rose. Her eyes were black and would shine like jet, and the same black sheen was in her hair." Legend says that her mouth was voluptuous, and she had the appearance of a dancing nautch girl of India.

Ching Yih signaled that he was ready for the untying of the girl. Although women did not amount to much in the Orient of the early nineteenth century, he decided that here was one who was different. But he probably did not realize what was in store for him, for the moment she was released, Hsi Kai leaped at the pirate chieftain and desperately tried to claw out his eyes.

She came close to succeeding, and her violent spirit delighted the veteran pirate. Then and there he decided that she was worthy of marrying him. Thus, instead of ordering her cut to pieces because of her assault, he offered her jewels, cosmetics, silk, and slaves for her bravery and gave her a glowing picture of what lay in store for her when she became his wife.

Eventually she agreed to marry him, but it was a long struggle. First she made Ching Yih agree to certain provisions which no one even dreamed he would accept. Regardless of what had been the Chinese custom, she demanded a full and equal share of all his money and a vital part of the supreme command. These she received. The union was a perfect one, as far as pirate marriages go, until one day a great typhoon hit the fleet, battering the flagship into wreckage. When the storm went down it was discovered that Ching Yih had been washed overboard and drowned. Hsi Kai was a widow.

As usual in such cases, a great meeting of all the sea ruffians was held to decide on the new leader of the pirate fleet. Just before the conference began, Hsi Kai appeared. She stepped out before the assemblage, magnificently arrayed in the glittering garb of a pirate chief. Her dress had embroidered on it dragons of gold, backed by gorgeous purples, blues, and reds. Into her wide sash she had secured several of her dead husband's swords,* and on her head was Ching Yih's familiar war helmet.

"Observe me, captains," she cried. "Your departed chief sat in council with me. Your most powerful White fleet, under my command, took more prizes than any other. Do you think I will give way to a male chief? Never!" And there she stood as an historian later wrote, a "goddess" of a woman with a record as good as that of any man. Of course, the captains rose and acclaimed her their chief of chiefs.

Because of the capture of an Englishman by Hsi Kai's forces, we are able to read of his impressions of her as she appeared in the month of September 1809. Mr. Richard Glasspoole, an officer in the British East India Company, was then in service aboard the ship *Marquis of Ely*.

After going ashore at Macao, he started back to his ship. Before he reached the *Ely* his cutter was caught in a sudden change of wind, and the adverse weather conditions forced his craft to miss the ship and to remain offshore for three days.

Suddenly a band of pirates appeared, surrounded the cutter, and captured Glasspoole and his sailors. Carried aboard one of Madame Ching's Chinese junks, the Englishmen were chained to the desk while the pirates gesticulated at them. They were put into servitude under the pirate colors, and a letter was dispatched to the port of Macao demanding $70,000 as ransom money. Before an answer could be received, Ching Yih's widow took several squadrons of the pirate fleet, estimated by Glasspoole as five hundred sails, on a cruise up the river.

During the voyage many minor engagements were fought, but resistance was usually limited and easily put down. Entire villages were wiped out in several cases, with men, women, and children slaughtered. Thus we see that a piratical enterprise which started because of a famine was now so changed that it had become a scourge even worse than the reason for its instigation.

---

*One of which was the famed cresse wielded by Hsi Kai in battle.

On October 28, 1809, Glasspoole received a letter about the ransom from Captain May, his superior officer on the *Ely*. May told him that he was offering $3,000 for the group's release, but was prepared to offer more.

Meanwhile, the Chinese mandarin government, aware that matters were going from bad to worse, again attacked the Ching pirates. During the encounter, Glasspoole and his sailors were forced to man one of the great cannons aboard Hsi Kai's own flagship. The pirate leader showed her interest in the young Englishman by frequently approaching him at the height of the battle and sprinkling him with garlic water, said by the superstitious Chinese to be particularly effective as protection against cannon shot.

The conflict ended with another defeat for the government, but in the confusion the ransom for Glasspoole failed to appear. During the next interval of peace the English captive had a chance to see how the pirates lived with their families aboard the junks. I quote from his observations about Madame Ching's sea highwaymen, whom he called the Ladrone Pirates:

> *The Ladrones have no settled residence on shore, but live constantly in their vessels. The afterpart is appropriated to the captain and his wives; he generally has five or six. With respect to conjugal rights they are religiously strict; no person is allowed to have a woman on board, unless married to her according to their laws. Every man is allowed a small berth, about four feet square, where he stows his wife and family.*
>
> *From the number of souls crowded in so small a space, it must naturally be suppo6zsed they are horridly dirty, which is evidently the case, and their vessels swarm with vermin. They are much addicted to gambling, and spend all their leisure hours at cards and smoking opium.*

Glasspoole also spoke of his unusual diet of white rat meat and caterpillar soup aboard the junk.

The period of peace was soon interrupted by other engagements, during one of which an English sailor in Glasspoole's party was killed.

Finally, on December 2, 1809, Glasspoole received a letter from Lieutenant Maughn, commander of the cruiser *Antelope*, saying that he had the ransom aboard and had been cruising for three days trying to find the captives. Arrangements were eventually made whereby Glasspoole and the sailors were to be sent in toward shore aboard a small gunboat to meet the *Antelope* coming out from port.

At four o'clock on the morning of December 6 the gunboat left the pirate fleet, and at one o'clock that afternoon the *Antelope* emerged. It was after dark when the negotiations were completed, however, and then the appearance of a Chinese government craft caused the gunboat to return with the captives to the pirate fleet. The following morning the Englishmen tried again to complete the transfer, but it was seven o'clock in the evening before contact was made and all the survivors of Glasspoole's group were safe aboard the *Antelope*.

One day, later in her career, possibly weary from her many raids, Hsi Kai decided to elect as her captain a trusted fighter, one Chang Paou.*
A clever leader who was considered by Hsi Kai to be a fine young man, Paou was soon occupying an important position in the growing armada. With his effective support, Madame Ching struck hard and often during the next few years.

Accounts of her great battle exploits are many, but perhaps more interesting to the reader today is this female fighter's ability to conduct the details of her piratical business with discipline and efficiency.

Her rules of conduct were unusual. No pirate was allowed to take plunder privately; all in his group must share equally. No pirate could go ashore by himself, and, if caught, his ears were perforated in the presence of the entire fleet. If he repeated the act, he was beheaded. No person was permitted to debauch, at his pleasure, captive women brought on board a ship; he first had to request the ship's purser for permission and then go aside in the ship's hold. To use violence against any woman, or to wed her without permission, was punishable by death.

To assure her great bands of pirate followers enough food and drink at all times, Hsi Kai Ching enlisted the services of hundreds of country people who did nothing but grow grapes, rice, and all other necessities of life for the sea marauders. This required the pirate chief to add another rule to her list, applying to farm products. If a pirate was caught taking "anything of this kind by force or without paying for it," he should be put to death. Because of Hsi Kai's clever planning, the pirates were almost never in want of gunpowder, provisions, or other important commodities.

---

*His name is now usually given as Chang Pao.—*Ed.*

By means of this remarkable organization, her pirate empire thrived for a long period. But finally came the time when the great overlords of China decided Hsi Kai was ruining the country, and they agreed to destroy her. As an old chronicler tells us, "on the seventh moon of the thirteenth year, the naval officer of the garrison at the Bocca Tigris, Kwo Lang Lin, sailed into the sea to fight the pirates."

Hsi Kai and Captain Paou were ready, however. Hearing of the approach of Kwo's navy, Paou prepared an ambush with relatively few ships "in a sequestered bay." As Kwo sailed by, the pirate vessels attacked. At the height of the engagement Paou sent three lines of his warships in behind Kwo's fleet to surprise the Chinese leader. Both sides fought furiously, but the pirate squadron soon surrounded the government craft. The entire engagement lasted from early morning until late at night. Eventually, when the tide of battle began to swing against him, Kwo found that it was impossible to escape, for he could not break through the pirate lines. He decided to die in battle.

Paou fought his way aboard the enemy flagship, saw Kwo in person, and then apparently was hit at close range. Everyone thought Paou was killed, but he had ducked the shot and soon stood "again firm and upright, so that all thought he was a spirit." Both sides fought on bravely, and the carnage was great. When hundreds had been killed on each side and the pirates had overcome almost all resistance, Paou asked Kwo to surrender. The Chinese leader refused, and then did something very strange. Smiling, he approached Paou. When he was close enough Kwo grabbed the pirate by the hair. It was a gesture of desperation with which he hoped to insult Paou and make the pirate kill him in return. But Paou only beamed tolerantly at the seventy-year-old man, for Paou had no desire to hurt him. Humiliated in his own eyes by this loss of face, Kwo grabbed a dagger and committed suicide.

This act horrified Paou, who told his leader that he would be blamed for the old man's death whereas he had not meant to harm him at all. "Every man will charge me with the wanton murder of a commander after he had been vanquished," Paou complained.

On the "eighth moon" another fleet commander of the Emperor, General Lin Fa, went out to fight the pirates. Finding them too numerous, he became afraid and attempted to sail away. It was too late, however, for the pirates caught up with him and, as it was calm weather, they swam across to his vessels, attacking the sailors and killing Lin Fa and most of his men. The forces of the government had been defeated again.

Finally, Hsi Kai decided to quit the tedious profession of piracy, and took up the greater art of smuggling, at which vocation she died several years later.

But it is said that she never forgot one incident which occurred in the last few years of her unusual piratical life, an event which some historians claim caused her to give it up for good.

One spring, as was the custom, the pirates went ashore in four groups for their annual plundering, and acquired a tremendous amount of clothing and other goods. In addition they carried away 1,140 captives of both sexes.

Then the pirates set on fire ten houses, and soon the flames were spreading all over the village. Some of the inhabitants had been able to escape by hiding themselves in the fields, but as the marauders were leaving one of them heard a child cry, and realized that more women must be nearby.

Crossing over into the field, the sea ruffian attempted to pick up the baby, but several of the women formed a cordon around him and he was forced to call for help. Rushing to his assistance, the pirates soon subdued all but one of the women, a beautiful girl who was said to rival in every way the attractiveness of Hsi Kai herself. This girl, Mei Ying, was the wife of Ke Choo Yang. By teaming up against her the pirates were able to tie her hand and foot, and finally deposited the bound prisoner on the shore.

Carrying her aboard the pirate craft, the men secured her to the yardarm, but she managed to get her hands loose and began battering any one who came near to her.

Finally one pirate decided to subdue her. He cut all of Mei Ying's fetters, pushed her to the deck, and hit her repeatedly with a belaying pin, shattering her two front teeth.

With blood filling her mouth, she twisted away from him and ran over to the side of the ship, which was unprotected from the water. He followed after her, but as he approached, she sprang at him and sank her teeth into his clothing. He grappled with her, but she twisted around, tripped him, and they both fell into the sea, with Mei Ying clutching him in a convulsive grip which ended in death for both, as neither came to the surface again.

The incident occurred in the harbor at Pwan Peen Jow. Some years later the Chinese writer Yung Lyn Yuen visited the scene. Impressed by the valor of the woman who pulled her tormentor to death in the sea, he composed a song mourning her fate, which I have quoted at the beginning of this chapter. The translation of that verse follows:

> *Cease fighting now for awhile!*
> *Let us call back the flowing waves!*
> *Who opposed the enemy in time?*
> *A single wife could overpower him.*
> *Streaming with blood, she grasped the mad offspring of guilt,*
> *She held fast the man and threw him into the meandering stream.*
> *The spirit of the water, wandering up and down on the waves,*
> *Was astonished at the virtue of Ying.*
> *My song is at an end!*
> *Waves meet each other continually.*
> *I see the water green as mountain Pei,*
> *But the brilliant fire returns no more!*
> *How long did we mourn and cry!*

The sword purchased by Snow that was said to have belonged to the infamous Chinese woman pirate is now in the possession of the Peabody Essex Museum of Salem, Massachusetts. At this writing it is not on public display.

One of Snow's chief sources for this chapter was the 1928 book *Pirates Old and New* by Joseph Gollomb. Unfortunately, this book has been shown to be largely fanciful and inaccurate based on recent research by Dian H. Murray, a history professor at Notre Dame University. The opening of Ching Dynasty archives previously unavailable to the public has made it possible to piece together much more primary source material on Cheng I Sao ("Wife of Cheng I"), as her name is now generally given.

Murray has written on Cheng I Sao and Chinese piracy extensively in her book *Pirates of the South China Coast, 1790–1810* (Stanford, 1987) and an essay entitled "Cheng I Sao in Fact and Fiction," which was included in the book *Bold in Her Breeches: Women Pirates Across the Ages* (London: Pandora, 1995), edited by Jo Stanley. In "Cheng I Sao in Fact and Fiction," Murray wrote that Gollumb's book and many other accounts were guilty of sloppy interpretation and sometimes outright fabrication, as in the case of the physical descriptions of Cheng I Sao. "Historical fiction has overtaken history," she wrote, "and much of what we think we know is more myth than truth."

Another of Snow's sources was *A Brief Narrative of My Captivity and Treatment Amongst the Ladrones* by Richard Glasspoole, who as Snow mentions was an officer on the *Marquis of Ely*. The word "ladrone" was a Portuguese term for pirate. Glasspoole's descriptions are largely corroborated by a book called *History of the Pirates Who Infested the China Sea from 1807 to 1810*. This volume was translated by Charles Friedrich Neumann from a Chinese text by Yuan Yun-lun. These two books give us many glimpses into the daily lives of the pirates.

Although the struggle for sustenance certainly played a role in Chinese piracy in the late 1700s, there's no evidence that a particular flood or famine in 1799 was to blame. The events described in this chapter took place in the vicinity of what is now Vietnam, and the sponsorship of the Tay-son rulers in power at the time had a great deal to do with the rise of highly organized pirate fleets. Cheng I Sao obtained much of her wealth from a massive protection racket, as she demanded "contributions" from every village within her reach.

Cheng I Sao actually negotiated the terms of her surrender in 1810. Those among her crew who voluntarily turned themselves in were allowed to keep their stolen wealth. Chang Pao was made a lieutenant and put in command of a fleet of twenty or so junks. Cheng I Sao died in 1844 at the age of 69.

Snow may have repeated some distortions written by Gollumb and others who came before him, but the basic facts of Cheng I Sao's incredible life as one of the most powerful pirates in history are true. Anyone interested in an in-depth examination of her life and times should seek out the works of Dian Murray.

CHAPTER 6

Consuelo

*I am a useful woman, you see, a veteran of great and glorious wars.
Therefore, if you please, be so good as to preserve my life. Ah, if you
knew how often I have ventured upon the fields of battle and braved
the bullets to carry assistance to our gallant men!*

Thus spoke Consuelo DuBois of Strasbourg, France, in the year 1816,
while she was on a raft of terror in the Atlantic Ocean. Even after a century and a half the weird fate of the French frigate *La Meduse*, her crew,
and her passengers is still shocking because of the human suffering
involved in the terrible disaster.

The trip of *La Meduse* became necessary when the final defeat of
Napoleon at Waterloo ended his dominance of Europe. Great Britain
decided to return to France the captured province of Senegal, on the
west coast of Africa between Cape Blanco and the Gambia River. Pirates
frequently went ashore here before the Napoleonic Wars and established their headquarters, while in later days slave ships often put
aboard their human cargoes at the Gambia River.

On June 17, 1816, *La Meduse*, a French forty-four-gun frigate, sailed
from Rochefort, France, for Senegal. The crew had been recruited for the
journey with a minimum of care, and as a result the officers were mostly
ill-suited for their positions of trust. Many of the seamen were little
more than city street rabble.

The passage, a relatively short one when compared with journeys to India and South America, was looked upon as a summer trip a short distance down the African coast where cargo and passengers would soon be unloaded. The latter were mostly French colonial officials and their families, people who were helping to reestablish the colony at Senegal.

The master was Captain de Chaumareys. A very agreeable shipmate, he was an indifferent seaman. As a leader of men in an emergency, it turned out that no one could be worse. When ten days from port, the captain discovered that his reckoning had set him almost one hundred miles off his course.

Instead of being more cautious because of his error, De Chaumareys ordered the ship's course in his same careless way as before, and the voyage proved to be one fatal mischance after another. When the frigate crossed the Tropic of Cancer on July 1, 1816, the captain felt he had an excuse for a holiday and took personal charge of the deck parties which he arranged. To have more time to supervise the entertainment, he gave over the command of the ship to one Monsieur Richefort, a civilian officer who had seen a little naval service.

As the festivities continued unabated with singing and dancing, a feeling of uneasiness developed among several of the officers and a small group of passengers who had seen marine service. Finally a chosen few reported to Monsieur Richefort, insisting that they were worried about the ship's position, but he laughed in their faces.

"There is at least one hundred fathoms of water under the keel!" he assured them, and told them how foolish they were to worry. Meanwhile, the celebration proceeded on deck.

An hour later, with a crash that brought the spars tumbling down about them, *La Meduse* struck the deadly sands of the Bank of Arguin, about forty miles off the African coast. The depth of water was only sixteen feet where they hit. She was a lost ship on that bright July day, for the men knew that *La Meduse* would pound to pieces in the first great gale of wind. As it was then very calm, the officers felt it was wise to start away at once. There was plenty of time in which to abandon ship and break out provisions and water barrels, but nothing was done in proper sequence. When it was realized that there were not enough lifeboats, valuable time was lost. There were carpenters and mechanics aboard the frigate and all manner of tools for the colony they planned to start again at Senegal. In times past hundreds of people had been saved from other ships in similar situations.

La Meduse only had six seaworthy boats, and they were launched and filled with people who wanted to save themselves. In one boat the governor of Senegal put his family. In another, four children and the wives of other officials were placed. Finally the officers decided that all was ready, and the six boats shoved off to wait for a raft which was even then almost completed. The men hoisted barrels of wine and water and bread onto the deck, but in the confusion, only the boats received them. Monsieur Correard, an engineer attached to the expedition, had volunteered to stay with his own men to build and launch the raft.

Not having lost his wits as had Captain de Chaumareys, Correard went to the captain and said, "Sir, have navigational instruments and charts been provided for the raft?" The captain assured Monsieur Correard that this had been done, and a moment later he scrambled into one of the boats and shoved off.

The raft was a contrivance of spars and planks held together by lashings. Sixty-five feet long and twenty feet wide, it was loosely put together so that it would give with every wave. But after it had been launched and placed in position for people to get aboard, trouble began. Almost two hundred attempted to climb onto the craft, and it started to

Survivors of the French frigate Medusa *(or Meduse), wrecked off the coast of Africa in 1816, are shown on their harrowing voyage aboard a raft.*

43

sink. One by one more than a score were forced back aboard *La Meduse*, but there were still about one hundred and fifty terrorized survivors on the raft.

It was still calm weather, and the ship remained in the sand. But no barrels of beef or bread and no water casks were put aboard the raft, and when it finally left *La Meduse*, there were only enough biscuits for one meal and a few casks of wine.

Sixty men remained behind on the stranded vessel, but a short time later a partly filled lifeboat returned and took off forty-three of them. The other seventeen were so drunk from having raided the liquor supplies at the time of the stranding that for the moment the fear of death did not trouble them.

It had been understood by the people who climbed down aboard the raft that it would be taken in tow by the six boas boats strung out in line. When the hawser was secured, the flotilla slowly headed for the African coast, but after a few hours of progress the wind freshened, and the towline between the captain's boat and the raft parted. Instead of making the line fast again, the captain ordered the oarsmen in the boats to abandon the raft.

Two men wrote about the disaster later—Monsieur Correard and Monsieur Savigny. They reported that when the survivors on the raft saw the boats forsake them and vanish over the horizon, they were stupefied. Clinging together, arms locked and bodies squeezed tightly so that they might not be washed off, the castaways despaired of the future. Consuelo Dubois and her husband were among them. But, as she said, she had been in battle, had gone through campaigns, and had shared in victories and defeats. she She was a *vivandière*, or sutler,* and with her husband had followed for twenty years the campaigns of Napoleon. Although she was worried, she encouraged her companions in their plight.

The first day passed calmly enough and several of the men talked with Consuelo and her husband concerning the manner in which they would save themselves. Consuelo sustained the hope of the soldiers by telling them that later they could revenge themselves on the captain who had abandoned them. In the evening she prayed and hoped for the best.

The wind came up that night. The sea soon was so rough that the waves roared across the raft, which in places was three feet under the

---

*Someone who follows an army and sells merchandise to the soldiers.—*Ed.*

water. A few ropes were stretched for the people to cling to, but by midnight many had been caught and killed between the grinding timbers. Others, perhaps more fortunate, were just swept off to vanish in the sea. by By dawn twenty of the one hundred and fifty had perished. Two ship's boys and a baker said farewell to their comrades and, in spite of everything that Consuelo did to persuade them to stay, threw themselves into the ocean as the easier way out of their misfortune.

All that night Consuelo struggled against death by keeping a firm grip on the spars which were bound together. She was tossed by the waves from one end of the raft to the other. Sometimes the action of the waves pulled her into the sea, but she swam back on each occasion, helped by her husband.

Finally the sun came up. It was a beautiful day, but several of the survivors had already been affected by the strain and exposure. They saw visions of the shore, of ships, and of loved ones at home. Consuelo watched one older man lose consciousness and collapse at the feet of the soldiers. His two sons raised him up, thinking he was dead, and their despair was expressed in the most affecting manner. He slowly revived, however, and was restored to life.

The sun described its parabola in the heavens, and darkness followed. Squally weather again hit the raft, with many more people crushed and drowned. Shortly after midnight soldiers and sailors broke into the wine casks. Then, bolstered with false courage, they attacked the other survivors in a battle which raged all night long. Sabers, knives, and bayonets were used. When the tide of battle was going against her side, Consuelo called the real soldiers of Napoleon together.

"To arms, comrades!" she cried. "Rally or we are lost!" Realizing the truth of her words, Monsieur Correard mustered a small force of officers and laborers, and Consuelo watched them as they charged. The rabble was pushed back to their part of the raft, and the crisis ended for the time being.

Again the next day was beautiful, and it was calm until dusk. Darkness, however, brought rough seas, and soon the waves were breaking over them almost every moment. The sailors took to drinking the wine again, quaffing it down on an empty stomach. For the second night they went out of their senses, and this time began to slash the ropes which bound the raft together. The officers again rushed forward. They killed one of the offenders and threw another overboard. But the mutineers outnumbered them and took what revenge they could by cutting up the sail.

The officers now made plans for a final assault against the rabble. At a signal the charge began. Many of the mutineers were killed, while others cried for mercy. The officers forgave them, but when order was apparently restored, the mutineers again began to start trouble, and organized a fresh group which began a charge against the officers. They came on like madmen, and such was the fury of the assailants "that they tore with their teeth into the flesh and clothing of their adversaries." There was no time for hesitation on either side, and a general slaughter took place, with no quarter given or asked. After the fighting ended the raft was strewn with dead bodies.

Suddenly several of the mutineers seized Consuelo and without ceremony threw her into the sea. Then they wrestled with her husband and threw him after her. Watching what was taking place, and even though he had been cut by several saber wounds, Monsieur Correard leaped into the sea with a rope and rescued Consuelo. Lavallet, the head workman, swam after her husband and hauled him back as well. Grateful Consuelo did what she could to show her appreciation, but all she had in her pockets was a little snuff. She gave that to Correard, but since he was unable to use it, he in turn handed it to a wounded sailor.

On the fourth day after the wreck twelve more died on the raft. The survivors, according to Consuelo, were "extremely feeble, and bore upon their faces the stamp of approaching dissolution."

A shoal of flying fish passed under the raft, and many were entangled in the timbers. More than two hundred of the fish were captured and placed in a barrel, and these were to serve the hungry people for several days. Some dry gunpowder was discovered. With the aid of a steel and gunflints a fire was kindled and the fish were fried and eaten.

That same night a plot was hatched by the Spaniards and Italians among the survivors to throw all the others overboard. Thus they would gain the security of the raft for themselves. The leader of the new plot, a huge Spanish laborer, placed himself behind the mast. Making the sign of the cross with one hand, waving a knife with the other, and invoking the name of God, he signaled the start of the battle.

Two French sailors, who had learned of the plans, rushed at the Spaniard and threw him into the ocean. They then cornered a giant Asiatic, another of the ringleaders, and tossed him overboard to his death. A third member of the group saw what had happened to his two comrades and followed them into the sea. The other mutineers fought desperately, but at last they were repulsed.

The carnage had been so great however, that only thirty of the one hundred and fifty were alive by dawn. That same morning two soldiers, caught stealing wine from the sole remaining cask, were put to death after a makeshift court-martial.

At the seventh day Consuelo noticed that the twelve-year-old sailor boy, Leon, was rapidly weakening. She watched him as he cried out in pain. Suddenly he sprang up. Running from one side of the raft to the other, he called at the top of his voice for his mother and for water and food.

The boy had been an inspiration to Consuelo because of his angelic appearance, his musical voice, and his courage. Just as darkness fell Leon climbed across the legs of the wounded and dying to reach his place at her side, where he collapsed. Monsieur Coudin raised the boy's head, but he died at that very moment.

Twenty-seven survivors now remained alive on the raft, and after a discussion it was decided to throw overboard all those who had been wounded in any way, thus allowing the fifteen persons who had not been injured more chance of survival.

As Consuelo and her husband had been hurt fighting the mutineers they were both slated for this fate, and it was at that moment that the brave woman made her statement which begins this chapter.

Shortly afterward, in spite of all that she had said, the two were thrown to their death in the ocean. Five minutes later only fifteen persons remained alive on the raft. Why Monsieur Correard was not thrown overboard with the other wounded survivors is a mystery.

On the ninth day a gleam of canvas was seen far in the distance, and soon a brig was identified. But the vessel sailed on, filling the hearts of the survivors with despair.

Then the craft was sighted again, making a long tack, and came toward them. Half an hour later she was alongside and rescued the fifteen men, six of whom died soon after reaching shore.

Of the six lifeboats which had abandoned the raft, only two arrived at Senegal; the other four landed safely at different locations along the coast. All lifeboat survivors eventually reached Senegal with the exception of three persons who died on the way.

Back on the stranded *La Meduse*, the seventeen abandoned men spent the next fifty-two days fighting and killing each other. Finally when a vessel went out to investigate only three were found alive. They were taken ashore, the last survivors of the terrible marine disaster which cost the life of Consuelo, the sutler of Napoleon.

Much of what we know about this disaster comes from a volume innocuously titled *Narrative of a Voyage to Senegal*, published in 1817 by two survivors, Alexandre Correard and Henri Savigny. The monumentally harrowing story is also the subject of a 1975 book (republished by Signet in 2000) called *Wreck of the Medusa: The Tragic Story of the Death Raft* by Alexander McKee, as well as a 1998 French movie called *Le Radeau de la Méduse*.

The episode was also the inspiration for a celebrated 1819 painting, *The Raft of the Medusa* by French Romantic artist Théodore Géricault (1791–1824). The huge painting (16 by 23.5 feet) hangs today in the Louvre. Géricault studied corpses at a morgue for research, and it's said that the stress of completing the work contributed to the artist's death a few years later at a young age.

Captain de Chaumareys was a customs officer who hadn't been to sea in twenty years. The captain received his appointment as a reward for his pro-Bourbon leanings, and French officials later tried to cover up the truth of the captain's incompetence and cowardice. De Chaumareys was acquitted in a courtmartial despite a public outcry. Some put much of the blame for the disaster on Colonel Julien Schmaltz, the new governor of Senegal. Schmaltz reportedly insisted that the ship take the fastest possible route, which took it far too close to shore.

An interesting side note is that after Schmaltz took charge as governor in Senegal, he quietly allowed slave trade to continue even though slavery was abolished in the English colonies in 1807 and abolition was a condition of Senegal's being turned over to the French. Correard, in a second edition of *Narrative of a Voyage to Senegal,* was extremely critical of this. Géricault shared Correard's abolitionist views, and he portrayed a black man prominently among the survivors on the raft in his painting. Many have seen the painting as an antislavery statement.

In 1980, the remains of *La Meduse* were located by a French expedition on the Arguin Bank, about thirty miles off the coast of Mauritania. The team, led by marine archaeologist Jean-Yves Blot, recovered artifacts positively identifying the wreck, including bottles, ceramics, cannons, and swords. Some of the recovered items were subsequently displayed in an exhibition at the Musée de la Marine in Paris. Charles Mazel, Principal Research Scientist at Physical Sciences Inc. in Andover, Massachusetts, was the technical director for the expedition.

CHAPTER 7

The Sole Survivor

Suddenly my mind became greatly disturbed. The feeling was one I never experienced, for I was a stranger to fear at sea. My mind was filled with horror; I feared the vessel would sink, or something terrible would happen.

Thus did a Methodist woman missionary, Mrs. Jones, write in the year 1826 while aboard a passenger craft which was taking her and several other missionaries to the island of Antigua.*

Although long a stopping-off island for pirates, Antigua in 1826 had become the headquarters for a group of Wesleyan missionaries sent to the West Indies from England, and when the lines which begin this chapter were written the party was returning to Parham, Antigua, to resume their regular island services.

On Thursday, February 2, 1826, Mr. and Mrs. Jones had sailed from Antigua, together with six other missionaries, Mr. and Mrs. White,

---

*Antigua today, with Barbuda and Redonda, forms one of the five presidencies in the Leeward Islands colony. It is fifty miles east of St. Kitts, and has two major ports, English Harbor and Saint John's. It was discovered by Columbus in 1493. He is said to have named it for a church in Seville, Santa Maria la Antigua. [*Editor's note*: In 1981, the islands of Antigua and Barbuda became an independent state within the British Commonwealth of Nations.]

Mr. Oke, Mr. Hillier, and Mr. and Mrs. Truscott, along with several children and two servants. Aboard a relatively decrepit missionary schooner, they were bound for the district meeting to be held on the island of St. Kitts. At seven o'clock that night they arrived at St. Kitts and went ashore. That evening they held the first prayer meeting. After many additional prayer meetings and hymnal services, the missionaries sailed for Montserrat, where they also arrived safely.

On Sunday, February 26, "Brother Hillier read the prayers and lessons for the day," and for some reason Mrs. Jones became deeply concerned when Mr. Hillier chose for his text II Corinthians 11:25, "a night and a day I have been in the deep."

As she later explained, she could "suffer anything but shipwreck" and not until "evening did I obtain relief from these horrible feelings." On Monday morning the same peculiar sensation of concern about their sea voyage returned. She asked herself the meaning of it all, as she had never before worried about anything connected with the ocean.

The weather became stormy that same afternoon, and because of the rough seas then developing, it was agreed by the missionaries that the party would be safer in returning to Antigua by the regular mail boat, *Maria*, which was about to sail rather than by the missionary schooner which up to that time they had been using.

After going aboard that evening, the older folks retired to their berths while the children were put to bed on mattresses spread on the cabin deck under the charge of their nurses.

During the night the wind rose and soon a gale of more than moderate force was upon them. By morning the seas were breaking so high that the group could not go out on deck, and the *Maria* was forced to sail directly into the path of the tempest.

It was not long before all but two passengers, Mrs. Jones and Mr. Hillier, were violently seasick.

At four in the afternoon Antigua was sighted, and Mr. Hillier happily proclaimed that all was well and they would soon be in their homes.

Another event now occurred which added to Mrs. Jones's uneasiness. To prepare for their happy homecoming Mr. White's son William opened the hymnal and the children sang a few hymns, after which William told the story of Jonah and the whale. This story gave Mrs. Jones further concern. Then the lad repeated the verse which began, "Though waves and storms go o'er my head," and it seemed a curious coincidence to Mrs. Jones that the boy had chosen that particular line to quote.

Suddenly Mrs. Jones's mind was filled with horror. "I feared the vessel would sink," she said later, "or something terrible might happen. I attempted to pray, but for the moment could not." After that an "oppressive anticipation of evil" hung over her.

Shortly afterward the *Maria* was hit by several terrific waves. Then, without further warning, the keel of the *Maria* crashed into an underwater ledge, and the vessel went over on her beam ends. Her last voyage had come to an end.

Washing down into the cabin, the seas engulfed everyone. The passengers tried to clamber up the slanting companionway to reach the deck. Mrs. Jones had been given the baby of Brother White to hold, and with her husband's assistance managed to get up on deck with the child.

A moment later a sailor leaped into the *Maria*'s small boat, but in doing so was knocked senseless by the swinging boom. Mate George Newbold also jumped into the boat, and both were carried away. Before long they were out of sight in the terrific seas then running. They were later saved by a French sloop off Nevis.

The captain now ordered the mast and the rigging cut away, but the ship herself began to break apart. Wave after wave crashed against the *Maria*, and soon the stern separated from the bow and began to float away. Brethren Hillier, Oke, and Jones clung to the bow, while Mrs. Jones, Brother White and his family, Brother Truscott and his wife and child, two nurses, one gentleman passenger, and several sailors clung to the quarterdeck. Almost at once the quarterdeck began to sink, and Brother Jones called to his wife, whose feet were tangled in the rigging.

"Put out your hand," he shouted, and when she did so he reached out and grasped it, pulling her to safety. All the others on the quarterdeck, after finding themselves in the sea, struggled to keep afloat, but one by one sank beneath the waves to their death.

When the seas subsided briefly, the captain noticed Mrs. Jones, and directed that she be brought up to the bowsprit.

"Let us cling to this part of the vessel," he told her. "It is the firmest, and will remain the longest time together." As she had lost her dress, the captain managed to locate an old jacket, and she readily put it on.

The great billows continued to sweep through the wreckage, and the hours of the night wore on. Shortly before dawn a large dog which was aboard attempted to climb on Mrs. Jones to save himself, but as only her head was out of the water the animal almost smothered her.

Submerging, she lost her hold. Desperately clutching a chain she just managed to clamber back to her position on the bowsprit. Again the dog climbed on top of her, and again she lost her hold, but this time the captain pulled the animal off and it swam away toward shore. Whether or not it ever reached there alive Mrs. Jones never discovered.

Finally, the light of morning appeared. It was Wednesday, March 1, and when the darkness had vanished, the seas appeared much calmer. The sun soon burst through the clouds, causing Brother Hillier to clasp his hands together and shout, "Bless God! I see the light of another day! Now, my sister, we shall soon have help!"

But help did not come. Although Mr. Oke and Mr. Jones removed their cravats, tied them to a long piece of wood, and hoisted the pole for a beacon no one paid them the least attention. As they clung to the bowsprit they figured that the estate owned by a Mr. Byam was immediately opposite to the wreck, not more than three miles away. The survivors knew that there was a telescope at the Byam residence, but as it turned out, no one used it that day.

The wreck of the Maria, *carrying a party of missionaries, off the coast of Antigua in 1826, of which Mrs. Jones was the sole survivor*

Bodies of their companions began to float by those still clinging to life on the bowsprit, and the captain ordered the rigging cut free so that the corpses would not be caught. Several vessels now sailed close to the wreck, but not a soul aboard these craft noticed it.

Soon a large schooner came bearing down on them. Brother Hillier took heart, and he gratefully said, "Now, Sister Jones, help is coming. I shall see my children again."

Nearer and nearer the schooner came. Then suddenly she tacked and sailed away, soon to disappear from view.

Of course the survivors were terribly discouraged at this turn of events. It was remarked at the time that the soldier stationed at Goat Hill Battery at Antigua should have noticed them. Actually, he had become lax in his duties and had taken unauthorized leave to visit the other side of the island on a personal errand.*

Some time later the cook and the steward weakened their hold and were washed overboard by the high billows which continued to sweep toward the distant shore. Mrs. Jones tells what followed:

> *We began to feel hunger. Brother Hillier complained of this, and seemed to want food the most. The day was now passing away; boats and schooners were still scudding along; but none approached us. The two remaining sailors were earnestly inquiring, "What must we do to be saved?" The missionaries pointed them to Jesus, and encouraged them to pray. They clung to the brethren, and would not be satisfied but when they were talking. Oh, how eagerly did they receive every word of comfort and instruction! One poor black man often cried out, "Massa! Massa! my great Massa! have mercy! have mercy!"*
>
> *Night was fast approaching; and as no help had arrived, we concluded it would be the last we should see. The sun set, the wind rose, the sea swelled, and the waves came with greater violence. This brought to mind the horrors of the preceding night; and I trembled at the thought of passing another night in that situation. We were seized with cold and sat shivering, clinging to each other to keep us warm. I shall never forget, so long as memory continues, the kind attention paid to me by the brethren and captain. This night was almost as bad as the former one; but truly it was a night of prayer. If ever I felt the real value of religion, it was then. How foolish, how empty was*

---

*When his negligence was reported, the soldier was removed from his position.

*everything besides! How valuable was the little which I had, in time
of danger!*

Daylight of Thursday came, but hopes were not as buoyant as they
had been the preceding morning. When the signal of distress was
hoisted again, the captain noticed that the seas had gone down considerably. He also noted an isle about a mile and a half away, called Sandy
Island.

"If it wasn't for the current, one might swim to Sandy Island," the
captain said, but no one paid much attention.

A short time later a schooner came sailing along, but again it tacked
away, probably because of the known rock in the area.

At high noon the sea became considerably calmer, and Brother Hillier
announced that now was the time for him to swim to the shore of
Antigua. Not believing that anyone could survive that distance, the captain suggested that Hillier try for Sandy Island instead. The missionary,
however, explained that he had been a strong swimmer as a boy and
believed that he could reach the further destination. Then he removed
his timepiece, giving it to Brother Oke.

"Here is my watch. If I should not succeed, and you should be saved,
give it to my wife."

He told the others that when he reached shore he would send out the
boats at once.

Plunging into the sea, he swam strongly at first for about forty yards,
but then encountering trouble, he attempted to turn back. He managed
to fight his way to within a few yards of the wreck, but then a huge
wave smashed into it, continued to roll toward shore, and caught the
unfortunate missionary in the process. Brother Hillier was soon
engulfed and lost forever.

"Brother Hillier's sufferings are at an end," remarked Mr. Jones,
shortly after the incident, "and we cannot live much longer."

Mrs. Jones steadily became weaker, but her thoughts were of poor
Hillier's family, who would never see him alive again. The minds of
those who still survived were on the subject: "Who will be next?"

Mrs. Jones continues her story:

*The want of food and water was almost insupportable, as we had
nothing from Monday night, and it was now Thursday. Our longing
for water was indescribable. The salt water washing into our mouths*

caused us to suffer more from thirst than we otherwise should have done. I now suffered also much from cold. Mr. Jones took off his coat, and insisted on my putting it on, as being a great coat, he thought it would keep me warmer. I availed myself of it, and he put on the jacket which the captain had kindly given me.

Towards sunset Brother Oke announced that there was no hope of our being saved, and asked the captain if he thought they could make Sandy Island, if they got on the mast that was floating by us. The captain said he had little hope, all of them being so weak, but he would try. He then laid hold of the rope; and the mast was brought to. While the captain and Brother Oke were making ready, Mr. Jones said to me, "We shall soon be alone." I asked him if he wished to try with them. He said, if I were not with him he would. I then told him, I would attempt it by getting on the other mast, or if he would make the attempt with the captain, I would remain clinging on the bowsprit. Mr. Jones replied, "No, my dear, I will not leave you! We will remain together as long as we can."

The wreck began to unjoint, and we expected before morning it would quite separate. We suffered much from pieces of wood with nails in them, which by the force of the water were driven against us and tore our flesh. On that day the sun greatly scorched me, for, as I had no bonnet to screen my face, both my face and hands were blistered, and afterwards the skin and my fingernails came off. I am astonished, that after all I still live, and possess the perfect use of all my limbs and faculties.

Mrs. Jones watched as the captain and one sailor attempted to climb on the mast to reach shore aboard it, but the spar began to twist and the captain was washed off, saving himself only with difficulty. Returning to the wreck with the sailor, he looked across at Goat Hill, where he could plainly see people walking, and laborers in the fields of an estate nearby. No one paid those on the wreck the slightest attention.

Another long night began, but the swells were not as strong as they had been, and the survivors hung on to their positions without effort. As Mrs. Jones did not feel sleepy, she supported her husband and Mr. Oke for several hours while they slept. Early Friday morning, however, Mrs. Jones began to feel terribly weak and experienced a violent pain in her stomach. She feared she was dying, but when the sun rose and its warmth reached her, she regained her composure.

As the sun reached its zenith, it burned them with great intensity, and Brother Oke could scarcely move his hand. Then a small boat was seen a short distance away, but although they shouted continually, no one in the craft appeared to notice them. Probably little of the wreck showed above the surface, and the distance was much greater than they believed.

The captain now suggested that they should all chew lead pellets, a supply of which he had, to relieve their thirst, and soon every survivor was chewing away. Mrs. Jones found that this relieved her considerably.

That afternoon the bodies of several of the children floated nearby. A short time later Mrs. Jones' husband became drowsy, and she could not awaken him. Washed overboard, he was floating away, but Mrs. Jones* managed to rescue him.*

Suddenly Mr. Oke announced that he was going to swim ashore. The others realized that in his condition he could never make it, and that he was probably delirious. Nevertheless, he shook hands with Mr. Jones and was about to say farewell to Mrs. Jones, who was asleep at the time, but her husband said not to awaken her. Brother Oke then plunged into the water, where after a few feeble strokes he sank to his death in the sea.

Then a sailor attempted to float ashore on a plank, but it went under and he perished before the eyes of the others. A short time later the last remaining member of the crew was washed overboard to his death.

Three persons now remained alive on the wreck of the *Maria*, Mr. and Mrs. Jones and the captain. Jones was probably dying, and the captain was not much better off. How Mrs. Jones was able to keep her strength for such a long period of time she never really understood, but she was then the strongest of all three survivors.

Every time a wave swept across the wreck it almost pulled Jones away from his wife, but she was able to hang on, although it had been three full days and nights since the disaster.

Then came the terrifying moment when a great wave pulled Jones off his perch, and Mrs. Jones had hold of him only by the collar as he floundered in the water. She knew that he would soon be dead unless the captain could help and cried for his assistance, as her story describes:

---

*Throughout her account Mrs. Jones maintains a strict custom of never mentioning the first name of any of the missionaries.

"Mr. Jones is drowning! Oh, if you can help me, do! Do not let him drown, for he is dying! Raise him and let him die in my arms!"

The captain turned around and attempted to assist, but could not. He was not able even to assist in lifting his foot over the bowsprit, but said, "It is all over! I am dead almost myself. I cannot, I cannot assist you!"

Then, by a last effort, I got his head upon my shoulder, but how I collected strength for the exertion, I cannot tell. I continued to hold him in my arms, but frequently thought I must yield him up. Then again I thought, "Oh, if I can but save him until death has ended his sufferings, I shall be satisfied!"

He spake after this, but I could not answer him for weeping, and I now felt as though my heart would break. Mr. Jones then gave a struggle, and cried aloud, "Come, Lord Jesus!" This he repeated three times, and then exclaimed, "Glory!" I held him several minutes, but he neither moved nor spoke afterwards. I spoke to him and begged him, if still alive, to move his hand, but life had fled.

I well remember feeling thankful, amidst all my sorrow, that I had been enabled so to help him as to keep him from drowning, and that he had not to struggle with death in the water. I had also the full assurance of his being admitted into Heaven. This was to me an indescribable consolation. Though exhausted, I could not yield him to the waves; my heart seemed to say, "Stop awhile before I let him go," but a wave at length washed him away, and he floated at my feet. The captain to whom I called was not able to speak, or even to stir, being then almost dead. My feelings now quite overwhelmed me. The last thing I remember was my saying, "Farewell, I shall soon be with you."

It is probable that Mrs. Jones lapsed into unconsciousness soon after this, for that same afternoon two men in a boat, Mr. Kentish and Mr. Ashford, noticed the wreck, saw her sitting on the bowsprit, sailed over, and found her still alive. Her face was resting on her hands, with her eyes looking out over the water.

"What do you wish?" Mrs. Jones asked in her delirium as the two men came aboard.

"We have come to assist you," was their reply.

"Bring my husband, Mr. Jones. He is there," was her answer, but when they examined the body it was that of the captain. Evidently Mr. Jones had floated off, and his remains had sunk to the bottom.

Carrying her to their own craft, they gave her a drink of "some cordials," and then started ashore with her. Her pulse almost stopped beating, but a Dr. Peddie was waiting on the beach and gave her first aid.

News of the wreck electrified the island, and an immense crowd of people were on the shore. Many of them, who knew Mrs. Jones, did not recognize her, so sunburned and bloated from exposure were her features.

Mr. Kentish carried her to his home, and there Dr. Peddie stayed for three days while bringing her back to strength. When she was carried to the house, there was little hope of recovery. But because of the unwearied attention of the doctor and with Mr. and Mrs. Kentish's kind care, her life was spared. Her final remarks follow:

> *Never shall I, as long as memory continues, forget their kindness and that of many others. When I think of the scenes I passed through, I wonder that I could sustain them; but I owe all to the grace of God, who brought me down to the grave, and has raised me up. It is mine to mourn the loss of an affectionate husband, and that of the missionaries and their wives, with whom I had rejoiced and sorrowed.* *

Mrs. Jones's account of her harrowing experience was published in 1827 as *The Loss of 5 Wesleyan Missionaries*. Mrs. Jones's first name appears to be lost to history, but her husband's name was Thomas. Thomas Jones (1802—1826) had been a minister in the Brigg Circuit in England before deciding to pursue missionary work.

---

*According to historian John Telford, a Wesleyan scholar, Mrs. Jones fully recovered and returned to England, where she later married a Mr. Hincksman. A child of the union became a major in the British Army.

CHAPTER 8

Azubah, the Whaler's Wife

On September 29, 1835, Azubah Bearse Handy celebrated her fifteenth birthday. The daughter of Captain Bethuel G. Handy, a coastal schoonerman, and his second wife, Mary, Azubah had been named for the captain's first wife.

At the age of fifteen, Azubah had taken a position as a seamstress in the local Cotuit Port tailor shop. One day, while she was stitching made-to-order garments, she was particularly attracted by a young man who entered to be measured for a suit. Deciding to take action, she hastily wrote out a note, "I hope I meet the dashing young man I made these clothes for!" Unseen by the tailors, the seamstress thrust the message into the pocket of the new suit, which was picked up by its owner a day later. His name was William Cash.

The Cash family of Massachusetts was well established. William was named for his grandfather, who had been killed by a whale on the first voyage in which he sailed as master. A resident of Nantucket, the grandfather left a wife, Phoebe Bunker Cash, two daughters, and one son, Alexander.*

---

*Captain William Cash had sailed away from Nantucket in 1796 as master of the whaler *Leo* of 217 tons. One day, probably in 1798, several whales were sighted, and Captain Cash was lowered in one of the longboats. At the first strike he was killed by a whale. His chief mate Joseph Allen then became the captain and after a long voyage the *Leo* returned successfully to Nantucket Island in 1800.

Alexander Cash entered the rope-making business at Mattapoisett. Having married Hannah Higgins at her parents' home, he returned to Nantucket later in life and became the toll-gate keeper between Nantucket and Siasconset. Hannah and Alexander had six children, George, Charles, William, Phoebe, Hannah, and Martha.

In spite of his relative youth, the man to whom Azubah wrote her daring note had already been a whaler for three years. At the age of sixteen, William had sailed on the ship *Catherine* of Salem under Captain Henry Paddock. Reaching Valparaiso, Chile, the ship's master was killed in a skirmish with the natives, and Goodrich, the first mate, became captain.

The *Catherine* continued her voyage but it was not the end of her hard luck. While sailing off Hawaii the whaler caught fire, burning to the water's edge. The crew took to the boats and reached shore at Honolulu.

Left without a ship, William and several others signed on aboard the whaler *Peruvian*, commanded by Captain Benjamin Cogswell. This cruise ended successfully. The *Peruvian* returned home in September 1835, and William soon made his way to Cotuit Port.

It was at this time that Cash went to be measured for a new outfit, which he took home a few days later. He tried the suit on, found the note, and met Azubah. A period of courting followed until with summer approaching, William shipped out again as boat steerer on the *Edward Quesnell* of Fall River, under the command of Captain William Wood.

Thirty-five months later, homeward bound with a heavy, rich cargo, the *Quesnell* was caught in a terrible gale and smashed ashore on Long Island between Montauk and Amagansett. Within twenty-four hours she had gone to pieces. The longboat in which young Cash escaped capsized in the surf, and of the eleven aboard, only four were saved. Only a few barrels were salvaged from the cargo of 2,300 barrels of oil. Thus within a day or two's sail from their home port the whalers lost many of their comrades and most of the wealth for which they had toiled three years. William recovered his strength, but the financial loss was a heavy one.

Reaching Cotuit Port late in May 1839, the young whaler went almost at once to Azubah's house, where in spite of his loss of funds, the two made plans for their marriage on July 8. The wedding occurred in the bride's home; the couple took a honeymoon of sorts; and after a few weeks William again made plans to go to sea. This time he was given the second mate's berth in the ship *Ganges* of Fall River.

Three days out the vessel was found to be leaking so badly that she was forced to put into Newport Harbor for repairs. Starting out again, William found the voyage relatively uneventful until the ship caught fire in the port of Talcahuano, Chile. Once more Cash watched unhappily as his whaler burned to the water's edge.

Left without a ship, William obtained a berth as second mate on the ship *Milton* of New Bedford. He was now to serve under the command of Captain Robert Ruckerman, a veteran whaler. It was a highly successful voyage which the *Milton* made into the North Pacific, and when they returned home in March 1842, the men of Massachusetts had been absent more than two years.

Azubah greeted Second Mate Cash with a new son, Alexander George, born May 9, 1840. Remaining home barely long enough to make the acquaintance of his family, William sailed again as chief mate of the *Milton* on May 28. This time Captain Lewis was master. Again it was a long, successful voyage, and the vessel arrived home in May 1844.

On July 17 of that year, he set sail once more, but now he was master of the *Milton*. The months dragged slowly by for Azubah, and she did not see her husband for almost three years. Arriving home in April 1847, he sailed soon as master of the ship *Gideon Howland* of New Bedford. This voyage lasted until April 1850. Again it had been a lucky cruise. By now, however, Azubah felt that she must speak her mind to her husband.

"You have been home scarcely twenty-six weeks in the eleven years of our married life," she reminded him, "or not much more than two weeks a year. I am going to do something about this if I can."

When he asked her what she intended to do about it, her answer astonished him.

"I am going to sea with you," she calmly replied.

Although other wives had sailed with their whaling husbands, William had never considered that Azubah was interested in becoming a woman of the sea. On October 1, 1850, however, she left Edgartown with her husband and their ten-year-old son, Alexander, aboard the ship *Columbia*.

Rough seas hit the *Columbia* almost before she was out of sight of land, and twenty days later a great storm was encountered off the island of Flores in the Azores. Narrowly escaping destruction, the *Columbia* outrode the gale in spite of the fact that both wind and current were driving her with almost irresistible force toward the dangerous shoals and cliffs of the island.

When morning came, the storm subsided, but it was found that they were uncomfortably close to the island's towering breakers. Although they had lost several boats and suffered considerable damage, there was no serious injury to the vessel herself, and an hour later the whaler was in calm seas and deep water. It was indeed a rough initiation at sea to which Azubah and Alexander were subjected.

Several more gales, accompanied by continuous rough weather, followed, but at last the seas went down. The *Columbia* reached the Pacific Ocean and eventually arrived at the Hawaiian Islands. Here Mrs. Cash, now expecting a baby, decided to go ashore with her son to stay at the home of a Hilo missionary.

There is no evidence that Captain Cash's logbook is still in existence, but a journal kept by Azubah, begun at sea, is a recent acquisition of the Nantucket Whaling Museum. Together with what we know about the missionary establishment of Hilo, the journal gives a picture of her existence for the next few months.

Landing at Hilo Mrs. Cash was received by a famous missionary, the Reverend Titus Coan, a native of Killingworth, Connecticut.* Reverend Coan had taken over the frame house at Hilo which had been built by Joseph Goodrich, who had not been paying enough attention to the religious aspect of the mission and had been sent home.

Mrs. Cash enjoyed living in the neat, two-storied dwelling, with its double rows of small windows. Painted red, the house had white trimmings and made Azubah nostalgic in more ways than one for her New England home far away.

Sitting on the wide piazza, she would look down at Hilo Harbor below, and admire the crescent-shaped beach and the blue ocean beyond. Often as she sat there, she thought of her husband far at sea, hunting the world's largest mammal. Her son, Alexander, was fascinated

---

*The life of this early Christian missionary at Hilo was exciting and varied. When the sailing captains and crews first came ashore after he had been established, Reverend Coan would make a point of admonishing them if they had chased whales on the Lord's Day. "Sunday is a day of rest," he would tell them.

Azubah Cash soon made friends with Mrs. Fidelia Church Coan, originally of Churchville, Connecticut, and later named her own child, a daughter, after her. The child's full name was thus Fidelia Coan Cash.

with the island, but Azubah was too concerned with the immediate future for complete relaxation.

Alonzo D. Sampson visited Hilo in 1855. Quoting from his *Life and Adventures [Three Times Around the World, Or Life and Adventures of Alonzo D. Sampson, 1867]* , we read that:

> Hilo has only some twelve houses and sixty inhabitants. It boasts one store and one hotel, saloon, or groggery, as you please to call it. The best and only really respectable looking house is that of the Mission, occupied at that time by Mr. Coan and family. Half the houses in the place were kept to rent to such skippers as wished to live ashore while in port. Beside the houses which I have reckoned as forming the town proper, quite a number of native huts were scattered along the beach for a mile or two each way. . . . The anchorage [is] two miles distant from the town.

Finally, on August 20, 1851, a baby son was born to Azubah at the residence of Reverend Coan. Two months later, with her husband's whaler *Columbia* in port, she took her family aboard and sailed from Hilo Harbor on October 27, 1851.

Although she had planned to keep a careful diary, Azubah did no writing for several months after going aboard the *Columbia* with her two children. Toward the middle of March, however, she finally arranged a schedule which allowed her to set down her thoughts on paper from time to time.

Infant mortality was terribly high in the mid-nineteenth century, and Azubah's anxiety concerning her son Murray, as he was called, is present on every page of her journal. Several of the first entries follow:

March 13th A.D. *1852*

William Murray Cash. Born at Hilo, Hawaii at the house of Rev. Coan, Wednesday, August the 20th, A.D. *1851, left there with his parents in the ship* Columbia *October the 27th. When 4 months old he began to put things in his mouth to eat, and at 5 months and 2 days his first tooth cut through and about two weeks after two more came through. He sat alone nicely at 5 months and at six began to get along a little and wished to stand on his feet a great deal. He will be 7 months if he lives a week longer and he creeps about nicely and gets up by things and tries to go along by things a little. He is a healthy* and active little thing at present and I hope will continue to be. A.B.C. [Azubah Bearse Cash]

[March] 21st—Little Murray appears to be very well, and seems to improve in creeping nicely, and likewise begins to show that he has considerable temper. He was seven months old yesterday and his father had a little trial with him in the morning. He took him to rock him to sleep, and he was disappointed thinking he was going on deck, and he showed great resistance for 15 or 20 minutes, but was conquered and awoke very pleasant. I had a similar trial with him this morning by bringing him down from the deck when he was not ready and making him sit in his little chair. It was [as] much as I wished to do to hold him there for some time for he showed great resistance, but after some time yielded and now is asleep. But withal he grows to be

Azubah Cash, circa 1860s (Nantucket Historical Association)

very knowing. I hope we shall be able to bring him up in a proper manner, to know and to love the commands of God and fear to disobey them.

[March] 28th—Murray gets along nicely but does not grow fleshy very fast, he weighs 17 1/4 pounds, 7 months, but he gets up by anything he can get hold of and gets along by things a little. He seems to be well and if we have moderate weather I think he will go alone quite young.

April the 25th—William Murray is very well and grows nicely at 8 months, he weighed 19 lbs. and he is very stirring. The cold weather seems to agree with him quite nicely. He is carried on deck nearly every day whether it snows or not.

William Cash (Nantucket Historical Association)

May the 9th—Murray grows nicely but has been rather worrying for a few days. I expect that he has some teeth that he ought to cut soon. He is quite forward as to helping himself, he goes along by things as fast as need be, or creeps either, and the little thing gets to the foot of the stairs very often and looks up very wishful for he is so very fond of going on deck, where he does go very often. He seems strong and healthy. I hope he will continue so for the present.

May the 16—Little Murray's health continues good and he is as lively as if he was in warm weather, he does not mind the cold at all. I believe he would stay on deck until he froze without crying, he creeps to the foot of the stairs often and says ah, ah, ah, as if talking to someone to take him up and he goes around from one thing to another as fast as he can creep and sometimes he appears to forget himself and lets go both hands and only leans. He understands a great deal that is said to him, when I say No, No, Murray he looks very hard and sometimes obeys instantly and again he will venture again. He is a pet and I hope he will be spared to us, he takes up time that might be spent less profitably. A.B.C.

May the 23rd—Murray is nine months old, he weighs 19 1/2 lbs. and is as merry as a kitten when well, but he has had days the past week of being feverish and wanted tending but he has got over it; he sleeps delightfully nights when well and is enjoying that rest at present.

From May 30, 1852, through the early part of September, Azubah speaks in great detail of Murray's progress in walking. By the time he is a year old, she reports that he walks fairly well, but in his teething he is somewhat slower. At one point she mentions that the boy is "in a great habit of screaming when things do not suit him, and I have to use the rod and then he tries to conquer, but I think he will soon get over that."

Azubah's diary continues:

September the 28th—Murray appears to be well at this time but he has [an] eruption on his face which looks rather bad and I cannot tell what it is....He grows very interesting and was 13 months old the 20th and weighed 21 3/4 lbs. and yesterday he went on shore with us a-berrying and had a fine time, was good as need be, he falls down, and up again, and when he creeps now it appears to be fun for him, but he has got his sea-legs on, as the saying is, nicely. A.B.C.

October the 4th, 1852—Murray is now sleeping to all appearances the sleep of health, although his face looks very red as if it might feel uncomfortable and no doubt it does sometimes (I wish I knew what it was and what to do for it). He has cut his eighth tooth through within a few days but he does not get them very fast, he is what I call a busy thing for he is about something all the time that he is up and loves to hang around me very much and will hug and kiss nice enough. I think he is quite forward for he understands so much that we say and will act so quickly from hearing a speck of things. I hope that God will watch over his little heart and guide him by His wisdom that he may walk in the straight path that leads to life everlasting, and may God assist his parents to teach him that which is right in His sight. A.B.C.

1852, Oct. the 20th—William Murray is 14 months old today and weighs 22 lbs. but it seems as if he had gained more than that during the last month, but our weights are not very good ones. He looks quite fleshy and appears quite well, except the 18th of this month he fell off the transom head first and struck his collar bone near the right shoulder against the stovebox, and broke it we think. It was very painful at first but he favored that arm for a few days, but soon used it as ever. All I could do was to put a bandage under his arm and round his neck and bathe it in spirits. The swelling has gone down but the bone sticks up quite large. His face has got better by trying a remedy for Ringworms which now I think they were. He seems to enjoy pretty good health and I hope by the blessing of God he will continue to. A.B.C.

Nov. the 12th—Arrived at Hilo, his birthplace and in quite good health, except a little trouble getting his eye teeth, weighs 22 lbs. rather slender, but naturally small, is perfectly delighted with all he sees on the land as it is all new after being on board a ship the greater part of his little life.

Far at sea aboard the whaler, Captain Cash was having his disciplinary problems. A member of the crew actually mutinied, and the captain could legally have executed him, but chose an easier method. The

Columbia was then off an island, and the mutineer was rowed ashore and marooned.

Years later young Alexander Cash, now grown to manhood, was visited at Hyannis by a grizzled veteran of the sea, who reported, "I am the one your father put ashore on the island. I heard his son lived in Hyannis and decided to visit him. That marooning was the best thing that ever happened to me. A ship called soon afterwards, and I told them I'd been put ashore because I'd had smallpox. I changed my evil ways, became a good sailor, retired from the sea, married, and raised a family. And your father was the reason for it!"

At times, strange as it seems, it was the very remoteness of Hilo which appealed to Azubah. Letters to the States often took a year and a half in transit, and there were not many people in the general vicinity of the mission home with whom she could freely converse. All articles of food, clothing, furniture, and medicine had to make the long trip from Massachusetts by sailing vessel around Cape Horn, a voyage of about six months, so that the provisions were stale before they reached Hilo, and the goods were often damaged. Although Mrs. Cash had been accustomed to hardships aboard the whaler, it was still a great disappointment to watch the barrels of flour, which had been unloaded on the Hilo pier, opened and to find the flour either mouldy or so hard that an ax or chisel was needed to split it apart.

Often the island schooners, themselves decrepit reminders of happier days on the mainland, would offer passage to other locations in the islands, taking four to six weeks to make a round trip to Honolulu, a total distance of about six hundred miles. Azubah took one of these journeys to Honolulu in November, and recorded her thoughts:

> *November 19th—-Left Hilo after being quite unwell at that place but health rather better at this time and bound for Honolulu, having it quite rough.*

> *November 22nd—-Arrived at Honolulu and removed [Murray] on shore with his parents and brother to spend a recruiting season, his health is not very good, is getting his double teeth, but when well is as quick as need be, as busy as a bee and grows more interesting every day, and mischievous withal, for yesterday he got Mr. Luce's inkstand and spilled it on his new apron and hands, such things will not be in his way long before he will take care of them.*

January the 17th [1853]—-After spending 8 weeks at Honolulu he is now on board of his old home, the ship Columbia, *where he has enjoyed himself well heretofore, he has had a fine time on shore and gained many friends (if their pretensions were sincere) and I hope he will continue to as long as he lives. A.B.C.*

Azubah and her children arrived back at Hilo, all "in good health after a cruise in the ship off Halekala where he went on shore a short time."

After landing at Hilo, Captain Cash soon left again on a cruise to the Okhotsk Sea. This whaling area lies between the peninsula of Kamchatka, the Kurile Islands, the Japanese island of Yezo, the island of Sakhalin, and the Amur province of East Siberia.

Continuing in her journal, Azubah writes:

Little Murray is quite well. His father left the 18th for a cruise to the Okhotsk Sea, with his mother and brother at Mrs. Coan's to board for a short time.

April 4th [1853]—-Murray grows very cunning, he improves very fast in talking. I think he will be a great talker by the time his father returns. This day a son is born in this house to Mrs. James Willis, the name is Henry A. Willis. If he and little Murray should live to be men, they would think of this place and I hope it will be as dear to them as to me. A.B.C.

May the 2nd—-My Murray is well and this day has removed from Mr. Coan's to a house belonging to Mr. Pitman with his mother and brother, expect to board there the remainder of the season. Mrs. Willis and son has removed likewise. He is very attached to Mrs. Coan's family especially Sarah. A.B.C.

July the 10th—-Our Murray is enjoying quite good health although he has had two or three ill turns since we came over to Mr. P's to board. When he is well he is trotting around, hardly ever still and now is a very great talker for a little one, he talks about his papa gone in a ship and I believe speaks of him with a great deal of pleasure. Yesterday we was to Capt. Worth's to tea, likewise Henry P. and Mrs. W. and he will remember Capt. Wort, as he calls him, because he gave him sugar which he calls candy.

August the 2nd—William Murray is about as well as usual today—has had an ill turn of a day or so but nothing serious, he is getting to be quite boy-like, for he has quite an idea of acting like larger boys. Today he has been with his mother (and most of the foreign residents here) over to a place called Keokea to a Chowder party given by Mr. Pitman and enjoyed it very much but got rather tired and coming back had a short nap in the boat, but has gone to bed pleasantly after repeating after me his little prayer Now I lay me down to sleep, etc. So ends the day. A.B.C.

August the 19th—William Murray has been well as usual the past week until yesterday, he was playing around where I had a fire in a furnace putting in some coal and got burned on his arm, quite a little sore. I used Painkiller and soon took the fire out, but made him most distracted for the time, I was obliged to hold it on his arm.

October 2nd [1853]—My little Murray is well at this time but has been quite unwell for one day during past week. He is now sleeping sweetly but has had a very merry time before going to bed. He went to meeting today with me but soon wanted to go outside with the woman, so she took him to the Native meeting, when that was over they came back and in M. walked and sat himself down on the floor side of Letty and in a minute or two he got up and went out, so I sent him home, but he says Now I lay me, etc. at night and Good night to us all and says he loves his brother best, once 'twas papa, but I suppose he thinks his papa has been gone so long he has a right to change his mind, he grows very interesting, and he talks as fast as English. God grant that he be carefully trained and help him to do right. A.B.C.

So ends the journal of Azubah Cash, who eventually returned to Cape Cod with her husband. William finally left the sea and devoted almost all his attention to his wife for the remainder of her life.

Their son Alexander became fairly important in Hyannis when he grew to manhood. Deputy sheriff and selectman, he erected a large business edifice on Main Street. Cash Block, the second building of the name, still stands at Hyannis. Years later, when President Ulysses S. Grant visited there, he spoke from the porch of the store. Alexander died around 1920. Where his home was located a hotel has been built, and the house has been moved back 300 feet from Main Street. After working in Brockton, his brother William Murray died in Augusta, Mine, of blood poisoning in 1942.

The Cash house in Cotuit Port still has markings on the wall of the heights of the members of the family which Whaler William and his seafaring wife Azubah brought into the world.

———————— ⌁ ————————

One of the earliest known instances of a whaling wife accompanying her husband to sea was in 1823, when Mary Hayden Russell went on a voyage to Australia on the English whaler *Emily*. Whaling wives have achieved some degree of prominence in recent years with the publication of such books as Joan Druett's *Petticoat Whalers: Whaling Wives at Sea, 1820—1920* and the popular novel *Ahab's Wife* by Sena J. Naslund.

Azubah Bearse Cash's journal is in the manuscripts collection of the Nantucket Historical Association Research Library at 7 Fair Street. The library also houses the William Cash papers (1852—1866).

In 1865 William Cash brought back the 18-foot jawbone of an enormous sperm whale taken in the Arctic. P. T. Barnum tried unsuccesfully to buy the jaw, which is now on display at the Nantucket Whaling Museum.

Azubah Cash in later years

CHAPTER 9

Emily Ballard

The story of Emily Ballard and Jewell Island is a strange one. Jewell Island lies in Casco Bay off the shore of Portland, Maine. There are about 112 islands in the bay which have been, or are, inhabited, and probably more than a hundred other islets or rocky ledges large enough to be identified.

Among the well-known landmarks of Jewell Island is the "Punchbowl," an indentation shaped like a half moon, located on the outer shore toward the northern tip of the island. Others include the two observation towers of World War II vintage, a small, often-inhabited offshore rocky ledge facing Cliff Island, two sea caves just east of the westerly tip of the island, and wave-swept Indian Rock, southeast of the World War II pier. A ruined building, which figures in our story, stands at the head of the tiny cove.

One hundred and twenty-five years ago the island was seldom visited, for only a few knew of the pleasant sheltering harbor in its lee, to the south of Rock Ledge Island. The tip of the insular promontory was less than a quarter mile from larger Cliff Island.

A few years before our war with Mexico began there were three residents of Jewell Island—a father, mother, and a girl of fifteen, who lived in the building at the head of the sheltered Jewell Island cove.

One August morning Emily, daughter of Martha and Ichabod Ballard, watched her father as he walked down toward his dory. A tall, angular man, he had immense, powerful hands, and could row rapidly, apparently without effort. His wife, inside doing the housework, had many creases on her weather-beaten face. She might be called a typical fisherman's wife, with faded eyes and iron-gray hair. Ichabod reached his dory, slid the boat into deep water, and rowed out to pull his lobster traps.

Another house had once stood on Jewell Island, but only the ruined cellar remained. The daughter of the Ballards had often visited the debris-filled cellar where she set up a sort of playhouse in the ruins. That morning she went there and soon was arranging her little make-believe room. She thought back to her earliest days on the island.

Her father had landed at Jewell Island when there was not another person living there, and he had managed to take enough timbers and boards from the other ruins to make the dilapidated house by the harbor habitable.

Neither of Emily's parents could be said to be uneducated. They spoke careful English and had several books which she had learned to read, among them a Mother Goose and a Shakespeare with illustrations.

Strangely enough, Emily had never gone to school, nor were school authorities on the mainland aware of her existence. She knew no other children. Faced with a desire for some sort of companionship, she made friends in the summer with the field mice and squirrels, but it was the birds with whom she pretended to share her innermost thoughts. There was a large, ancient dog which did little more than exist, but on the rare occasions the animal showed enough energy to accompany Emily on a hike, she soon left it far behind.

The song sparrows; the great white owl; the blue herons uttering their weird, uncanny squawk; the wild loon; all fascinated her, and once in a while the eagle and the egret visited the island briefly. The flock of sheep which roamed the meadow had less interest for her.

This true child of nature knew practically nothing of religion or theology. Her parents did not teach her to say her prayers nor encourage discussion of Biblical stories. There was a large family Bible which had belonged to her mother's grandmother which Emily read from cover to cover, but somehow only a few of the stories appealed to her, and when she asked her father for explanations of them, he suggested that her mother tell about them, and she never got around to doing so.

Emily did enjoy the simple story of Ruth, and the legend of Tobit in the Apocrypha appealed to her. Jonah, of course, became a favorite, for on occasion she saw the giant mammals spouting right off her island, and could therefore understand what a miracle it was for Jonah to escape from the belly of a whale.

All her life, for fifteen long years, she had lived on Jewell Island, and she had never been taken ashore to the great city of Portland whose spires and tall buildings on many days she could see clearly outlined against the sky. Often, on dark nights, she was able to see the welcome flash of Portland Head Light off to the south.

Emily was perplexed by the fact that her father almost never went to Portland itself, usually preferring to go ashore at a small mainland hamlet nearby known as Maiden Cove. She accompanied him on these twice-yearly journeys and enjoyed the all-too-brief visits to the small variety store, which had the usual assortments of dry goods and groceries. No one ever came to the island, however.

Emily spent much of her time on Jewell Island exploring the shore line, gamboling with the breakers during the storms and running along the rocky ledges in calmer weather when the tide was low. Often she watched the clipper ships and the schooners as they sailed by on their way into Portland or toward the various ports of the world.

The annual question whether or not Emily should go to school always came up in the late summer. Her mother thought that it would be wise to send her to the mainland for her education, but her father always disagreed with such vehemence that his wife would back down, and year after year Emily stayed on the island. So it was that she was taught by her parents and never left the island except on those rare occasions when she would go to Maiden Cove with her father for supplies.

One day when she was eleven she had noticed her father acting in a furtive manner down on the shore near the little wharf which he had built. His behavior was so peculiar that she began to be genuinely concerned about what he was up to.

She noticed that he had a shovel with him. When he started investigating the ruins of an older stone pier which in colonial times had stood near the site of his newer one, Emily decided not to let him know that he was being watched.

Making careful visual checks with distant objects, he finally concentrated on a section of the old pier near the head of the ruins. First he moved one large boulder and then another, after which he began to dig with his shovel in the earth, but not for long. He stopped digging, knelt down, and pulled up a heavy mildewed leather portfolio. Undoing the thongs which bound it, he opened it carefully. Emily could not see inside the portfolio, but watching carefully, she saw him withdraw eight golden coins. Then he retied the thongs, lowered the portfolio into the earth again, and sat down, exhausted, for it was a heavy leather case.

Placing the coins in his handkerchief, he tied it up and pushed it into his trouser pocket. Lifting the two boulders into their original position in the ruins of the wharf, he glanced around carefully to see if he had been observed.

Emily waited no longer. Crouching low, she scurried away from the scene, and soon was on the other side of the island where her mother found her hours later when gathering driftwood for the evening fire.

She did not mention the incident to her father, but often considered visiting the old wharf when he was off the island to examine the cache herself. She never did, however.

And so it was that Emily reached the age of twenty without ever entering a school building or meeting young people her own age. She had never seen a railroad train or visited a large city. Strong and fearless, she was as wild as a seagull and as brave as the Indians for whom the rock offshore near her home had been named. During the summer that she observed her twentieth birthday an even occurred which changed all this.

Although some of the fishermen had, throughout the years, made clumsy attempts to go ashore at Jewell Island and be sociable, they had met with no success. Of course, at first there was gossip about its strange inhabitants, but fishermen of Casco Bay always respected the individuality of others, and left Emily's family alone. Of course, if they met, as sometimes happened on the fishing ground or at the little store in the cove on the mainland, they would in passing say "how do," talk about the mackerel shortage, or the poor run of menhaden, "pogies" as they called them, or the sad fact that lobsters were so scarce.

The younger fellows stared at Emily if she chanced to be with her father, but she had nothing to say to them. One rather bold lad went ashore on the island to make her acquaintance, but he landed at the wrong time, and old Ballard warned him off in such a manner that he never tried it again.

Emily had her daydreams, and one of the young fishermen whom she had seen appeared as romantic as the characters in the Shakespeare volume. She expected some day to have someone fall in love with her, but he would have to be a prince, she thought.

Whenever great storms battered the cliffs of Jewell Island the sea would rise up twenty or thirty feet and the spray, fifty feet. Emily would go down on the rocks and quote, "If by your art, my dearest fellow, you have put the waters in this roar, allay them. The sky it seemed would pour down stinking pitch, that the sea mounting to the welkin's cheek, dashes the fire out." And then she dreamed that some day perhaps some "brave vessel" with some "noble creature" in her might be dashed upon that rock-bound isle. The very moment he saw her the prince's heart should fly to her service and then she would sail back with him to Naples, or wherever her father's lost kingdom was. Minor inconsistencies she minded not. What, to her, was the lack of riches? Her imagination invested what she had with poetic glamor.

Strangely enough she did not like a long run of good weather. Emily wanted the storm, the lightning, and the dreadful thunder claps. In her opinion her lover would never appear under the light of the moon or when the sky was bright and the sea calm.

One July morning when she was out pulling lobster traps, she noticed a sail coming out from the bight of Cliff Island. The craft came right toward the tiny island off Jewell. She saw in the sailboat an elderly man and a younger one. They were not attempting to hide in any way. The elder, with a powerful physique, a long black beard, and a straight nose, had shaved only his upper lip, which gave him a pious look, or so Emily thought. He had coal black eyes and delicate hands with slender fingers. His companion was apparently an artist, much younger, with light, wavy hair. He wore a mustache typical of the period and had a sort of devil-may-care look about him. Getting close to Rock Ledge Island, they ran the dory up on the beach and began unloading it. Observant Emily noticed many bottles and flasks, and all the appurtenances of a summer camp. They brought half a barrel of water, provisions of various types, and one particularly heavy package of which they were rather careful.

As the weeks went by that summer Emily noticed that the two men were rarely seen fishing even for rock cod or cunners, but she did not pay much attention to them the first year. They came back the second year, and the third, when she was twenty.

Of course the fishermen of the area knew that someone had gone ashore on Jewell Island to take over the old Donnell place, as it was called. But what they did not know was that two counterfeiters had chosen tiny Rock Ledge Island as an ideal location for turning out their product, half dollars.*

It was that third summer that the artistic young man crossed over and landed on the point. Wandering around the island without being seen himself, he noticed Emily sitting by a tree overlooking the ocean and

---

*Counterfeiting in this period, which ended shortly before the middle of the nineteenth century, was much more prevalent than is usually imagined. Stephen Burroughs, about whom I wrote in the *Romance of Boston Bay*, was an expert in this field.

reading aloud. Gradually, he stole closer to her so that finally he stepped out into view. With a cry of alarm she jumped to her feet.

"Don't go," he said. "I won't harm you. Calm down and tell me what you are reading."

"Shakespeare."

"Do you live here?"

"Yes, in the house. My father, Ichabod Ballard, would not like me to talk with you."

"Why not?" asked the young counterfeiter.

"He doesn't like strangers to land on his island."

"Well, don't be afraid of me."

"I'm not afraid of you. I don't even know who you are."

"My name is Cosmo Primetti. I live over on the tiny island there."

"No one lives there."

"I do. I have lived there for three summers."

"What do you do?"

"Oh, I camp out."

"Why?"

Primetti threw himself down on the slippery ground, and the girl noticed that he was handsome, but he was not her ideal. Emily felt that she ought to be going, but she stayed. Cosmo took the volume out of her hand and glanced at it.

"So you like Shakespeare?"

"Indeed, I do. I know some of his plays by heart. When you surprised me I was reading *The Tempest*. Gonzalo tells how he would run a kingdom. I was sort of comparing it to our own island here, what with

> *treason, felony, sword, pike, knife, gun or need of any engine*
> *Would I not have; but Nature should bring forth*
> *Of its own kind, all poison, all abundance.*

"That is all right, but it is socialism. Have you always lived on this island? Where did you go to school?"

"I've always lived here as long as I can remember, but I never went to school anywhere. Mother and Father taught me what I know, I'm afraid."

"How about my visiting you from time to time? I am very lonesome over there on the island."

"Father would not allow it, but I'll ask him."

The young man rowed back to the rocky ledge, where his older associate awaited him, somewhat upset at the long time Cosmo had been away. He had watched with a telescope, and was angered because he had seen Cosmo talking with the girl.

"You know that we will get into trouble if you start anything with that girl, and that will be our finish. Now no more of that."

A week went by, during which time Primetti, ignoring his companion's admonitions, made several visits to Jewell Island. Emily watched for Cosmo carefully. Every time she saw the dory start from Rock Ledge Island to Jewell, she hid herself away, and the young visitor did not see her during the entire week.

Finally she relented, and Primetti asked her why she had avoided him.

"I might as well tell you the truth. My father would probably do you bodily harm if he found the two of us together on the island, and I really have been keeping away from you for that reason."

"Your father! Well, if I told you what I know about him, you would realize that he is on this island because he's afraid to go ashore. I've heard he was a pirate in the West Indies during the '30s, and saved quite a lot of gold, but I won't give him away!"

Seizing her hand, he pressed it to his lips, and then leaped into his boat and rowed off. She watched him until he landed at Rock Ledge Island, strangely stirred by what he had done.

The next morning she was down on the shore, but Primetti failed to come. The weather had changed. A storm was brewing. Soon she could hear the roar of the surf on the outer ledges. She walked across the island and went out toward the headland. On her way she encountered her father shearing sheep.

"Where are you going, girl?"

"Over on the other side!"

"In this storm?"

"Yes. It isn't raining. It is just windy."

Emily continued until she reached the low trees at the edge of the precipice and watched as the wind bent them toward the ground. Soon she was alone on the rocky headland, with the great surges of angry water crashing below her. Leaning against the wind, she stood looking out toward Halfway Rock three miles distant, where the surf was booming, with the spray going up fifty and sixty feet.

Far in the distance she saw a sail. The vessel was making a wide-circle approach to Portland Harbor and was scudding along under bare poles.

An hour later Emily realized that the schooner was heading for trouble, sailing straight for Mink Rocks, some distance off the eastern tip of Cliff Island.

She watched, horrified, as the craft struck the underwater ledges and ripped across them. As the vessel began to break up Emily ran back toward the house, shouting the news to her father. He rushed out and accompanied her to the eastern shore, where already material from the wreck was being driven by the northeast storm.

Suddenly Emily screamed in her excitement. "There's a man's head!" Sure enough, a man could be seen bobbing up and down in the ocean just off Jewell Island's Punchbowl on the northern tip.

The two watchers saw that the waves were taking the survivor toward shore just beyond the ledges. Barely clearing the final ledge, he floated into the Punchbowl, and Emily managed to clamber down the rocky shore until she was just a few feet from where the waves would take the floating survivor. Her father scrambled down and tied a line around her waist.

Then, just as the next billow was about to break, the man's body came by, two feet away, and she leaped in. Encircling him with her arms, she was pulled to safety with her burden by her father.

Five minutes later all three were up above the reach of the sea, and Emily was eagerly scanning the man's features for signs that he still lived.

"He's dead, I'm sure," said the father, but Emily would not give up so easily.

"He's not dead, father, he couldn't be." As if in answer to her words, the man's body shook convulsively, and daughter and father began to revive him. A moment later the young man opened his eyes inquiringly. They told him that he was the only survivor of the shipwreck, but he found it hard to believe. After a few minutes' rest he began to talk.

"There were ten of us," he explained, "my cousin and eight others beside myself. Couldn't it be possible that someone else came ashore at one of the other islands?" They agreed that it was a remote possibility.

A short time later a boat which Emily recognized as Primetti's was seen approaching. Cosmo had seen the tragedy and crossed over to find out if anything had washed ashore on Jewell Island. He explained that some wreckage had been swept by Rock Ledge Island, but none had come ashore. Whatever material there was in the vicinity had piled up on Cliff Island instead.

Later search at Cliff Island, however, revealed that no one else had been saved. The young man, Ralph Lancaster of Boston, was the only person rescued from the *Leda*, the schooner yacht which had broken to pieces on Mink Rocks. Word was sent to the mainland, and newspapers soon relayed the message to Boston.

Later in the week Lancaster appeared well enough to be taken ashore to the mainland. Before her father rigged his boat for the trip to Maiden Cove, Emily and Ralph managed to have a long talk.

"I'll be back," Ralph promised, "but first I have several things to do."

He then went aboard the sailing dory, and they soon were out of sight. Later that afternoon Ichabod Ballard returned to Jewell Island.

The months went by without word of any kind from Ralph. That following autumn was a bad one, but Emily was more concerned with why Ralph had not returned. Fall had given way to winter, and then troubles came to the family and kept Emily occupied.

First the old dog died. Then Emily's mother weakened, and her death came within a few weeks. Next her father fell ill. During a great blizzard all the sheep perished. Snowstorm after snowstorm hit Casco Bay. When spring came, Ichabod Ballard told Emily that he could not continue on the island. He explained that now that Martha was dead, he was going ashore and face whatever punishment might come his way because of his earlier life of piracy, for there might still be those who would recognize him as a highwayman of the sea.

"What if I die?" he reasoned. "You'll be left here all alone. We are moving ashore, and we'll just have to face it.

"I have enough money for us both for a few years," he explained, "and you'll not have to worry. I am sorry to leave the island, but it is all for the best."

A short time later Ichabod told Emily about the gold. They dug it up at the old stone pier and made final plans to leave the island. One night, before they departed, he told Emily details of his early days of piracy in South America, where he said it was in reality privateering.

After transporting their meager belongings to the mainland, they moved to a small cottage on the outskirts of Maiden Cove, but Emily's thoughts were of Ralph Lancaster. He had promised to return. How would he know what had happened if he did return? On the other hand, several months had gone by already. Possibly, if he were coming at all, he would already have landed at Jewell Island.

In June, Ralph did return to the island, going ashore from the yacht *Aliona*. The only one he could talk to was Primetti, who together with his partner had moved across to Jewell Island to occupy the Ballard dwelling.

Because he did not like Lancaster, Primetti decided to lie and said that so far as he knew Emily had died and her parents had moved off the island and gone out West. Overwhelmed by the news, Lancaster returned to Boston. Three weeks later, however, reading in a Boston paper, he learned that a counterfeiting pair had been apprehended by the crew of a revenue cutter at Jewell Island and that Primetti was one of those captured. Ralph decided to return there to make sure that Primetti had told him the truth.

The following week he was again at Jewell Island. Searching for some clue, he wandered out toward the Punchbowl, where Emily and her father had rescued him the summer before. There he found a cairn of rocks and a wooden burial marker, but the inscription cut into the wood read *Martha Ballard*, not Emily.

Thus Ralph knew that for some reason the counterfeiter had deceived him. Anxious to trace Emily and her father, he went across to Cliff Island, where he learned from the inhabitants that once in a while they had seen Ballard in the store at Maiden Cove, but never at Portland.

With new hope Lancaster sailed toward the mainland. Three hours later he visited the variety store at Maiden Cove and found that his search was about over. Directed to the Ballard cottage, he knocked at the door. Old Ichabod answered him. Emily had not been well for several months, actually grieving for Ralph, but of course her father had never suspected the reason.

Emily's happiness at seeing Lancaster again was so transparent that old Ichabod realized that his daughter was in love with the Bostonian.

"Why didn't you come back?" she asked when they were alone, after the old man had gone to purchase supplies for the evening meal.

"There were two main reasons," Ralph explained. "First, I had to go back to Boston to find out if the girl I'd been going with was still really interested in me. She had left on a trip to Europe. Two and a half months later she returned, and we both then knew we were not interested any more in each other, so that problem was settled.

"The other reason was that I had to decide whether or not to ask my father for work in his bank. I did, and then told him about you. A short time later I sailed up to see you.

"Then, when I did visit your island, Primetti told me you were dead, and it wasn't until several weeks later that I read that Primetti was one of two counterfeiters and that they had been arrested and sent to prison. I realized then that I'd better go back and retrace my steps, and it's lucky that I did, for I found that Primetti had lied about your death. Why he did, I'll never know, but I never did like him."

Ichabod Ballard told Ralph of his privateering activities off South America, but Ralph assured him that the United States now officially recognized the countries with which Ichabod had been associated and that all his worries were needless.

A week later Emily had recovered enough to be up and around, and when Ralph proposed that they should be married in a month she readily agreed. It was a proud father who walked down the aisle with Emily at a prominent Boston church that fall to give his daughter away to the man she loved. Surely it was a happy ending to the saga of Jewell Island.

In recent years the nonprofit Maine Island Trail Association has had resident caretakers on 221-acre Jewell Island, a popular spot for daytrippers. The Punchbowl is used by many kayakers as an entry point.

Some say that Jewell Island got its name from a fisherman named George Jewell, but the island's name, sometimes spelled "Jewel," has probably played a part in the treasure stories and other romantic tales associated with it. Various legends tie Jewell Island treasures to Captain Kidd and female pirate Anne Bonny. There are even legends of hauntings attributed to supposed piratical activity on the island.

But Peter Benoit, author of the privately published book *History of Jewell Island, Maine*, has found no evidence that the story of Emily Ballard is more than a wonderful legend. Benoit feels that Snow was likely working from "oral reports of past events that had been substantially corrupted through the many retellings."

A nineteenth-century owner of the island, Captain Jonathan Chase, had two daughters. One of Chase's daughters was named Emily, and this might have been a partial basis for the Emily Ballard story. Also, in 1846, close to the time frame of this chapter, a schooner called the *Active* was wrecked on the island in an October storm. All hands were lost, and Captain Chase buried six of the victims in a field on the island.

In his book, Benoit mentions a Jewell Island "woman of the sea," Mary Sinton Leitch. Leitch, the daughter of an owner of the island, married a Scottish sea captain. She became a poet of note and published her memoirs in 1950 as *Himself and I*. The book includes material on Jewell Island life.

CHAPTER 10

Nantucket Women

Without question no other island area in America the size of Nantucket has produced so many remarkable women. Local conditions often tend to influence the eventual success in life of a man, but if Nantucket is a criterion, this is even more true of the so-called weaker sex.

Down on Nantucket, at almost any period until 1880, except during the earliest days, the women outnumbered the men four to one, and at times five to one. There was an overwhelming number of spinsters most of the time, and the married women were often separated from their husbands for periods of from one to five years during long sea voyages. Normal home life was almost unknown. Since there never were half enough suitors to go around, the girls of Nantucket just had to hope and pray. In a very real sense, they were women of the sea.

Because of these unusual conditions, popular ideas concerning women had to be changed. In their essentially manless world, the wives were forced to work out a new mode and philosophy of life. They prided themselves on what they could accomplish around the house and what they could do to defray expenses. For pleasure, they visited, drank tea, and walked. The result was a practical, forceful type of woman, described by an 1815 visitor from Nova Scotia as "homely and ungenteel." Regardless of what was thought on the mainland, these women were highly intellectual and outstandingly moral. They won fame as mathematicians, abolitionists, philanthropists, suffragists, and reformers.

In this chapter I tell the story of several well-known Nantucket women. However, I am not overly emphasizing the careers of women who have already been given recognition in several books still in print.

Let us begin with Mary Coffin Starbuck. Mary Starbuck, the seventh child of Tristram and Dionis Coffin, was born in the year 1645 at Haverhill, Massachusetts, and her family took her to Nantucket when she was fifteen. At the age of seventeen she married Nathaniel Starbuck, and their daughter was the first white child born on Nantucket. As the years went by nine other children graced the happy household.

Becoming increasingly noted for her unusual gifts of mind and character, Mary assumed such an important position in the community that her advice was often sought. She was a woman of strong character and exceptional intelligence. She took an active part in town affairs and was regarded as a leader and judge. In 1701 she adopted the religious faith of the Friends. The first meeting of this society was at her house, and the Friends continued to meet there for the next four years. The house stood on what is now known as the W. R. Swain farm and was called the Parliament House.

Although she followed the prevailing seventeenth-century ideas on women's place and never gave an opinion without modestly prefacing it with "my husband and I think," her husband meekly took the part of consort.

Known as the "Great Woman" of Nantucket, whenever she spoke out in meetings Mary left her hearers spellbound. This "Oracle" of Nantucket died in 1717. Historian William O. Stevens says that when she passed away her place as the uncrowned queen of the island was never filled. But there were many other women who have impressed us with their unusual accomplishments.

For example, there was Keziah Coffin, a girl who descended from Peter Folger. Although she did not have Folger's scientific knowledge, she inherited most of his practical ability and his fearless character. She did not care "a tuppence about other people's opinions," and was excommunicated from the Quaker church for allowing her daughter to learn to play the spinet, which she kept in her house. She made no excuse about this matter after she was "set aside."

Her activities during the American Revolution have often been discussed, both favorably and unfavorably. She wrote to Admiral Digby, who commanded the British squadron on the coast, expressing her own loyalty to the King and intimating that many other loyal Tories lived at

Nantucket. Describing their plight, Keziah begged permission to have her own vessels trade between Sheburne and New York. Admiral Digby granted permission and gave Keziah a complete monopoly in this unusual trade. Keziah set up a room in her fine town house as a store and did a "land-office" business, taking mortgages on wharves, warehouses, homes, and anything her desperate customers could put up. Nevertheless, her monopoly was broken when the Island of Nantucket issued an official proclamation of neutrality which subsequently permitted the inhabitants to trade and obtain firewood and fish. Keziah's prices tumbled, and she soon lost most of her fortune.

Shortly afterward Keziah's husband returned from a long whaling voyage and managed to salvage a few pieces of property from the disaster so that they could begin once more, but she never again became wealthy.

Those who should know claim that Keziah had been cheating King George by smuggling, accomplished by means of a tunnel between her house and the shore, but the tunnel is not known to the present generation. When she left the island, she did not plan to return. Later, when her daughter brought her back to Nantucket, Keziah immediately began lawsuits to recover some of the property she had lost. Although her lawyer told her she had not much chance, she did not agree. "I want thee to keep this in court as long as I live," was her admonition.

One day, while she was hurrying downstairs to attend court, she slipped, fell heavily, and when they picked her up they found that she was dead. Keziah Coffin had broken her neck.

Lucretia Mott, probably the earliest American champion of women's suffrage, was born on January 3, 1793, the daughter of Thomas and Anna Folger Coffin. A direct descendant of Tristram Coffin on her paternal side, Lucretia claimed Peter Folger as an ancestor through her mother. Leaving Nantucket when she was eleven, she settled with her parents in Philadelphia. In 1811 she married James Mott, and five of their children reached maturity. Time itself has made her position stronger in the field of philanthropy and politics, for today she is known as the "bright morning star of intellectual freedom in America."

Maria Mitchell, born August 1, 1818, had a father who was "addicted" to the "dismal science" of mathematics. At the age of twelve Maria was assisting her father with his calculations in his study of astronomy. For years she helped him prepare his nautical almanac and was expert in her ability to correct the navigating instruments of the sea captains.

On the night of October 1, 1847, with a relatively small telescope, Maria made the discovery of a new comet, and Harvard University was notified at once. Two days later, on October 3, astronomer DeVico also observed the new comet in the heavens, and on October 7, W. R. Dawes sighted it, but Maria had been first and eventually received full credit and proper acclaim. Later the King of Denmark gave her a gold medal for her discovery.

On the opening of Vassar College she was invited to fill the chair of mathematics. When she accepted in 1865 she took full charge of the observatory there. She made photographs of the sun and a special study of Jupiter and Saturn.

Maria Mitchell died in Lynn, Massachusetts, on June 28, 1889. In 1893 the new Boston Library was completed, and the name of Maria Mitchell was important enough to be engraved on its stone frieze along with other great people of art, science, and literature. Miss Mitchell was elected to the Hall of Fame in 1905.

The Reverend Louise Baker, next to be included among Nantucket's unusual and outstanding women, was born on October 17, 1846, the daughter of Captain Arvin Baker and Jerusha Baker of Nantucket. On December 12, 1880, she accepted the pastorate of the North Congregational Church, continuing as the preacher there until February 14, 1888. During her ministry she attracted the largest congregations ever known in the church, and for years after her death, which came on September 19, 1896, the Reverend Louise Baker's sermons were remembered by those who had been in her audience.*

Of course, many other famous women were from Nantucket. In addition to the scores of school teachers with Nantucket backgrounds who became outstanding teachers all over New England, there was Anna Gardner, important in the antislavery movement. Abiah Folger, mother of Benjamin Franklin, was born on Nantucket August 15, 1667.

I have reserved for the last part of this chapter the names of three Nantucket women—Deborah Chase, Phebe Horrox Winslow, and Mildred Jewett.

---

*Another woman of Nantucket achieved fame of a different sort early in the nineteenth-century, when it was announced that Dorcas Honorable was the last full-blooded Indian woman on Nantucket Island. Dorcas died in the year 1820. The last man with any substantial amount of Indian blood died in 1854. He was Abram Quarry.

DEBORAH CHASE

Deborah Chase was born at Nantucket Island in 1760.* By the time she had reached womanhood she weighed 350 pounds and could "fling a man of 160 pounds weight upon a house top," according to F. C. Sanford.

Her brother, Reuben Chase,† who was known for his service at sea with John Paul Jones, was a giant of a man, but his sister was fully as large.

Legends about Deborah rival those about her later and small counterpart, Madaket Millie (see page 90). One day during the Revolution Deborah realized that the family was in need of water which had to be obtained from the nearest pump on the island, but Deborah was warned that the British guards then at Nantucket would prevent her from reaching the well.

Nevertheless, Deborah told her father that as they needed water, she was going to get it for the family.

"Don't," her father admonished, "or thee will get a bayonet in thee!"

"I'd just as soon die one way as another," she shouted as she left the house. Her family watched her as she neared the corner, carrying a heavy wooden pail in each hand.

Reaching the square, Deborah approached the spot where the sentry stood. Her six-foot-five height overwhelmed the Britisher, who was about to make his challenge, which was never given. Before he had opened his mouth, Deborah's bucket described a parabola which ended against the sentry's head, knocking the man unconscious.

Deborah then walked calmly to the pump, filled both pails, and returned to the house, stopping only to see that the soldier she had knocked senseless was still alive.

On another occasion several years later, when a shipment of flour arrived on the island, Deborah was challenged by the storekeeper to buy a whole barrel.

"If thou buys a barrel and carries it home, thou shalt get a special price," the Quaker merchant promised.

---

*The book *Nantucket: The Far-Away Island* by William O. Stevens gives her birth year as 1750. If, as Snow says, she was married in 1770, the earlier date seems more likely.—*Ed.*

†Chase was the Long Tom Coffin of Cooper's novel, *The Pilot.* He served both on the *Ranger* and the *Bon Homme Richard.*

Undaunted, Deborah approached the barrel, which was out on the sidewalk, put both hands on the top, and tilted it toward her body. Then, with a quick motion, the Nantucket woman got her shoulder under the barrel. Straightening up, Deborah steadied the heavy object and started to walk away from the store, the barrel firmly placed on her broad shoulders. Her road home was uphill all the way, but it is said she did not put down her load once until she reached the house.

One morning in 1789 a teamster irritated Deborah by driving too close with his huge dray as he passed the corner of her home, so that the wheel scraped against the foundation. The next day she made it a point to observe him as he approached with his heavy span of horses. Sure enough, again he bumped the corner of the Chase mansion. Her remonstrances fell on deaf ears, just as many discussions with truck drivers do today.

On the following morning Deborah was outside the house calmly waiting for the teamster to arrive. About fifteen minutes before she expected the wagon she stationed herself in full view at the corner, and a short time later the dray hove in sight. As he neared the Chase home, the teamster's sardonic grin was easy to see. Whipping up his horses, he drove toward the edge of the road, and aimed straight for an inevitable collision with the underpinning of the Chase mansion.

But this time Deborah was ready. As the team rumbled along the cobblestone road to crash into the building, she grabbed the back of the dray and lifted it up several feet. Then, with split-second timing, she overturned the heavy wagon with a final twist in the middle of the street. Luckily the driver jumped clear, but it is said that he had to recruit six men to put the dray rightside up again. Having learned his lesson, he never again attempted to crash his heavy wagon into Deborah's residence.

Adventures with the opposite, and in her case the weaker, sex were many, and two of them will be included here.

Down near North Wharf there was a tryworks on the beach where the oil from blackfish was extracted, and open vats for the temporary storing of the oil were located a short distance away. One day Deborah was in the vicinity, and when lunchtime came one of the men sent a little girl up the street to obtain the lunches.

Deborah, realizing that the lunch basket for all the men would be too heavy for the little girl, volunteered to carry it. As she returned with the heavy load, she was accosted by a young man who still wore the wedding coat in which he had recently been married.

It may be that he had not yet recovered from the effects of the wedding feast, but in any case Deborah was the object of his affections of the moment. Sidling up to her, he asked her for a kiss.

"Don't try any nonsense on me," she admonished, but the bridegroom of a few days was persistent, and strenuously tried to kiss her. Putting down the heavy lunch basket, she decided to teach him a lesson. As he approached again, she reached out and grabbed him by one foot and one arm. With a quick motion she tossed him squarely into the huge oil vat. Coming to the surface, blubbering and screaming, the bridegroom scrambled out as best he could. Subsequently, it is said, he became so fed up with taunts that he shipped on a long whaling voyage just to get away from those who had embarrassed him.

On another occasion Deborah distinguished herself in an encounter with a man by grabbing the unfortunate victim by his hands and feet and throwing him up on the roof of a nearby house. What an Olympic champion she would have made with either the shot put, discus, or hammer.

In 1770 Deborah married. Unfortunately the interesting details of this union are lacking. She was twenty-two at the time.* There are many missing chapters in her life, and at present we do not even know where she is buried.

PHEBE HORROX WINSLOW

Mother love is indeed wonderful. Possibly one of the outstanding examples of this affection was found in Phebe Horrox Winslow of Nantucket. On many occasions I have stood at her grave in the South Cemetery on the island, thinking of the strange story connected with this woman who married Benjamin Winslow early in the nineteenth century.†

The son of the union, Charles F. Winslow, was born June 30, 1811. His mother idolized the lad as he grew into manhood, and Charles was trained by her in such an expert manner that he easily outdistanced every other pupil in the Nantucket school. His mother arranged it so that later

---

*This would mean she was born circa 1748, rather than 1760 as stated earlier by Snow. William O. Stevens wrote that she was married in 1772.—*Ed.*

†Benjamin was born August 2, 1768. He died December 12, 1839. Phebe Horrox was born July 11, 1767 and died June 10, 1847.—*Ed.*

he studied at Harvard Medical School, from which institution he graduated in 1834. Some time after this Dr. Winslow attended school in Paris.

His mother kept up her careful guidance of the young man, and eventually he became a doctor, a lawyer, and an advanced student of astronomy and the nature of the universe. In 1853 he published a book* in which he discussed his theories of atomic reactions. These theories later were expounded in his correspondence with the great English scientist, Michael Faraday.

During his career Dr. Winslow traveled for the State Department. When he visited Europe in this capacity he is said to have astounded the learned men of the continent as well as the English scientists by his advanced, precise theories of the universe and the world.

During this time, however, his thoughts were often of the mother on Nantucket who had brought him into the world. After his wife's death in 1874, Dr. Winslow made his will. It was unique.

Evidently concerned because his mother had been buried at Nantucket and his wife interred at Mount Auburn, in Cambridge, Dr. Winslow thought long and carefully about his own burial plans. He finally decided that he would leave directions in his will that after death his heart should be cut from his body, placed in a glass vessel, enclosed in a double box filled with cork dust, and sent across to Nantucket Island, where it was to be buried "in the grave and over the remains of my dear and venerated mother."

His body was then to be cremated and the ashes placed beside the remains of his wife in the Mount Auburn Cemetery.

Thus did Dr. Winslow solve one of the problems of his unusual life. In the year 1947, on July 14, a group of relatives and others placed a marker on the grave of Mrs. Phebe Horrox Winslow. The marble marker reads:

The Heart of Dr. Charles F. Winslow Lies Buried Here

MADAKET MILLIE

Mildred Jewett, known as Madaket Millie, a present resident of Nantucket Island, likes to call herself a "female hermit." Born on Nantucket, September 24, 1907, she is the daughter of Mr. and Mrs. Walter Jewett.

Cosmography, or Philosophical Views of the Universe.

From her earliest recollection, she remembers two things, her ability in feats of strength, and her deep love for animals. Millie is of stocky build, has an extremely muscular frame, and is of medium height.

When I talked with her in February 1962, she admitted that there were many island legends concerning her interesting career, but she would only verify those which others had told me and would not cooperate when I suggested that she might voluntarily recall a few for this chapter.

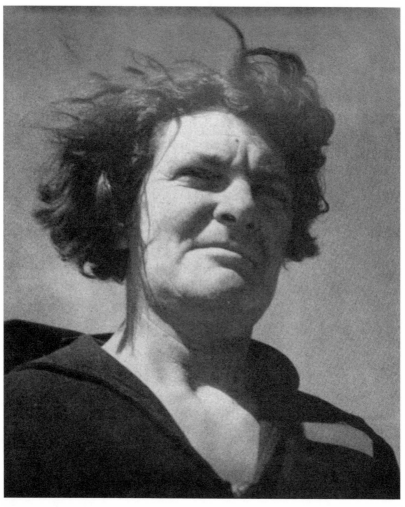

Mildred Jewett, Madaket Millie, who has spent her life on Nantucket Island and is an honorary member of the Coast Guard with the rank of warrant officer

"I'm not going to blow my own horn," she explained, "but anything you have heard I'll either admit or deny. It's one thing if some coast-guardsman or islander has told you a story about me, but it would be boasting if I told you it myself." Millie agreed to listen to the reading of these remarks about her, and her final approval was expressed simply: "It happened that way."

One of my best sources of information about Madaket Millie was the late Lawrence Cummings whose many references to Millie were confirmed by his friends as being extremely accurate.

Mr. Cummings once told me that by the time Millie was eleven years old she was equal in strength and ability to any two coastguardsmen at the Madaket Station, and they realized it. She could roll over a dory, launch it, fish with the best of them, and could handle any sort of craft in almost any type of blow.

Early in Millie's life, during World War I, a steamer was stranded at Madaket, and she has never forgotten this experience with disaster at sea. Although she did not tell me much concerning her own activity during that stranding, rest assured that Millie was in the thick of the excitement even though she was a young girl.

The 382-foot steamer *Ruby*, laden with supplies for France, had been caught in the blizzard of Sunday, February 3, 1918, and was fifty miles off her course when she hit the Nantucket shore near the Madaket Coast Guard Station. A German saboteur, serving as quartermaster, purposely stranded the *Ruby*, according to evidence revealed later.

The *Ruby* carried a heavy cargo which included 1,900 barrels of badly needed lubricating oil. On the day following the stranding Millie's father aided in getting the barrels ashore, after which they were brought to town by local teamsters. At the time, ten-year-old Millie did not participate much in the handling of the cargo, but she always remembered the great barrels as they were rolled ashore and into the drays.

After several days of planning, salvage craft freed the *Ruby* and towed her across to Newport, where she was eventually repaired. Millie told me that the *Ruby* was hauled off "bow first."

Millie's real love has been animals and birds. She is able to speak to them in a language all her own, a tongue which they understand. From the time she could walk unassisted, friendless dogs, stray cats, and all types of birds seemed to realize that here was a human being who would help them.

Millie's home and the surrounding area was a haven of refuge. It can be said, and Millie agrees, that never did she turn away an animal or bird in distress. Sometimes, when the larder at that particular moment was low, Millie would go without her own dinner so that a hungry animal could be fed.

Her World War II activities include an episode which was told as long as the Madaket Coast Guard Station remained at Nantucket.

One day in 1945 four young coastguardsmen from the Midwest, recently drafted and sent down to Nantucket for training, were walking along the sandy beach near the station.

Millie was training her dogs nearby and casually noticed the four men. When the boys stopped to inspect a good-sized log, Millie put the dogs inside the enclosure and began to watch the young men.

Apparently they were interested in picking up the log, but were unable to do so. First the boys got down on their knees and slid their hands under the log, after which they all strained to lift it. The log, however, which later tipped the scales at 283 pounds, did not budge. Then they stood over it, and attempted to encircle the trunk with their arms. Lifting in unison, they failed again.

By this time almost every other coastguardsman at the station was watching, and when Millie started across the road toward the log, the onlookers knew that they were in for an event which would be remembered.

Madaket Millie, of course, has gone beachcombing ever since she could remember, first with her father and then alone, and logs were the natural prey of a good beachcomber. Her yard was filled with driftwood of almost every size.

As she approached the scene, the four men were still trying in their embarrassed attempts to move the huge object, but it simply would not be lifted from its bed in the sand. Millie stood it as long as she could and then spoke to the coastguardsmen.

"Stand back," she commanded, "and let an Islander try it!"

Not knowing just what Madaket Millie was planning, the men stepped off to one side and watched as she strode slowly toward the log.

Millie stood at one end of the heavy tree trunk, reached down, put her hands under the tip end, tightened her powerful muscles, and slowly but surely raised it to her shoulders.

Then, with a quick motion, she tossed the 283-pound log across her shoulders and walked away from the others, her load apparently not bothering her a mite!

Those who saw the feat of strength never forgot it, but most of them believed that they had witnessed something that really could not have taken place!

On another occasion our group visited Millie at the stand near her residence where she sold things on an honor system. One of our party, Francis Forrester Haskell, was anxious to meet her. First, however, I took her aside and explained that Mr. Haskell, a life member of the Boston Young Men's Christian Union, an organization which still sponsors weight lifting and other feats of strength, was anxious to try her handshake.

Of course, I exaggerated, as Mr. Haskell was not anxious to try his handshake against such a fabulous woman, but Millie felt that her handshaking abilities were in question, and when they did shake hands she put on quite a show, actually forcing Mr. Haskell to his knees!

Millie remembers a strange coincidence. The old Madaket Coast Guard Station closed in 1947 because of what the Coast Guard called the lack of need for a station at the southwestern tip of Nantucket. The very same day a great steamer stranded a short distance from the old Coast Guard quarters. Millie always thought that this occurrence was merely to prove that the Coast Guard was mistaken and the station should have been kept open.

The date was Friday, January 3, 1947.

"I was the first one who spotted the freighter *Kotor* on the beach," Millie explained. "We had been opening scallops that afternoon. The Coast Guard had closed up Madaket Station forever only a few hours before, and I remember it had been very foggy all day.

"Darkness came on, and with the fog, it made things pretty hard to see. Shortly afterward I saw something that didn't belong down on the beach, a huge shape with lights fairly high in the air. Realizing that it was a ship in trouble, I telephoned Brant Point Coast Guard Station and was told to walk as far as the cable house to check.

"My father and I went down and sure enough, it was a large craft. Then a man from the crew of the Brant Point Station, Jules Serpa, arrived in a jeep, and we went out to the vicinity of Sheep Pond. There was no question, a great ship was on the beach. Others from the Brant Point crew reached the old closed station and then sent for help by radio. My father and I found out what had happened later.

"At about five that afternoon, approximately the time I noticed her lights, the *Kotor* had hit bottom just off Sheep Pond. She had sent out an

SOS, and the captain thought that he had struck on Davis Shoal, more than forty miles southeast of Nantucket. The *Kotor* was owned and operated by the Cunard White Star Line under Panamanian registry."*

On confirming Millie's report, Coastguardsmen Frank Massaschi, John Kittila, and Melvin Chambers started out from Brant Point and at Madaket picked up a small dory which they placed in their truck.

Reaching the scene, they launched the dory successfully on the third try and Massaschi, Chambers, and Serpa rowed out to the unknown craft. There they found she was the same ship, the *Kotor*, erroneously reported forty miles away in the Davis South Shoals area. Shortly before this, explained Millie, Tommy Giffen and Gordon Turner had arrived and called their paper, the *Nantucket Inquirer and Mirror*.

Meanwhile, Gus Bentley, a "ham" operator of WISU on the island, and Pitman Grimes, who had a broadcast receiver, both heard the distress messages from the wreck. In this way it was ascertained that Captain Dracatos of the *Kotor* did not know his ship's position until long after he had stranded, although the fog had lifted two hours before. The real trouble was that the radio operator aboard knew very little English.

Millie recalled how cars were arriving at Madaket throughout the night. Ablaze with lights in the lifting fog, the *Kotor* was a beacon visible for miles. Automobiles soon began to line the bank at the head of Sheep Pond, for the ship, a spectacular sight, was only about a hundred yards offshore.

By Saturday morning, because of the heavy traffic, the road to Millie's residence was a bog of mud, and soon the drivers found that the moor itself was much easier to navigate, especially near the Massasoit Bridge.

Madaket Millie watched as the lights of Coast Guard cutters began to appear. Soon the *Mendota*, the *Algonquin*, the *Kaw*, and the *Hornbeam* were offshore. Millie estimates that the lights of the *Mendota* were visible about nine-thirty that evening.

Particularly impressed with the huge twenty-four-inch signal light aboard the *Mendota*, Millie watched as the entire scene was illuminated with what she suggests was the brightness of the sun itself.

---

*The *Kotor* was built at West Hartlepool, England, in 1904. She was operated before the war under the name of *Eurymedon*, and ran between Boston and India. When she hit at Madaket she was carrying Australian wool as well as a general cargo, and was running for St. John, New Brunswick, from New York, where she had discharged part of her cargo.

The glow made the *Kotor* stand out in silhouette, and Millie saw the two craft exchange signals with their blinkers. Soon afterward the *Mendota* sent across a small boat, and men went aboard the *Kotor* to discuss the situation.

With the coming of dawn Saturday morning, five rescue ships were on the scene, as were a large number of townspeople who lined the shore, but it was not until afternoon that any great progress was made in getting the vessel off. Aircraft had a field day over the scene all morning, and New England Central Airways changed the course on flights to and from Boston, giving their passengers an aerial view of the "wreck." But soon the rescue craft pulled the freighter off, and the show was over.

After the *Kotor* incident ended, the Madaket residents wondered if their Coast Guard station could not be reopened. It had been established in 1891 with Thomas Sandsbury as keeper. The station had to be moved back toward the center of the island several times because the sea, as the years went by, cut steadily into the shore, and by the time of decommissioning the original location of the station was well beyond the surf in deep water. The station had given occasional help to small boats, but not for years had a serious wreck occurred in the area.

In spite of the *Kotor*, however, the Coast Guard did not reconsider. The years went by and recently the station building was torn down.

Millie continues to live in the area, all alone with her pets. Her nearest year-round neighbor, Mrs. Chauncey Chappell, was of great help in allowing me to use her communication facilities.

In my final talk with Madaket Millie, she gave a little of her philosophy of life. Of course, her feats of strength are part of Millie's memories, but she explained to me recently that she would rather be remembered for her friendship and management of the dogs she trained in World War II than for anything else.

> *I was born on Darling Street, Nantucket. When I was four we moved to Madaket, where we lived with Grandmother Etta Jewett. I've lived on the island all my life and wouldn't live anywhere else.*
>
> *I've always trained dogs, ever since I can remember. They seem to speak to me in a language I understand. Cats, geese and ducks are the same way.*
>
> *My big chance came in World War II. I tried to get into the service but was turned down because of my eyes. I did the next best thing, training dogs for the war effort. The Coast Guard needed dogs for*

many duties of patrol and the like, and I soon began to accept them and train them down here at Madaket.

If I had to remember one dog in particular of the many I've trained, it might be Bob Stark's great St. Bernard. Before I took him over the dog had to be penned in, and every time someone went by the yard, the dog apparently would go for him, but of course the fence kept the animal from doing any harm, if that was his intent.

Bob gave me the dog, and I trained him into harness successfully. I taught the war dogs about everything. The Government training system, as I recall, was to teach the fundamentals, which consisted of the six following major training orders: (1) Come; (2) Stay; (3) Sit; (4) Heel, which means walking beside you; (5) Crawl; and (6) Climb (ladders). When I finished with a dog he could do anything required of a service dog and quite a little more. I'll always consider my work with the dogs as one of the high points of my life.

The first dog I trained for the war was Buddy, a chow shepherd I got at the age of three weeks, and he was the first to be shipped away.

I had read in the New York papers how they needed dogs for war service, and finally I received instructions to ship the dogs to Dogs for Defense at the Dedham kennels. For the rest of the war I trained the dogs, and paid all expenses, including, on occasion, the shipping charges as well. I never received a cent for food.

When meat became rationed, I used all my stamps for the dogs' meat, and ate nothing in that line myself. I have never received any money for all my expenses during the war in training the dogs.

To keep things going, I had to have money, so I worked as a plumber, well-digger, and everything which would earn me an honest fifty cents. I still work at scallop opening, but have not been able to work since last December, as my scallop shanty needs repairing.

This end of the island is known as the W.E.C.S. of the Coast Guard, or West End Command Station. It is also the outpost for the State Police.

"In the wintertime I usually see no one else all day long," she told me.

I had a stand in the summertime where people could buy things in an honor system, but it just didn't work out. I open scallops, as Dad and I used to do together, but since mid-December there's been nothing to do, although it should start up again soon.

They finished tearing down the old Coast Guard station in January, last month, and now the beach area looks so barren. But I live with all my pets, and have seven dogs, quite a few cats, and countless geese and ducks.

My dogs are Scottie, Scamp, Orphan Annie, Brus, Yappie, Shortie, and Babe. My cats are all black, and Termite might be called the pest of the neighborhood, as Termite will bite anyone. I trained him that way so he couldn't be stolen, as others have. The other cats and my wild geese and tame ducks keep me busy.

I have often been asked if expenses are not high. Indeed they are not for me, for I don't drink and I don't smoke. Putting aside the money the average person uses in drinking and smoking, I can buy a twenty-five-pound bag of food for my pets and be no poorer.

One year, at the Fair Grounds, I was thrown from my horse and suffered a fractured skull, broken nose, and other injuries, but was out of the hospital in record time and still love horses in spite of my injuries.

I go shopping once a week for the pets and myself. The rest of the time I am alone, and keep out of everyone else's hair.

Millie has been made an honorary member of a branch of the Coast Guard, and now carries the rank of warrant officer. I cannot think of anyone who deserves it more than Nantucket's Madaket Millie.

Mary Coffin Starbuck and her eldest son Nathaniel are credited with making Quakerism the leading religion of Nantucket. Today an 1838 Quaker Meetinghouse on Fair Street is owned by the Nantucket Historical Association and is open to the public as a historic site.

William O. Stevens, in his 1936 book *Nantucket: The Far-Away Island*, wrote that most of the proper ladies of Nantucket would have looked down their noses at Deborah Chase, but "not in a literal sense unless they climbed to the second-story window." According to Stevens, Chase died in 1818.

In this chapter, Snow doesn't hint at his great personal involvement in the story of Dr. Charles Winslow and his heart, which is described in detail in his 1979 volume *Tales of Terror and Tragedy*. He first learned of the Winslow heart buried on Nantucket in 1934, and in 1946 he set out to learn more about the bizarre story.

Since many disbelieved that the doctor's heart was truly buried in his mother's grave, Snow went so far as to have the box disinterred. After permission was granted by Winslow's relatives, the box was opened. There was the heart in question, reportedly still intact.

On July 14, 1947, in the presence of Helen Irving Oehler of Texas, the great granddaughter of Dr. Charles Winslow, Edward Rowe Snow had the marble marker mentioned at the end of this chapter placed on the Winslow burial plot.

Among Madaket Millie's friends in her later years was summer Nantucket resident Fred "Mister Rogers" Rogers. Soon after she died on March 1, 1990, the Coast Guard held a remembrance ceremony in Millie's honor. According to an article by Captain Russell Webster in the United States Naval Institute *Proceedings* in August 2003: "More than 300 people from all walks of life, from seaman to admiral, from laborer to lawyer and politician, attended. A military ceremonial platoon rendered honors, and a bugler played taps. Flags at Coast Guard facilities were half-staffed in her honor. . . . At the end of the ceremony, the Coast Guard helicopter crew carefully spread her ashes over Hither Creek, forever commending her to the place she loved so dearly."

Madaket Millie's memory has been honored in a number of ways. The commodores of the Nantucket Anglers' Club established the Madaket Millie Award in 1991 to honor a woman who helped the U.S. Coast Guard "above and beyond the call of duty" during the previous year. A forty-seven-foot motor lifeboat at the Coast Guard's station at Brant Point is named the *Madaket Millie*. And in 1997 a children's book, *Madaket Millie*, was published.

CHAPTER 11

Wives of Good Samaritans

Although maritime courtesy has long been practiced out on the ocean, at times kindness at sea has ended in disaster.

Two women whose husbands were Good Samaritans each had reason later to regret certain deeds of marine benevolence performed by the men they married. Mrs. James Dawes and Madame Desnoyer, whose unhappy experiences at sea will be recorded in this chapter, often looked back on these kindly acts with sadness. In the case of the first wife it meant substantial financial loss and practical bankruptcy, and for the second, the death of the husband she loved.

In August 1847, Captain Christiansen sailed the new 1,000-ton ship *Mameluke* from New York, bound for Liverpool, with sixty-four members of the ship's company aboard. Shortly after leaving port, the *Mameluke* was overtaken by a southwest hurricane, and Captain Christiansen kept her before the wind under close-reefed topsails and reefed foresail.

When the gale increased, the fore and mizzen topsails were taken in, but scarcely had they been furled than the ship broached-to.* A tremendous sea now swept right across the deck to throw the ship on her beam ends, but she righted herself at once. Green water crashed into her deckhouse and swept forty-two persons overboard to their deaths within a few minutes. The mizzenmast was broken halfway up, the mainmast

---

* Broached-to means to lie broadside to the waves.

just below the top, the fore topmast and jib boom at the caps, and the foreyard was left a-cock-bill.*

The hurricane continued with unabated violence. The waves frequently rolled over the poop so that the survivors had to hold on for dear life to keep from being washed away.

During the next two days several vessels passed. One came so near that a man was seen on her quarterdeck surveying the *Mameluke* through a spy glass, but he did not offer help, and "passed by on the other side."

At last a small brig, the *Belize*, commanded by Captain James H. Dawes, crossed the *Mameluke's* stern, and the master of the brig hailed her.

"Be of good cheer," shouted Captain Dawes as his wife stood at his side. "I will lie by you as long as I have a stick standing." Carrying a close-reefed foretopsail and close-reefed fore-and-aft mainsail, the *Belize* rounded under the lee of the wreck, but of course the sea then was far too rough for any small boat to survive, if rescue had been attempted. Captain Dawes stayed in the company of the *Mameluke* all that day, the following night, and the next morning. Around noon the gale slowly began to moderate. The sea was still very rough, but Captain Dawes decided to make the attempt at rescue as all indications were the *Mameluke* would not stay afloat much longer.

Now hove to, Captain Dawes hoisted out the tiny brig's only boat. Manned by the mate and three seamen, the boat left only the captain, Mrs. Dawes, and one sailor on board the *Belize*. Two ladies and two men were first saved, and when Mrs. Dawes helped take the women into her quarters, they fainted from sheer exhaustion. She comforted them as best she could, after which she returned to the deck to watch the continuing rescue efforts.

Unable to take more than four or five persons at a time, the brig's boat made six trips before all were saved. Captain Christiansen was the last to leave the wreck, which shortly afterward sank beneath the waves.

Captain Dawes and his wife surrendered their berths to the ladies and slept on cots. The *Belize* sailors gave up their forecastle quarters to those survivors who were suffering from exhaustion, and joined the others sleeping on deck, but most of the men from the *Mameluke* had

---

*At an angle with the deck.

to remain on deck all the time, as there simply was not any more room below.

Captain Dawes and his wife were now faced with a difficult decision. Bound from Boston for Port-au-Prince, they realized that there was only a small amount of food aboard for such a great number of persons, and they decided that the voyage would have to be delayed while they put the survivors ashore at New York, the nearest port.

All that the captain, his wife, and crew could do as the *Belize* sailed for New York was to make the shipwrecked people comfortable, and finally the survivors were landed at their New York destination. Early the next month the brig reached Port-au-Prince, but of course long before this news of the thrilling rescue became known. Upon her return to Boston the blow fell. The party who had engaged her refused to pay the charter because the *Belize*, regardless of the reason, had deviated from her course. In vain Captain Dawes proved that most of the people he had saved would have died from exposure had he attempted to take them to the West Indies. The charterer was unrelenting, for he had "the law on his side." Captain Dawes sailed the brig on shares, so he sued the charterer, who employed Rufus Choate to defend the suit. In the meantime the *Boston Post* exposed the story.

Mr. Choate told his client that the case must be settled by arbitration, for though he had the law on his side, humanity was against him, and after the article in the *Post* no jury could be found to decide in his favor. The case was referred to arbitrators, but they confined their considerations to the financial question alone and stripped Captain Dawes and his wife of all they possessed. The captain's humanity cost him almost three thousand dollars and resulted in his bankruptcy.

After such an experience one would naturally suppose that Captain Dawes would, like many others, find it convenient to notice wrecks or ships in great distress as little as possible. To his lasting honor be it recorded that hardly had he again been placed in command before he saw a vessel in distress and went out of his way to give her relief. It was the brig *Ciudad Bolivar* in a sinking condition. At great risk he took off all hands, twelve in number, and landed them safely at a West Indian port.

Subsequently, while in command of the ship *Matchless* of Boston, of which he was part owner, Captain Dawes fell in with the Bath-built ship *Japan*. Commanded by Captain Emmons, the sailing vessel was afire off Cape Horn on her journey from Cardiff for San Francisco. Captain Dawes ran off his course and rescued all hands.

For the remainder of her life, however, although Mrs. Dawes was proud of her gallant husband, the money which he was forced to give up because of his heroism at sea was sorely needed by this Good Samaritan of the Atlantic and his wife.

In the year 1767 a French family named Desnoyer, then living at Samana, San Domingo, planned to move back to Cape Francois, where the climate was more agreeable to Madame Desnoyer, who suffered because of the warm, dry winds which constantly blew in the Bay of Samana.

Before they could sail along the coast to Cape Francois, on August 7 a mighty hurricane hit the West Indies, throwing vessels ashore up and down the coast of San Domingo. At the height of the great storm an English vessel, name unknown, smashed to pieces not far from Samana, fairly near Monsieur Desnoyer's residence. With the assistance of Monsieur Desnoyer and his associates, the entire crew of eight was saved, although the ship became a total loss. Thus, as has happened on countless occasions, the shipwrecked, penniless sailors were left stranded on a foreign shore, and Desnoyer, the Good Samaritan of San Domingo, made plans to aid the Britishers.

The kindly people of the French settlement were anxious to help the Englishmen return to their native land. Arrangements were made whereby six of the crew could leave Samana on a small French sloop. Captain John, commander of the wrecked vessel, and his mate, Mr. Young, were to accompany Monsieur Desnoyer, his wife, two children, and a servant girl in the Desnoyer sloop to Cape Francois. There it would be easy for the Englishmen to obtain passage home.

Being a kindly man, Monsieur Desnoyer provided the two shipwrecked officers with clothing from his own wardrobe, giving them the best of his linen and other wearing apparel and paying all their traveling expenses as well. Outwardly overcome with thankfulness, the two Englishmen volunteered to sail the sloop themselves, thereby saving Monsieur Desnoyer the expense of hiring two native sailors he had planned to engage for the voyage.

Departing from Samana, the sloop soon reached the port of Grigri, a league from Puerta Plata. There, in a small sheltered harbor, they decided to spend the night. Since it was warm and oppressive, everyone slept on deck. Palmetto leaves were cut to cover the afterdeck, an awning was arranged to shelter Madame Desnoyer from the sun, and a palaisselike mattress on which to sleep was provided. A mosquito netting was spread as a cover for the lady, her two children, and Catherine, the servant.

As soon as Madame Desnoyer had been made comfortable for the night, her husband placed a mattress at the foot of his wife's bed, lay down, and went to sleep. The two Englishmen had sleeping quarters forward.

At midnight the baby began to cry lustily. Desnoyer took a bottle to the ship's goat, milked her, and fed the child.

Three hours later Madame Desnoyer suddenly awoke from her deep slumber and sat up. Something was wrong, and she was frightened. She was sure that she had heard a loud thump nearby and grabbed Catherine's arm. Just as she did so she heard a terrible groan from her husband. Trembling with fear, she whispered to the maid, "Good God, Catherine! I'm terribly frightened—I believe someone has struck my husband!"

Madame Desnoyer then lifted back the mosquito netting to look at a scene of horror which she would never forget. Captain John of the shipwrecked English vessel was standing less than three feet away with a hatchet in his hand.

"I'll kill you if you try to get up!" he whispered. "Put down the netting and nothing will happen to you!"

Madame Desnoyer

Captain John then turned his attention to Desnoyer, striking him two more terrific blows with the hatchet. Desnoyer gave a final moan and expired.

Hoisting anchor, the Englishmen then bent on the sails, and Captain John ordered Mr. Young to take the wheel. By daybreak the sloop was two leagues from shore.

Now that he was far enough from land, Captain John returned to the afterdeck, picked up the dead body of Monsieur Desnoyer, and carried it to the side. Then he went back for the blood-stained mattress, threw it into the water, and tossed the lifeless body of his Good Samaritan benefactor upon it. The mattress soon began to float away with its grisly burden.

Next the English murderer summoned Madame Desnoyer.

"Make yourself easy, madame," he said, "for your husband is merely taking a sound nap."

Shortly afterward a breeze sprung up, and within an hour the mangled body on its strange bier drifted out of sight.

While Mate Young kept his post at the wheel of the sloop, Captain John began to rummage about the cabin. Several hours went by with the sound of utter confusion coming from below. Finally the captain returned on deck where Madame Desnoyer was awaiting him.

"Where are your husband's keys to his strong boxes?"

The good woman, realizing the futility of resisting, handed the keys to the murderer. Then she summoned courage to speak.

"Why under God did you repay our kindness with murder? Have you an answer which can possibly explain the killing of the man who saved you from shipwreck and death?"

"Of course I have," came the reply. "I wanted to get this ship and that was the only way to do it. Can't you understand that?"

The captain went below, returning shortly afterward with food, tea, and chocolate, which he offered to the widow.

"I can never break bread or drink with my husband's murderer!" exclaimed Madame Desnoyer and turned away.

Later she relented in order to keep her strength and provide help for the rest of her party. Finally, in an effort to save her children, she even gave in to the advances of the pirate.

That night, as the two women again huddled under the mosquito netting with the children, they heard the Englishmen arguing violently near the foremast. Captain John was attempting to persuade the mate that he would have to take the slave as his mistress since he, the captain, had already taken Madame Desnoyer for himself. But neither man would give in. They secured the helm for the night and were soon asleep, their argument unsettled.

Near her side, Madame Desnoyer felt the girl, Catherine, stirring uneasily.

"Madame," she whispered. "I have a long nail with which I can put out their eyes. Shall I try now?"

But Madame Desnoyer, realizing that Catherine would probably fail in carrying out her plan, told her to give it up.

At dawn the next day Captain John appeared again and Madame Desnoyer implored him to let her go ashore. Smilingly John explained that he would permit her, her family, and her worldly goods to go aboard the canoe* which was on deck and he would have his mate paddle them ashore that very afternoon, for they were not yet out of sight of land.

"Pack up your linen in a bundle," Captain John instructed, "and get everything out of your trunks which you wish. There isn't room in the canoe for anything but the four of you and your bundles. Make haste now!"

The Englishmen then put aboard the craft a small mattress, four biscuits, a bottle containing four quarts of water, six eggs, and a few cuts of salt pork.

An hour before sunset the little family was taken across to the stern. Mr. Young first put the children and the servant and then Madame Desnoyer in the canoe, after which he stepped up onto the deck of the sloop. The two women looked up at the ruffian, their faces reflecting great apprehension.

"Aren't you coming to take us ashore?" Madame Desnoyer implored.

"Sorry, but I changed my mind. It's easier this way," answered Young, as he pulled out a sheath-knife and severed the line holding the craft to the vessel. Both Madame Desnoyer and Catherine began to shriek at the inhumanity of this villainous act, but the ship soon left them behind. Around dusk they saw the last of the vessel, miles away, sailing into the reflection of the rising moon.

All that long night the two women tried to console each other in their misery, but shortly before dawn Madame Desnoyer collapsed. She did

---

*A West Indian canoe is considerably broader of beam than its American counterpart.

not revive until noon. When she regained consciousness, she realized that this was no nightmare, that she was alone indeed with her two children and Catherine on the West Indian Ocean.

Late in the afternoon the wind, which had been fairly calm, increased in strength, and soon the little canoe was bouncing up and down on the ocean, buffeted by every wave.

Then Madame Desnoyer saw that they were drifting toward a shoal, where waves were breaking. For a time they thought they would escape, but suddenly a gigantic comber swept toward them, slid over the gunwale, and filled the canoe. With a foot of water in the boat, everything floated around in confusion. Before they could rescue anything, however, another wave came rushing at them, still more dangerous with its foaming crest. Madame Desnoyer clutched her baby while Catherine held on to the other child. The second billow swept over them and went on, leaving them safe for the moment, and the two women began frantically to bail. They did not realize for some time that the waves had swept overboard their fresh water and their biscuits, leaving only the salt pork and eggs.

That morning the sun rose hotter than usual, soon beating down with great force on the little party alone in the sea. Madame Desnoyer prayed that she might be spared to bring her children ashore alive, but night came without help of any sort.

Another day brought no relief. That third night adrift the last egg was fed to the children, and only the salt pork remained.

By this time the baby was crying piteously in its need for milk and water. Madame Desnoyer thought of opening a vein in her arm to allow the baby to drink her blood, but she decided to wait until the last possible moment before carrying out this desperate scheme to keep her child alive.

Finally, on the seventh day after they had been adrift, Madame Desnoyer told Catherine her terrible plan to save the infant.

The girl cried in alarm, "You cannot do such a thing, mistress, for your life must be saved for the sake of your children! Please, Madame Desnoyer, wait just a few more hours."

That very afternoon Madame was slumbering as best she could when Catherine's voice awakened her. "Quick, madame, a sail!"

Indeed it was a sail, that of a merchantman. Within the hour the great ship with its white sails was bearing down on the little canoe, and its passengers soon knew without question that they had been seen.

Unfortunately, the wind had freshened meanwhile and when the merchantman drew alongside it was dangerously rough. The ship was brought about, and two sailors leaped into the canoe to help the survivors clamber aboard to safety.

Readily giving up his quarters for Madame Desnoyer, the captain listened in horror to the story he heard from her lips. A few days later the mainland of Louisiana was in sight, and the next noon the ship's anchor rattled down in the New Orleans roadstead.

The plight of the pitiful little group was made known, and a relative, Monsieur Bougeot, was sent for. When he arrived at the ship, he embraced the members of the Desnoyer family and promised that he would do what he could to aid them. Taken to his home, Madame Desnoyer, her children and Catherine slowly recuperated. A week later they learned to their joy that the inhabitants of Louisiana had raised a subscription for their relief.

Before the month was over Madame Desnoyer had regained the strength she had lost during her terrible ordeal. Deciding to liberate Catherine, she was told by the bonded servant girl that she would have none of it.

"Nothing but death will part us now," the faithful Catherine announced.

A complaint had been lodged with the officials at New Orleans by Madame Desnoyer, together with a careful description of her husband's vessel, the two Englishmen, and the planned destination of the craft, but nothing further was ever heard of them. They probably sailed right to Bermuda, where they were able to repaint the name of the craft and sell her.

For the remainder of her life Madame Desnoyer never forgot that year of 1767, when the shipwreck of an English vessel on the shores of San Domingo brought eventual tragedy as a consequence of a Good Samaritan's help to shipwrecked sufferers.

CHAPTER 12

Navigator Hannah

Hannah Rebecca Crowell Burgess, a native of Cape Cod, Massachusetts, had the rare distinction of taking charge of a full-rigged clipper ship and navigating her off the coast of South America.

Her story begins in 1850, at the time when a young mariner, William H. Burgess, first met her. Hannah was then fifteen. After due consideration she decided that she liked the attractive Cape Cod sailor. The two promised to correspond during his coming voyage to India, and he soon sailed away aboard the ship *Herbert*, then commanded by the famous Captain Bangs Hallett of Yarmouth. Twenty-one-year-old William was the first mate.

The *Herbert* had a successful voyage. While at sea William wrote Hannah, whom he called Rebecca, several letters, including in them his vows that he would attempt to give up swearing, which was one of the principal objections Hannah had to him as a suitor. According to his letters he was also saying his daily prayers which Hannah had stressed as very important for the success of their future relationship.

Returning to Cape Cod after the voyage, William went at once to Hannah and told her that as he was to be captain on the next voyage of the *Herbert*, he was anxious for her answer to a very important question. Would she marry him? She accepted his proposal, and when he sailed away from Boston on September 17, 1851, William was a happy, engaged man.

On the voyage out he carried away his flying jibboom and split the sail-ends a short time later when he encountered "brisk breezes from the S.S.E." The *Herbert* arrived at Sand Heads off Calcutta in 119 days. Starting back to Boston on February 5, he successfully completed his voyage on July 17, 1852.

His log, now in the Sandwich Glass Museum on Cape Cod, tells us that he performed the voyage in "10 months to a day." He goes on to say that having been "mate of said ship 18 months and Master 10, I now resign her to her former and able Commander, Bangs Hallett, Esq., wishing her pleasant and successful voyages."

He hurried to Sandwich and his intended bride. It was agreed that their marriage would be performed by Reverend Benjamin L. Sawyer on August 5, 1852. Before the wedding took place, however, William was offered the command of the *Whirlwind*, a great clipper ship then building at Medford, Massachusetts, and he accepted at once.

The happy couple were married as scheduled and went to Boston for their honeymoon, moving into rooms at Fountain Place, off Hanover Street. Hannah started her diary that very day. The first page has been cut from it, and the first existing entry reads as follows:

> *Boston, August 7, A.D. 1852*
>
> *After dinner William hired a horse and carriage and took me out to Medford. The ship* Whirlwind *is building in that town. I enjoyed my ride very much. He introduced me to Mr. George Curtis, the ship-builder's son, and in company with him I went to his mother's. . . . The ship is now far along. The owners are Mr. Newell, Mr. Charles, and Frank Whitmore. The shipbuilder James O. Curtis is a very pleasant man. Opposite to Mr. C. is a very ancient building owned by an old lady. In front it is surrounded by a very high wall, and is situated some distance from the road. Beautiful trees and shrubbery engage the attention of the passerby. I was much pleased with the general appearance of this town.*

On August 11 came the day "distinguished in the annals of history by the celebrated Cape Cod Association of Provincetown," according to Hannah. This was the occasion for an annual trip to Cape Cod made by people who were born there.

That Wednesday morning it rained furiously, but two boats were waiting at the Boston pier for the long sail across Massachusetts Bay. The first boat, the *Eastern City*, had already been filled to capacity when the bride and groom arrived, and so they took the second.

"I was rather sick, but not having eaten any breakfast, I could not vomit," writes Hannah. "There were several ladies on board and we got along finely. First one would run to the closet and heave, then another. Real sport."

The sun came out as they rounded the hook of the Cape, and the waves went down almost at once. Hannah later recorded that she never enjoyed herself "in one day better in my life."

All the passengers were welcomed by James Gifford, one of Cape Cod's leading citizens, whose remarks of welcome were answered by visiting Chief Justice Lemuel Shaw.

The parade marshal, Colonel John L. Dimmock, soon had the order of procession arranged, and the entire assembly then marched through the town to a natural amphitheater, which was surrounded on three sides by hills. Here a mammoth tent had been set up, and scores of beautifully decorated tables were awaiting the visitors. As soon as all were seated, the pretty Provincetown waitresses began serving the food with great promptness, impressing Hannah with their charm and friendliness.

After the banquet and the program which followed it, William took Hannah for a walk, but she was not attracted to the sandy barrenness of Provincetown.

"They have plank walks so in this point they are rather in advance of their sister towns, but I did not observe any horses, so I suppose their plank sidewalks were as a substitute."

The stormy morning had somewhat cut down the attendance at the celebration, but Hannah estimated that there had been several thousand present. At seven-thirty that evening they took the *Eastern City* back to Boston. The young bride found it still very rough and was seasick.

"I was so dizzy it took two or three men to steady me while reaching the settee," she writes. "A gentleman wishing to do all he could for the afflicted gave me some brandy, which he said would ease me, and it did for I vomited quite well. Yes, lost all my nice dinner for which we paid $2."

Hannah explained that in spite of one of the members giving her brandy, the object of the Association "was to encourage industry and temperance," and it was composed for the most part of merchants in Boston who had formerly lived on the Cape. "It has been the happiest day of my married life," Hannah concludes, "may I be thankful for this privilege to God." The *Eastern City* did not get back to the Boston pier until one o'clock in the morning.

Hannah often commented on the restless nature of her husband. On August 16, the occasion of her first arrival at her home after their marriage, she stated that "William must go directly to the village to hire a carriage to go to Brewster." The very next day, William "could not content himself to stay in the house, so he gets Grandfather Howes to go down in the meadow and get a load of hay."

On August 18 Hannah became indoctrinated with some maritime customs. While they were visiting at the Brewster home of Captain Joseph H. Sears, her husband cautioned her that when addressing masters of ships she must not say "Mister" but "Captain."

"I tried to please him," she writes, "but once in a few minutes it would be 'Mr. Sears.'" She learned from Mrs. Sears that she "had been to sea, but she said she did not like it. There was a monotony, nothing to look at but the blue waste of waters. No one to converse with and see; no one but the sailors. Ah! . . . I should wish for no better company than my husband. He is the best of all to me."

On Thursday evening, August 29, the couple took a ride out to Medford to see the *Whirlwind*, the following Monday having been set for the launching from the Curtis yard. They inspected the beautiful figurehead "which was the Goddess of the Winds, holding a torch."

On Monday morning, at nine o'clock, the *Whirlwind** slid down the ways and into the Mystic River, "stopping in the stream." The terrific excitement associated with the launching gave way to a relatively dull afternoon, and Hannah did not enjoy herself, being "quite lonely," for her husband and Mr. Curtis had gone out to Spy Pond. "How can a country girl amuse herself without anything to employ her hands about?" she asked in her logbook. One thing she did do, and that was knit. While visiting one day at a Mr. Dillingham's she began knitting a white stocking. "I suppose I lowered myself in their estimation a great deal by this act. Mrs. Dillingham said she never knit a stitch in her life, but would like to knit just one stocking just for the name of it. It is not considered an accomplishment for a city lady to know how to knit."

By Thursday the clipper ship had been taken to Charlestown where her spars were being set. An accident occurred a short time later when the *Whirlwind* keeled over, and it was several days before all was well again.

---

*Her measurements were 185 feet long, 38 feet beam, with a 21-foot draft. Her tonnage was 960 44/95.

On November 9, as the sailing date for San Francisco neared, William asked Hannah to visit the *Whirlwind* to see the cabin where he would spend the greater part of the next year. Hannah was enjoying her visit when it was discovered that they would have to spend the night aboard, as the clipper had just grounded. Hannah records:

> I was very much disappointed on learning the boat had left the shore and we would have to pass the night on board, but I had rather be with my husband let it be where it would be.
>
> I was ready in the morning to leave the ship. I did not like the sight of it, since on it my best and truest friend was to leave me. . . .
>
> William went on shore with me on Wednesday morning, but on going to the store* found Mother B. and the girls there awaiting our arrival. It was a sober time for all of us. I could not weep but the girls showed their sorrow on parting with their only brother by weeping profusely. They bid him farewell and went to school, but did not see him again.
>
> William left the store, saying he did not think he would sail that day, but at 1 P.M. Mr. Crocker, the ship keeper came to the house with a note saying that William had indeed started on his voyage.
>
> I then felt bad. We had not even said farewell, but he had gone. I took to my room, and sitting by the window reflected on my situation. Thought I, many lonely hours I shall pass e'er my William's return, but I shall trust in the Lord. . . .
>
> While there reflecting Uncle Louis Howes came in, and in a few minutes the doorbell rang again, and it was for me—a note in the handwriting of my dear husband.
>
> Oh, how my heart leaped for joy on opening to learn he wished me to come immediately to the ship. He was becalmed, and let the cost be what it would, I must come.
>
> I enjoyed myself in the company of my husband, knowing that my stay must be short, but became quite interested in the passengers going in the Whirlwind. They appeared very pleasant and agreeable. One young lady, Miss T., would suit me for a companion, but I am not going.

---

*The store, Benjamin F. Burgess & Sons, was located at 28 India Wharf. It was a commission house.

Thursday, Nov. 11, A.D. 1852

This morning at 8 o'clock my husband sailed for California.* According to agreement the steamboat came for me. . . . It was truly a solemn moment to us all. Never did I witness such a scene before, nor wish so much to be with my husband, but it was of no avail. Much as I love him, we must part.

William stepped on the deck of the boat to bid me farewell, and never shall I forget his countenance. For four months we had been nearly all of the time in each other's society, and since our marriage had not been separated even for one night.

It seemed like a dream, that it could not be in reality that William could be gone so long. The passengers were straining their eyes to notice how the captain's wife appeared, but I think they were disappointed as she did not manifest her feelings. We parted—William to traverse the trackless deep, I to return to my native home until his return.

A page has been torn from the diary, but as the dates often leap back and forth the exact time of the page which is missing can only be approximated.

---

*Captain William H. Burgess was about to participate in one of the great mass clipper ship races of all time. When he sailed the *Whirlwind* from Boston for San Francisco on November 11, 1852, he entered the Golden Gate classic clipper ship derby.

Others in that never-to-be-forgotten sea drama were Captain George Putnam of the *Wild Pigeon*; James Miller of the *Dauntless*; Ashbel Hubbard of the *Flying Dutchman*; Joseph P. Johnson of the *Westward Ho*; Freeman Hatch of the *Northern Light*; Justus Doane of the *John Gilpin*; Edward C. Nickels of the *Flying Fish*; Elias D. Knight of the *Queen of the Seas*; Daniel McLaughlin of the *Grey Feather*; Nathaniel Webber of the *Trade Wind*; George W. Pousland of the *Telegraph*; W. E. Brewster of the *Contest*; Lewis G. Hollis of the *Game Cock*; and Samuel W. Pike of the *Meteor*.

Captain Burgess's showing was neither the best nor the worst. His time was 121 days. *Flying Fish* made the passage in ninety-two days, four hours and won the derby. Hannah later recorded that at least the *Whirlwind* beat the *Queen of the Seas* by a full week.

On arriving home I found Uncle Louis. Mary Emma and Lydia Abby were crying at a great rate. M. says to me "Why Rebecca, don't you miss William. I should think you would cry, too." Of course she loved her brother and felt bad on learning of his departure, but she little knew the deep anguish that filled my breast on parting with my husband. She was young and inexperienced and has yet to learn that "light sorrows speak, great grief is dumb." This afternoon seemed long indeed. I wept and smiled by turns, but I was lonely.

Boston, November 18
This morning I went to visit my uncle in Louisburg Square. . . . It was a lovely day and all nature seemed to rejoice. . . . My mind was ever on one subject, my absent husband. Right glad I was when the Common appeared in sight, when the State House and at length the well-known Mall which indicated my journey was completed. . . . I always felt contented and at home when at Uncle B's and now more than ever it did seem good. . . . I felt calm for the first time since William sailed to enjoy myself. . . . As I was seated with Uncle and Aunt in the evening I suffered my thoughts to dwell upon this aged couple. I looked at Uncle and thus soliloquize, "Thou art passing away, but many are the years of thy sojourn on this earth."

Hannah Rebecca did not write in her journal for almost a year after that above entry. Her next entry was on the last day of October, 1853:

October 31, 1853
West Sandwich. Silently and surely moves the wheel of time as I take my pen. Indeed. . . . I pause, for long is the time between my former date and the present time. Winter, stern winter, which was then approaching, has come and past. Spring . . . in its turn swept by, succeeded by the happy summer. Summer, too, has left us, and now autumn's rude blasts are heard. A year will soon have passed since that trying hour when I took the parting hand of my beloved husband and dropped the silent tear. . . . William will soon return.

William did return, and the couple were so overcome at seeing each other again that after a happy second honeymoon it was arranged for Hannah to go with her husband on his next trip aboard the *Whirlwind*. Hannah now tells us about her life on the bounding main.

On board the ship Whirlwind at sea, February 24, 1854
N. Lat. 13:550 Long. 35:09 West.

It was just three weeks ago today since I left the City of New York
to spend a short time on the ocean. It seems impossible that it could be
so long, so pleasantly has the time passed. I delight to think of the
happy past, for my life thus far has been one of joy and contentment,
but it seems to be I never was more blest than at the present. . . .

It has been very pleasant today, and we have made some progress
in our voyage to California. The Whirlwind is a first-rate sailing
ship. Only give her favorable winds, and I think her accommodations
are very good. . . . We shall soon be at the equator.

I expected to be seasick, and in fact I had made up my mind to
experience all the horrors attendant upon this affliction, but it so happened I had my sickness on the land and therefore escaped the worst
of all feelings, seasickness. I was sick, confined to my room a week
before I came to sea and went out of it the first time on Saturday morning, February 4, the day the Whirlwind sailed. . . . Today my husband is twenty-five years old.

February 26, 1854

Lat. 10.13 N., Long. 33.28 W. It is Sunday evening, the fourth
Sunday I have passed aboard the Whirlwind. Oh, it is a delightful
evening to me with a good breeze. We are sailing along at a rate of
ten miles an hour, and I enjoy it very much. It is warm and we may
expect it to be much more so. I do not like warm weather, but can get
along very well I think.

For breakfast I had a nice treat consisting of a flying fish fried. It
came, or rather it flew on board and was caught. I never ate anything
so nice, and should esteem it a great luxury should we have them at
our wish. We have an excellent steward. He cooks better than I can,
I am confident. The ship is supplied with provisions of every kind,
and I am enjoying myself as well as any person can who has their
husband's society and everything else convenient and comfortable. I
delight to be on deck and watch the motion of the sea. Oh, it
impresses me sensibly with an assurance that God is a just and holy
being.

As I gaze on old ocean's heaving bosom, I feel to exclaim in the language of the Holy Writ, wonderful are thy works, Oh Lord, in wisdom has thou made them all.

Another sabbath has rolled on and how different does it seem on this sacred day at sea from what it does at home. It seems hardly possible that it can be Sunday. How rapidly the time passes away on board the ship. Why, it seems but yesterday that we left New York, and we are many miles from that city. The last 24 hours the ship has sailed 270 miles. A good day's work. How pleasant it would be if we sailed at this rate all the way to California. I hope we shall have a short passage and meet with no disasters, particularly as the captain has his wife with him, and I have often heard it remarked that they bring bad luck. For my own part, I see no reason for the saying.

Two weeks ago today was the first time I went on deck. It was blowing very hard, and I thought I should never get used to the motion of the ship. I remember well how reviving the sea breeze felt and I think it very healthy to inhale it, and would like to sit in the house and meditate on the situation. Am I in truth on the sea? I sometimes think of my native home and get so wrapped up in the scenes gone by that I imagine I am still there and not that countless miles separate me from my youthful home. Once in no other place than my native town could I be happy. No other friends could please me but my parents and relatives. Now where my husband is, there is my home. May it ever be thus. Again am I permitted in the kind providence of God to resume my favorite occupation, that of writing my thoughts.

Later Hannah recorded the names of the officers aboard the *Whirlwind*. The first officer was Charles F. Moury, the second Jacob Versus Whittemore, and the fourth officer Charles Isaac Gibbs, but she did not record the third officer's name after leaving a space for the information. There were twenty-four men before the mast making in all "33 persons aboard the *Whirlwind* bound for San Francisco, California."

Hannah was particularly homesick on February 27. "Oh, I wonder what the folks are doing in good old Scusset tonight. I should like to step in for a few minutes and greet them," she remarked.

On Friday, March 31, the *Whirlwind* was abeam of the Jasons, part of the Faulkland [Falkland] Islands, from which Captain Burgess and his wife worked out a new departure. By this time Hannah was expert at taking the sun and figuring out the intricate tasks of navigation, which her husband willingly entrusted to her. This knowledge was to prove very important later. She writes that she had "been looking over all the books I can find, to get instruction regarding these islands and find by reference to *Maury's Sailing Directions* that since 1831 they have been taken possession of by the British Government."

At seven o'clock on Sunday, April 2, a ship was sighted which proved to be the *Tinqua*,* commanded by Captain Whitmore.

On Monday, April 3, the land of Tierra del Fuego was sighted. At 2 P.M.., "wore ship offshore, at 8 closereefed topsail, steered courses, at 9 P.M. took in fore and mizzen topsail, split the foretopmast staysail, unbent it and bent new one," Hannah wrote.

During the period of calm on Sunday, April 2, the *Whirlwind* and the *Tinqua* sailed along side by side, and Captain Whitmore decided to visit the *Whirlwind*. Unfortunately, while he was aboard, the wind came up, and he did not venture to leave the clipper to return to his own craft for some time. Meanwhile the *Whirlwind*'s second officer had gone aboard the *Tinqua* for a visit.

Hannah remained on deck for two hours watching the movement of the two craft and enjoying it to the utmost, for as she recorded, "What can be more exciting than to meet another ship when far out on the ocean?"

When night set in Captain Whitmore, nervous about losing his own command, decided to accept the offer to sleep on the cabin sofa. Hannah watched him carefully as he tried to adjust to the situation.

"I could not help smiling at each lurch of the ship to see Captain Whitmore roll off the sofa. He would take the berth for a few minutes and then try the sofa again."

Indeed it was rough that Sunday night off Cape Horn. They did not sight the *Tinqua* all day Monday, but Whitmore was relieved when on Tuesday, the 4th, his ship again appeared in view, bearing down at a brisk clip on the waiting *Whirlwind*. Hannah writes:

> *At 5 P.M. a boat left her bringing on board of the* Whirlwind *our second officer [and returning] Mr. Whitmore and two men that left with him. Captain Whitmore was glad to see his ship again I'll bet. We felt it to be almost miraculous, as we had not seen the* Tinqua *for 24 hours.*

Tinqua was launched at Portsmouth, New Hampshire, October 2, 1852. Her measurements were 145 by 31.9 by 19 and her tonnage 668. Named for a merchant of Canton, the *Tinqua* proudly wore as figurehead a ferocious dragon. Captain Jacob D. Whitmore superintended her construction and became her commander. She was lost on Cape Hatteras in 1855.

Captain Whitmore left the Whirlwind *as soon as the boat reached our ship, and discharged her passengers. . . . We stood on the deck and watched the boat as it bounded over the waving billows, and I could hardly repress a sigh as it rose on one wave, then seemed to descend and for a moment was hidden from my view. . . .*

I was quite confident that we should keep company with the Tinqua, *but it proved otherwise. We saw her until 11 P.M., after which it was thick and objects were indistinguishable.*

Mr. James Whitmore, the first officer of the Tinqua, *sent me a book entitle* Japan *and a bottle of port wine. . . . Mr. W. brought a little kitten off with him. Oh, it is a darling little thing and answers very well for a pet. We have now a dog and a kitten in the cabin.*

Hannah did not like Cape Horn at all. " 'Ease her when she pitches!' is the command to the man at the wheel. We go along for about five minutes very well, then it is Pitch! Pitch! and away flies everything movable," she reports.

Enjoying regular meals off Cape Horn was especially difficult. Sometimes, Hannah explained, one might be telling a story while at dinner when suddenly the ship lurches. A combination of hot tea and soup "is running on your clothes."

She wrote of a fearful Sunday night when the storm staysail split. "I should have liked to have been on deck then," she admits, "even though it meant being lashed to the rigging."

Hannah spoke of the terrible cold weather off Cape Horn and the necessity of wearing a shawl and furs nearly all the time. The only way to really get warm, she wrote, was to go to bed.

On May 15, 100 days out, they crossed the equator, but everyone by that time had given up all expectation of a quick passage to California.

On Friday, May 19, they were 104 days out. Hannah mentioned the beautiful sunset of the night before. Saturday, May 20, she was busy all day making William a pair of linen pants, a job that she had never attempted before but one at which she admits succeeding admirably.

Several dolphins were sighted May 21, and one was caught. Hannah speaks of the enjoyable breakfast of fried dolphin meat. That afternoon William "caught" a large quantity of water and put his clothes in to soak. Hannah also mentioned the baffling wind, which shifted and veered about from every quarter and then settled down into a calm again. The afternoon ended with roast beef for dinner.

The days went by with no favorable winds, and the clipper practically crawled toward her goal. On Saturday, June 3, a ship appeared in sight. She proved to be a Dutch vessel with no royal yard, and so the officers said that she could not possibly keep up with the *Whirlwind*. They were right, for soon she was hull down astern.

Hannah did not write in her diary between Thursday, June 8 and June 13, 1854, her last entry in the log, dated at San Francisco. She often left blank spaces and planned to fill them in, but she seldom did.

The *Whirlwind** returned east, and the couple went back to Cape Cod. Details of this period are lacking. Captain William Burgess was given a new command, the extreme clipper ship *Challenger*† which had been launched by Robert E. Jackson at East Boston. Captain T. Hill had already made the first voyage in the *Challenger*.

Hannah decided to make another trip with her husband, and this decision led to the most important and unusual event of her life. By this time Hannah was an expert navigator and, according to her husband and the other officers, could calculate her position at sea with the best captains of the period. Day after day she took the sun and recorded her calculations with exactness and speed. But she did not write in her new journal until eight days at sea from Boston. As usual, she left many blank pages in the new logbook, but never filled them in.

The *Challenger* had sailed on June 2, 1855, and Hannah's initial entry mentioned that they left at 11 A.M. "Cast off steamer *Enoch Train* and made all necessary sail." Hannah recorded:

> *On board the ship* Challenger *at sea June 10, 1855*
> *Lat. from Meridian Observation 39-45 north 44-51 west. Sunday the day set apart from the foundation of the world as a day of rest and sacred to the Lord finds me again on the broad ocean and with a thankful heart to the giver of all good. I have taken my pen to commence my journal.*
> *It is a very pleasant day and I feel as happy as ever in my life. I*

---

*She was last reported at Calcutta, November 27, 1860, and nothing further is known of her.

†Launched December 19, 1853, the *Challenger*'s measurements were 206 by 38.4 by 223. Her tonnage was 1,334, old style.

should very much like to attend divine service but praise the Lord. A
lovely afternoon, going ahead at ten knots.
We have an excellent cook and steward.

Hannah spoke later of Miss Sarah C. Taber, a passenger for Washington, and then began to put down the distance sailed since leaving Boston, but did not fill it in. Her next important entry, however, included a note of danger.

June 10, 1855
All in cabin appear in good health, but there are a number of sailors
sick. And we think one has the smallpox. This infectious disease, once
on board, has been known to wipe off an entire crew. . . . sick on
board ship is not like being sick at home. One year ago we were in
San Francisco. Where shall we be another year? I am finding it very
difficult to write today as I can scarcely preserve my equilibrium. I
think I must try to be a little more punctual in writing my journal, or
my journal will not be filled. Nothing has occurred since we left
Boston. I like the Challenger *very much. She is a much better sailor*
than the Whirlwind *and 400 tons larger. My writing looks so bad I*
will not write any more today.

Sunday, July 29, 1855
Time in its hasty strides has brought us to see the commencement of
another week. All well. We have had many changes of wind and
calm. We are a long way astern of the Whirlwind's *last voyage.*
Fifty-five days from New York we made Jason Island, one of the
Faulklands. It is too bad to have such hard luck.

October 8, 1855
Made the Farralon [Farallon] Islands, distance eight miles. At 8:30
came to anchor on the bar and laid all night. One hundred thirty-three
days passage from Boston and very glad that it is no worse.

Going ashore in San Francisco, William and Hannah probably enjoyed visits to the principal places of interest, but there is little in her journal concerning this. In fact, she did not write in it again until the following month, when she was starting another long voyage with her husband on the *Challenger*.

Certain thoughts concerning him have been recorded by Hannah from time to time. "I am happy in the love of my husband," she once wrote, "yet one thing grieves me; he does not carry out those principles he once professed to sustain. In his letters written to me at sea, he appeared to enjoy sweet communion with his God. Oh, that he might again experience this happy feeling!"

On another occasion, after working on his vocabulary for three months in her campaign against his swearing, she recorded that he was doing better, and his swearing was not so frequent. Nevertheless she noticed that her husband was fond of planning work "for others to do," but admitted that his patience was improving.

The *Challenger* sailed toward the Far East from San Francisco on Friday, November 9, arriving at the Hawaiian Islands on Tuesday, November 20. She departed from Honolulu on Friday, November 23, and Hannah continued her chronicle:

> *Having got into the writing humor this evening, I think I will spoil the looks of another side of my journal. I do not think of writing so long when I commence, but it is seldom I get a chance to write, the ship rolls so.*

Mrs. Doris Kershaw with a picture of the clipper ship Challenger *which Mrs. Hannah Rebecca Burgess navigated safely to port in 1856 following the death of the captain, her husband*

We have agreeable companions in the persons of Mr. Alden and a lady, passengers to China. Mr. Jackson, the gentleman who came out to San Francisco in the ship is still with us, and we have quite a curiosity in the form of a Chinaman, a cabin passenger from Honolulu.

Sunday evening, 9 P.M. Thursday November 29th, 1855.
A day set apart for public Thanksgiving and praise with us on board. It was a day of some note. At 12 o'clock we were in Long. 179.30 W. and of course in sailing west we gain time and must drop a day. So Thursday, Thanksgiving Day at our home, witnessed our departure from west into east longitude. We had no Friday, but passed over it.

Hannah's health had been poor for about two months. Several in the crew were also sick. Her own sickness was finally conquered, as the next item indicated:

One thing which I wish particularly to speak of is my health. I am happy to write that it is very much improved and now feel well. We had a turkey for dinner and since leaving the Sandwich Islands I have eaten twelve little pigeons. Well I think I have done well to write so long. I will now cease for the present. . . .

Sunday evening, December 2, 1855
We are now on our way to Hong Kong having on board 350 Chinese passengers. They are very peaceable and quiet, and we get along finely. I am anticipating having a fine time in China, yet I don't think it possible to enjoy myself better in any part of the world than during my last day in San Francisco. I enjoyed myself during the twenty-six days we lay at that port as much as it is possible for you and I to enjoy this world's gifts. It is six months ago since we sailed from Boston. How rapidly time passes. We left Boston the second day of summer and passe into cold weather. Now the second day of winter we are in warm summer weather while at home it is cold.

On December 18 occurred the first of three deaths on board the *Challenger*, the final one of which would affect Hannah's future existence. Hannah's words follow:

Lost from the main topmast rigging, Frederic D. Magoun, seaman. He was at work setting up the ratlines. In his descent he passed through the mainsail, which was clewed up and injured himself by contact with the spars, as to sink in a moment. No assistance could be rendered. Poor fellow he is gone, in a moment hurried from time to eternity. He was a lovely youth and oh, how much would I sacrifice to bring him back to life. Oh, I loved that young man, a very interesting youth of twenty years. May he be at rest with God is my desire. How uncertain is life, and yet how unmindful we are of death.

Hannah's next entry was made on December 19, 1855, after the arrival of the *Challenger* at Hong Kong, and is a recapitulation of the trip to that city:

November 9th, sailed from San Francisco for Hong Kong, via Honolulu. Friday discharged pilot at six o'clock in the afternoon. November 20th arrived at Honolulu Tuesday, took a pilot at 2 P.M. November 21st, sailed from Honolulu at four in the afternoon. November 30th, Lat. 19.26 N., passe from west longitude to the east. We are 36 sailing days from San Francisco, have had pleasant weather and sailed 5,051 miles, averaging 200 miles a day from Honolulu and from San Francisco to this port, 7,000 miles, averaging 200 miles a day the whole time. The greatest day's work we have made is 290 miles.

Her next entry was from Wampoa, which is on the Pearl River, not far from Canton.

January 9, A.D. 1856

On board ship Challenger *lying at Wampoa Beach, Thursday evening. We are still lying at this place, although ready for sea. The* Challenger *arrived in Hong Kong three weeks ago yesterday and sailed for Wampoa on Christmas Day, Monday, December 25, A.D. 1855. We are now bound to London direct and we hope we get away on Saturday. I do not like this place at all, and feel no regret in leaving it. Captain Burgess has just returned from Canton for the last time. I was in Canton Monday. It is a disagreeable place in my estimation.*

She speaks of four craft:

> N. B. Palmer, *Captain Charles P. Lowe from New York direct,*
> *120 days; ship* Fleetwing, *Captain Howes, arrived yesterday, going*
> *into dock; ship* Rabbit, *Captain Richard Corning, is loading for New*
> *York with tea.*
> *The ship* Highflyer, *Captain Waterman, is supposed to be lost.*
> *She sailed some twenty days before us from San Francisco. The Cap-*
> *tain had his wife with him.*

The *Highflyer* was a medium clipper ship, launched from Currier and Townsend's yard in Newburyport in 1853. Her measurements were 180 by 38 by 25, and she was of 1,195 tons, old style. She left San Francisco on October 25, 1855, and was never heard from again, but evidence indicates that she was captured and set afire by Chinese pirates who may have made up part of the 300 passengers.

In any case, a wreck similar in size and shape to the *Highflyer* was later found stranded and burned. On inspection, the searchers discovered a telescope which was identified as belonging to Captain Gordon B. Waterman, the *Highflyer's* master, but the evidence was not conclusive. No American aboard was ever seen again.

Finally the *Challenger* sailed for London. Hannah's words follow:

> *Sunday, January 20th*
> *Out six days. Sunday afternoon. We are again on the seas, but not*
> *as yet on the ocean, but trust to the providence of God to be in the*
> *Indian Ocean e'er many days. I can hardly realize that we have vis-*
> *ited the celestial empire so short does the time seem since we were in*
> *San Francisco. But it is ever thus. Time is progressing and waiting for*
> *no man.*

The second of the three deaths to which I have referred occurred the second week in February.

> *Sunday, February 10th*
> *Died on board ship* Challenger *of dysentery, James O'Neil, sea-*
> *man. He left nothing to designate his nativity. Has been sick since*
> *leaving Wampoa and was reduced to a skeleton. How sad the thought*
> *to die in a strange land and among strange people, but ah, how sad*

to die on shipboard. Indeed the sailor's life is a singular one, a life spent on ocean's bosom, and often he finds it his long home. Oh, that I may not share the fate of the man and be at rest beneath the swelling tide. The deceased has probably followed the sea from early youth. Of his history we know nothing.

Sunday, February 24
Forty-one days from Canton. During the past week we have experienced much squally weather. I have just been on deck and I see a little flaw having struck us. An English ship is way astern.
Spoke the whale ship Eliza L. B. Jenney. *Three weeks ago Capt. Marsh got his boat out very early and came on board of us. William returned with him and came back at four P.M., when a little breeze springing up, we sailed right past her leaving her at dark hull down. The* Eliza *belongs to Fairhaven.*

On reaching London the *Challenger* was soon loaded for a trip to Callao, Peru, after which a stop at the Chincha Islands for guano was made.

On November 22, 1856, Captain William Burgess was taken seriously ill and put to bed in the cabin. After a "conference with Chief Mate Henry Winsor" Hannah agreed to navigate the *Challenger* on the journey to the nearest large port, Valparaiso. Henry Winsor agreed to "take the sun," but gave the greater responsibility to Hannah, that of making all the calculations to determine the ship's position.

Now an expert navigator in her own right, Hannah recorded and charted the route of the clipper ship day after day as they sailed toward Valparaiso. Hannah prayed by the side of her sick husband every spare moment she had, and read passages to him from the Bible. She stayed close by him in those last fleeting hours of William's life, and watched his strength slowly leave his body. Less than forty-eight hours from port, on December 11, 1856, she writes: "Nineteen days from Chincha Islands, 250 miles from Valparaiso, and in sight of Juan Fernandez Island, at 11 P.M. my dear husband departed this world apparently at peace with his maker and in no pain. His age was 27 years 9 months 14 days."

In those days it was customary to bury the dead at sea, but Hannah could not bear the thought. Her will prevailed, and her husband's remains were brought into Valparaiso aboard the *Challenger* on Saturday, December 15.

Hannah Burgess wrote that "on Sunday the remains of my beloved were interred in the Pantheon, receiving Christian burial, the service performed by an Episcopal clergyman." There William's body would rest until arrangements could be made for transportation to his homeland.

Although a Cape Cod writer in 1940 claimed that Hannah returned to this country with her husband's remains, such was not the case.

On Tuesday, December 16, Hannah wrote:

> *Dec. Tues. 16, 1856*
>
> *Left Valparaiso in steamer* Bogota, *Capt. James Wildes, bound for U.S.A. The steward [David Graves] of the* Challenger *at my husband's request accompanies me. Mr. Burroughs, a gentleman from N.Y. gives me assistance. Mr. William Hobson also helped. Mr. Marvin, our consul, also came out in the boat with his wife to bid us farewell.*

The steamer reached Iquique, Chile, at 7 A.M., Sunday, December 21, and later Hannah transferred to the steamer *Illinois* and proceeded to New York. On January 27, 1857, Hannah wrote that she was one hundred miles from New York.

Early in February she reached West Sandwich and awaited the arrival of her husband's body. On May 1, 1857, Hannah received a telegram stating his remains would arrive on the ship *Harriet Ewing*. Finally came the day of the funeral.

After the services she had the body interred in the West Sandwich Cemetery where she often visited as the years went by. Hannah Burgess lived for the rest of her life in Sandwich, where it is said that she had fifty-six offers of marriage, all of which she refused. When she and Captain Burgess were married, he had made her promise never to marry again, and the promise was inscribed in her ring: "I will never marry again."*

Hannah died in 1917 at the age of eighty-two and is buried under a small gravestone by the side of her husband's larger monument.

The Bible from which Hannah read to her dying husband had a strange history. When Hannah left the ship, she presented it, with an

---

*The ring is still on exhibition at the Sandwich Museum, along with many other mementos of Hannah. A painting of the *Challenger* is also at the museum. The *Challenger* was afloat as late as 1875. Captain Winsor was her master until she was sold to Peru, where she was renamed *Camille Cavour*.

appropriate inscription, to the mulatto steward, David Graves, who had been faithful to the last in accompanying her back to New England. Graves, for the next six years, kept the Book constantly with him, but in a shipwreck and subsequent looting by Chinese pirates he lost it.

After the pirates had sailed away from the wreck, a sailor named Dennison from another vessel went aboard and found the Bible, evidently abandoned by the Chinese pirates as not worthy of their consideration. Noticing the inscription, Dennison decided to send the Book to Richard Henry Dana, author of *Two Years Before the Mast*, with the suggestion that Dana might forward it to Mrs. Burgess. In due time the Bible arrived in West Sandwich, and Mrs. Burgess kept it for the rest of her life. This same Bible now rests in the rooms of the Sandwich Historical Society, along with many pictures and the extremely interesting diary of Hannah Burgess.

Some of the items mentioned here are still on display at the Sandwich Glass Museum. According to Eliane Thomas of the museum, "We also have many items such as a lace collar, paintings, ornaments, her wedding skirt and veil, a compass, and other assorted items and mementos in our collection. This lady of outstanding character is very well known and admired, so much so that we have several people interested in her and her life who do research here on the subject."

In 1999 a carved sandalwood box given by Captain Burgess to his wife one Christmas season in Canton, China, was donated along with other items to the Bourne Historical Commission by William Madison Ripley. Ripley's mother was the niece of Hannah Rebecca Burgess.

Another woman with a very similar story was Mary Ann Brown Patten of East Boston, not far from Edward Rowe Snow's birthplace in Winthrop, Massachusetts. Her husband, Captain Joshua Patten, fell deathly ill during a voyage around Cape Horn on the clipper *Neptune's Car* in 1856. Mary took full command of the ship at the age of nineteen, while pregnant, and brought it safely to port in San Francisco. Her incredible story has inspired novels (*Captain, My Captain* by Deborah Meroff, and *The Captain's Wife* by Douglas Kelley) and several children's books.

CHAPTER 13

Abbie Burgess

Lighthouse heroines have often been the subject of chapters in former books which I have written. In other volumes I have mentioned such women on lighthouses as Celia Thaxter of the Isles of Shoals and Ida Lewis of Lime Rock Light in Newport, Rhode Island, but the haunting story of Abbie Burgess at Matinicus Rock Light more than one hundred years ago has always fascinated me.

Abbie Burgess was one of the most dedicated women in American lighthouse history. Born in August 1839, she went out to Matinicus Rock with her father, mother, and the younger children in 1853. Soon she was running the light herself, allowing her father to fish for lobsters and sail his catch all the distance into Rockland, Maine, where he could get much higher prices than at Matinicus Island.

In January 1856, Keeper Burgess was forced to go to Rockland to purchase supplies and food. He said farewell to his invalid wife and took Abbie aside to tell her that it was extreme necessity that prompted this trip, as the lighthouse cutter had not made its regular September call for some reason.

Abbie watched as the sail disappeared, but almost before it was out of sight the wind veered to the northeast, and the storm which followed was a terrible one. Her brother had left the rock months before, fishing on the Bay Chaleur, so Abbie was alone with her younger sisters and her mother.

For three days the storm increased in intensity, and on the morning of the 4th it was so violent that she was glad she had moved her mother

A nineteenth-century engraving of Abbie Burgess

into the lighthouse itself. A few hours later, at high tide, the waves broke right across the island and destroyed the old dwelling where the family had previously lived.

Let us quote from Abbie's pen at this time:

Dear Dorothy,

You have often expressed a desire to view the sea out upon the ocean when it was angry. Had you been here on the 19 January, I surmise you would have been satisfied. Father was away. Early in the day, as the tide arose, the sea made a complete breach over the rock, washing every movable thing away, and of the old dwelling not one stone was left upon another.

The new dwelling was flooded, and the windows had to be secured to prevent the violence of the spray from breaking them in. As the tide came, the sea rose higher and higher, till the only endurable places were the lighttowers. If they stood we were saved, otherwise our fate was only too certain.

But for some reason, I know not why, I had no misgivings, and went on with my work as usual. For four weeks, owing to rough weather, no landing could be effected on the rock. During this time we were without the assistance of any male member of our family. Though at times greatly exhausted with my labors, not once did the lights fail. Under God I was able to perform all my accustomed duties as well as my father's.

You know the hens were our only companions. Becoming convinced, as the gale increased, that unless they were brought into the house they would be lost, I said to mother: "I must try to save them." She advised me not to attempt it. The thought, however, of parting with them without an effort was not to be endured, so seizing a basket, I ran out a few yards after the rollers had passed and the sea fell off a little, with the water knee deep, to the coop, and rescued all but one. It was the work of a moment, and I was back in the house with the door fastened, but I was none too quick, for at that instant my little sister, standing at the window, exclaimed: "Oh, look! look there! the worst sea is coming."

That wave destroyed the old dwelling and swept the rock. I cannot think you would enjoy remaining here any great length of time for the sea is never still, and when agitated, its roar shuts out every other sound, even drowning our voices.

Abbie

Abbie's father returned after the storm and was happy to see that all was well.

The years went by. Finally when Mr. Burgess did not vote for Abraham Lincoln, he lost his job, and Abbie stayed at the light to operate the beacon for the new keeper, Captain John Grant, who had four sons.

Isaac H. Grant, one of the sons, married Abbie and they continued as assistant keepers at the light. Finally, after four sons were born to them, they moved to White Head Light, where poet Wilbert Snow came to know them, as his father was a coastguardsman there for forty years.

In 1890 the Grants moved to Massachusetts, settling in Middleboro, but soon the call of the sea lured them back to Maine, where Isaac obtained a position at Portland in the Engineers Department of the First Lighthouse District.

Abbie became ill the following year, and the last letter which she ever wrote includes a sad thought:

> *Those old lamps [at Matinicus Rock] . . . I often dream of them. . . . I feel a great deal more worried in my dreams than I do when I am awake.*
>
> *I wonder if the care of the lighthouse will follow my soul after it has left this worn out body. If I ever have a gravestone I would like it to be in the form of a lighthouse or a beacon.*

The twin lights at Matinicus Rock, which Abbie Burgess kept burning while her father, the keeper, was stranded on the mainland for four weeks during a storm.

Unfortunately, her last wish was not granted for many years, and it was not until more than half a century had elapsed that it was my privilege to bring together all of the relatives and friends of this lady of the lights. In the presence of poet Wilbert Snow of Spruce Head and other prominent residents of Maine, I unveiled a little lighthouse on her grave, and now I trust that her soul rests in peace.

Wilbert Snow later wrote a poem about Abbie Burgess, of which I quote the last part below:

> *For twenty days she trimmed the wicks, and kept*
> *A vigilant care over her hapless brood;*
> *The gruelling seas kept up their thundering rage*
> *Unceasingly, kept her as much marooned*
> *As if she dwelt upon a distant planet.*
> *For twenty days Starvation climbed the crests*
> *Of those cold waves distraught by undertow,*
> *But met its match in Abbie. She doled out*
> *One cup of cornmeal as their daily ration,*

Poet Wilbert Snow and Edward Rowe Snow placed a small lighthouse at the grave of Abbie Burgess, honoring her wishes.

And, thanks to the rescued hens, a welcome egg.
And, on the afternoon of the twenty-first
When a landing could be made without disaster,
Her father's dory, loaded to the gunnels,
Rowed in amid the daughter's joyous shrieks,
Shrieks like Cayista's swans in unison.
Young Abbie was the swan pre-eminent,
The friend and guide of sailors through dark nights,
Her father's pride, her mother's shield and stay;
And not long after she was certified
*First woman light-keeper of the Western world.**

———————————— ⌒ ————————————

Snow's text doesn't make it clear, but there were two lighthouses in service on Matinicus Rock in Abbie Burgess's time. Following is the complete text of Abbie Burgess Grant's final letter:

Sometimes I think the time is not far distant when I shall climb these light-house stairs no more. It has almost seemed to me that the light was part of myself. When we had care of the old lard oil lamps on Matinicus Rock, they were more difficult to tend than these lamps are, and sometimes they would not burn so well when first lighted, especially in cold weather when the oil got cold. Then, some nights, I could not sleep a wink all night though I knew the keeper himself was watching. And many nights I have watched the light my part of the night, thinking nervously, what might happen should the light fail.

In all these years I always put the lamps in order and I lit them at sunset. Those old lamps—as they were when my father lived on Matinicus Rock—are so thoroughly impressed in my memory that even now I often dream of them. There were fourteen lamps and fourteen reflectors. When I dream of them it always seems as though I had been away a long while, and I am trying to get back in time to light the lamps before sunset. Sometimes I walk on the water, sometimes I am in a boat, and sometimes I seem going in the air—I must always see the lights burning in both places before I wake. I always go through the same scenes in cleaning the lamps and lighting them, and I feel a great deal more worried in my dreams than I do when I am awake.

I wonder if the care of the lighthouse will follow my soul after it has left this

*Copyright 1960 by Wilbert Snow. Reprinted with permission.

worn out body. If I ever have a gravestone I would like it to be in the form of a lighthouse or a beacon.

The Burgess/Grant gravesites, including the little lighthouse on Abbie's grave, were refurbished by the American Lighthouse Foundation in 1995.

In 1997 a 175-foot buoy tender named the *Abbie Burgess* was launched in Marinette, Wisconsin, one in a series of state-of-the-art "Keeper Class" tenders built for the Coast Guard. The vessel is homeported in Rockland, Maine.

Poet Wilbert Snow called Abbie the "First woman light-keeper of the Western world," but in actuality she was one in a long line of female keepers dating back to Hannah Thomas at Plymouth Light in Massachusetts in 1776. Many of these women replaced their husbands or fathers as keeper upon their deaths.

CHAPTER 14

Alice on the Bark Russell

One wintry night in the year 1907, when the snow was swirling around our Winthrop home and great icy flakes were beginning to bounce against the window panes, I watched and listened as Grandmother Caroline played the guitar to accompany Mother's zither.* I experienced my usual fascination at the speed with which Mother's hands flew over the zither strings.

As they often did during the long winter nights, Mother and Grandmother had promised each other that they would play some tunes after the dishes were done, and Mother had interspersed the songs with stories of her unusual experiences on Robinson Crusoe's island and out on the high seas, aboard the bark *Russell*, of which my Grandfather Rowe was captain. Then came the moment when the music of the stringed instruments swung into "Good Night, Ladies," as they had often played it with each other at sea, and I knew there would be no more entertainment that evening.

When the last echoing chord faded away, Grandmother got up from her chair, stood her guitar in the corner, and slowly climbed the hall stairs to her room.

Ever since I can remember anything I have been able to recall my mother's zither and my grandmother's guitar being played in our

---

*The zither was given to my mother in Chile, and she was taught to play it by a Dr. Harvey, an officer of a British frigate.

spacious Winthrop parlor. The earliest stories I can recall are of Mother's adventures at sea and ashore in foreign lands.

That particular evening, Mother took me aside to tell me about my family tree. For at least five generations, with one exception (my own father, a Boston businessman) all my male ancestors had been sea captains. Probably these sea captain ancestors go back for at least one or two generations more on the Snow, Nickerson, Rowe, and Keating side of the family than on the others. Of one thing, however, I am very sure—both my mother and her mother were "women of the sea" whose only real homes were on sailing craft for most of the first twenty years of my mother's life.

For Mother, then Alice Rowe, her sea experiences began in 1869, when at the age of eleven months she made her first trip on the *Village Belle*, captained by Grandfather Rowe. Eventually she learned to walk on that schooner. Later, when she went ashore, she found she could not keep her balance, because the land did not roll with the motion of a ship. Grandmother told me how Mother's first vain attempts to walk dropped her to the floor. She cried in terror, and Grandmother Caroline had to teach her to walk all over again.

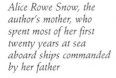

Alice Rowe Snow, the author's mother, who spent most of her first twenty years at sea aboard ships commanded by her father

In the first years of her life, Mother's parents were her only companions at sea and her teachers as well. Grandmother Caroline gave her instruction in the usual school lessons, guitar music, and sewing. Grandfather Joshua Nickerson Rowe taught her how to box the compass, steer the ship, and even "take the sun." As Mother and Grandfather paced the deck every day for exercise, he told her story after story of his own career on the clipper *Crystal Palace*, and of unusual shipwrecks, strange pirate adventures, and his own service at sea during the Civil War. Often he would sketch little pictures to go with his stories. Mother soon followed his example, making her own illustrations for her stories as she wrote them down. Of course there were cameras in those days, but they were not instruments which the average person could take on a sea voyage with any hope of success, so Mother used pencil and paint brush and did the best she could.

At one time Mother, Grandmother, and Grandfather lived on a banana plantation located on the island of San Domingo, which Grandfather ran for about a year. Captain Rowe shipped the fruit on fast sailing vessels to Boston and New York. Then at the height of his relative prosperity, a revolution occurred, which resulted in Grandfather's capture. The following morning, just as the revolutionists were holding a kangaroo court to decide whether they should shoot Grandfather or hang him, an American man-of-war came around the cape a short distance away. This saved his life, as the rebels fled into the forest at once. After this experience Grandfather lost his interest in the plantation and decided to take his family to a safer place.

Becoming master of the brig *J. Bickmore*, Captain Rowe sailed with his family to the British Isles, entering Queenstown Harbor some weeks later. As they were coming in toward the anchorage, a great square-rigged sailing vessel smashed into the stern of the *J. Bickmore*.

After the excitement was over Captain Rowe repaired his brig, and traveled to Liverpool for the lawsuit to recover damages. During this interval he was forced to put another master on the *J. Bickmore*. The new captain was not a dependable sailor, according to Mother. He wrecked the ship, and they never saw her again.

Without a vessel, Grandfather Rowe was forced to enter business in Liverpool, but the longing for the sea, as Mother expressed it, made him accept an offer to command the English sailing bark *Russell*. Putting his family aboard her, he sailed away on a voyage which lasted four and a half years, with his first objective Santos, Brazil.

We still have Mother's diary of her adventures, which include the journey from Liverpool to Lima, Peru, and back, with stops along the way. Mother was just the age when the prospects of such a voyage delighted her. Let us look over the shoulder of this fourteen-year-old lass as she opens the writing book which her father has bought for her. Alice Rowe dips her pen into the ink and begins the account of her trip from Liverpool to Santos, Brazil:

Tuesday, January 16, 1883
I feel so happy; I just want to shout right out and tell everybody that I am going on a long sea voyage with Father and Mother. All the boys and girls I know think I am lucky and want to come, too. I wish they could, but of course they can't. Although I am only a little girl, I will write a book all by myself and make pictures, too. Then when I come home my boy and girl friends can find out what I have been doing. I wonder, oh, how I wonder what will be written in this book! The first picture is the Bark Russell, *all under sail. She is our floating home.*

My father is the captain, usually called Skipper, and they say the sailors call me the Skipper's daughter. It seems very funny to me.

Wednesday, January 17th.
Our ship is rolling. Mother and I are awfully seasick. I can't write any more, and perhaps I never can, as I feel terribly bad! I will climb into my bed, or bunk as the sailors call it, and stay there forever, maybe. Oh, dear, I said good-by to the land today, but now I guess I'll say good-by to the world!

Friday, January 19th
I am still sick, but I must just write to say that Harry Kidd is a stowaway on board! He is dreadfully seasick, and I guess by the way he looks and groans, he doesn't think there is much fun in going to sea. If only the ship would stay still one minute, but she tosses and rolls, creaks and shivers and makes us all miserable. Lucky are those boys and girls who didn't come! The wind has increased to a gale and is dashing the spray across our skylight. Our cabin is under the deck, not built on the deck as some are, so when the waves roll over the skylight, we are in darkness. Our ship only has one sail set, while the others are all furled. As this is a sailing vessel, we have no steam, but just depend on the sails.

January 19th, later.

A ship just went by us going the same way, and has disappeared into the mist ahead, and the storm grows worse.

Still later. Something awful has happened! The mist cleared a little just in time for us to see waves hitting the rocks. The ship that had passed us was going to pieces in the surf.

The poor men clinging to the masts were helpless as the waves were roaring and rolling, making it impossible for us to save them. At that very moment when we saw the danger before us and it would have been fatal to have gone any farther, we heard a splitting, crashing noise over our heads which sounded above the shrieking of the wind and the thunder of the surf, then down to the deck fell the fore lower topsail, mast and all, thus instantly stopping our headway.

So by this accident we were saved from going on the rocks and being shipwrecked. We are all very thankful. I do feel dreadfully sorry for those poor sailors, but my father says that if we tried to save them we would surely be drowned, too, and that would do them no good.

Alice Rowe Snow at age fourteen

January 21st.
Calmer today. Saw the Isle of Man where the Manx cats with no
tails come from. Can also see the coast of Ireland.

On the next day, the 22nd, my mother recorded that another gale of
wind arose. She was back in her bunk and she mentioned that two
drawers under her bunk jerked out, as well as a shelf with charts and
books. Then she commented that Harry the stowaway was made cabin
boy, and told of many things that happened on deck.

Two days later, on the 24th, because the ship was leaking badly,
Grandfather Rowe started back for Liverpool, and my mother could
hear the pumps going and the water pouring out on the deck. As the
men pumped, they were singing a song which sounded very pretty.

January 25th.
We just sighted the coast of England. Now we are peacefully sail-
ing up the River Mersey. Harry did not want the ship to go back, as
he might be made to stay ashore, but Father said he would keep him
as cabin boy.
Liverpool once more. How astonished our friends will be when we
call on them this evening! We hear that more than a dozen ships were
lost during these two terrible storms. How fortunate we were not to
have shared their fate.

Other craft which encountered great trouble included the schooner
Orange of Liverpool, which put back into the Mersey after losing her
boom and fifty feet of the topgallant bulwarks; the schooner *Jim Crow*,
commanded by Captain Horea, which became a total wreck at Redca
Rock, and is probably the craft Alice mentions; the schooner *Norfolk Tar*,
whose captain was Tillson, which also crashed on Redca Rock; and the
abandoned smack *Margaret Elizabeth* of Caernarvon.*

---

*The *Times* of London for January 27, 1883, reports: "The *Russell*, British
barque, which left Liverpool on the 18th inst. for Santos, laden with machinery,
has returned to the Mersey, and the master reports having experienced heavy
gales. The vessel appears to have strained badly and is leaking considerably.
Her topsailyard, several sails and nearly all her running gear have been carried
away."

That is the end of my mother's diary of that time. They stayed in Liverpool an entire month while the ship was being repaired and started off again on February 25. On the 26th, they saw the south coast of Ireland.

And then the days began to go by during which nothing really important happened. On April 10, Alice writes in her logbook: "We are a little world to ourselves. I have my lessons, my meals, and my daily walk up and down the deck with my father for exercise."

Then came the day when her father called her to look at a whale, which was near the ship. He told her it was her chance to make herself a real sailor by dropping a piece of wood on the back of the whale.

> *He passed me a short, thick stick, and I held it in my right hand, while with the other I held onto the rigging. My father held on to me and then we waited for a whale to come close. Soon one did so, and the ship rolled way down nearer and nearer. I was just as scared as could be, but I didn't let Father know it. The whale was very near, right under my nose, when I let go of the stick. Down it went, with a little bump on his back, and gave a bounce up again. One great eye glared at me, and I thought he might be about to open his awful big mouth and swallow me down, like Jonah. For a half minute I thought he would do so. I planned to kick tremendously when I got into his tummy. Suddenly our ship rolled back with a lurch, and I was safe in my father's arms, and wasn't I glad? And I'm still glad.*

The arrival of the bark *Russell* in the Sargasso Sea, which is nearly always calm, reminded Mother of the tales that the *Flying Dutchman* was still visible there if you looked in the right place. Grandfather Rowe never believed "such silly stories," but he took Alice in the boat, rowing among the long lanes of seaweed, some of which my mother gathered up to press between sheets of blotting paper. Among the seaweed she discovered tiny crabs, equipped with queer paddlelike hind legs, clinging to it.

One day the *Russell* crossed the equator, and Grandfather Rowe suggested that Alice might enjoy picking up the telescope for a look through it. Sure enough there was the line of the equator indicating that the *Russell* had reached a point halfway down the face of the world. Indeed my mother was surprised, but when she put the telescope down and a little later picked it up, she noticed that the equator had tipped up into the air. What had happened, of course, was that Grandfather Rowe had placed a long hair across the lens to fool his daughter, and as she said later, "Father and all the rest laughed, but I didn't."

But she was worried when she realized that she had never crossed the equator before and therefore was among those who might be subjected to the traditional visit of Neptune, the King of the Sea. Noticing a very old man with a long white beard climbing over the rail of the ship, asking for his victims, Alice followed his movements with extreme concern. Then Harry Kidd was given his initiation, which included being shaved with a barrel stave and dumped over backward into a trough filled with seawater. Alice became so absorbed in the ceremony that she soon forgot the threat of her own initiation.

Suddenly, one of Neptune's aides stepped forward and respectfully addressed Captain Rowe.

"I understand the young girl on board has never crossed the Line before." Terrified, Alice fled to the deepest, darkest locker that she could find. There she hid, listening intently, and remained quiet as a mouse. Finally she must have fallen asleep, for hours later she heard her mother's voice calling, "Alice, Alice! Where is that child?" and she answered by saying, "Is he gone?"

"Is who gone?" asked her mother.

"Why, that awful King Neptune."

"Of course he is gone. He went long ago. You don't suppose your father would let him hurt you! Oh, no, your father bought you off with something nice." Out came Alice, crumpled and embarrassed, with a tear-stained face. It was obvious that she was glad to be safe after such a terrible experience.

The voyage continued for several days without incident until Sunday, April 22, when Alice records in her diary that she and Harry had landed on a sandy Brazilian beach with the older people. The two of them rushed on ahead, eager to see all the strange things. Suddenly Harry spoke.

"Say, Alice, I don't think we had better go too far. There are lions, tigers, bears, boa constrictors, or something, and we might meet them."

"Oh, Harry, don't be a scared cat," Alice answered. Just then she stepped across a snake. She screamed, stopping so abruptly that she nearly knocked over Harry, who bumped against her. They both ran from the spot as fast as they could, but the snake did not seem bothered by them.

Caroline Alden Keating Rowe, mother of Alice Rowe

At last, back in the harbor, the cargo was unloaded from the bark and their visit in sunny Brazil ended. Then the *Russell* sailed toward Cape Horn, on her way to Peru.

While rounding the Cape they had terrific storms. Day after day frightful mountains of water lashed the ship. It soon became so cold that the spray froze everywhere. A thick sheathing of ice formed in the rigging, while layer after layer coated the deck. One morning an overwhelming blast of wind snapped off the foretopmast, and soon the bowsprit split asunder.

Shortly afterward the vessel sprang a leak that kept the crew pumping nearly all the time. Meanwhile the poor cook had his troubles with the ocean; every time he lighted the galley stove the spray would sweep in and put out the fire. Finally he gave up trying.

On her terrifying journey, battered by the storm, the *Russell* went sixty miles south of Cape Horn. She eventually rounded it but described a loop in her track while doing so. Alice did not enjoy her memories of the Cape, but I do not suppose anyone can blame her as storm after storm struck the unfortunate bark. Finally latitudes below sixty degrees were reached, and the *Russell* sailed alone in the Antarctic Sea. Alice was

Captain Joshua Nickerson Rowe in a Civil War uniform

emphatic in her feelings, and her comment "I don't like it" expressed her sentiments of the ordeal.

On August 13, her father had her all bundled up and brought on deck for a distant view of the "wonderful Andes Mountains." The next day the wind went down, and they were able to set more sail.

Later Alice wrote, "How happy I was when Father let me put on oil-skins and go on deck to see an immense albatross soaring in a stately manner overhead. He had a wicked look in his eye." The bird was about twelve feet from tip to tip of his great, widespread wings. Alice did not like the way he glared at her as he kept winging back over the deck time and again, until she decided he looked hungry. Then she went down into the cabin, where she felt safer.

On August 24, off the coast of Chile, the *Russell* took on a pilot and a short time later anchored in the harbor of Valparaiso. Alice tells us that the bay was a mile and a half wide by a mile and a quarter long. She observes that the city was built on many little hills and was rather bare of trees in contrast to the heavily shaded Brazilian cities. The same day there was a substantial earthquake in Valparaiso.

Later in the day the sailors started repairing the bark's leak and putting on a new bowsprit and a new foretopmast. The days went by rapidly, and the work was eventually finished. Finally the ship was ready for another cargo, and then came a moment that Alice Rowe never forgot.

Her father called his daughter and wife into the chart room.

"Where do you think we are going, young lady?" he asked. Alice guessed and her mother guessed, and then they both gave up. Finally Grandfather Rowe smiled and pointed to the chart of the South Pacific Ocean.

"We are going," he began, "to Robinson Crusoe's island." Of course this statement astounded everyone, and Alice inquired, "Father, did Robinson Crusoe really live near here, and isn't it a made-up yarn anyway, like Little Red Riding Hood?"

"No, it is not," replied Grandfather Rowe. "His real name was Alexander Selkirk, and he lived on Juan Fernandez, 360 or more miles west of this city. I have promised to take a freight of two masts to the island for a small ship they are building there."

And so it was that Alice and her mother, two Yankee women of the sea, received the news of their amazing luck. They were going to fabulous Robinson Crusoe's Isle. After a sail of three days with a fair wind all the way, those aboard the bark saw a great purple cloud on the horizon, which gradually changed to what appeared to be a huge pile of rocks as they sailed nearer. Later the pile took a definite shape, and it proved to be a towering mountain peak called the Anvil, 3,040 feet high.* The island itself spread along the horizon for about fifteen miles.

Eventually the ship reached the anchorage, and before the hooks finished rattling down, a boat was seen approaching. The governor of the island, Count de Rodt, was aboard, bringing fresh vegetables and some delicious goat's meat. He stepped up the gangway and aboard the bark to introduce himself. The food was soon unloaded, and Count de Rodt was shown around the ship.

Finally, after a conference, the Rowe family were invited to go ashore with the governor, who gave them permission to explore anywhere they wished. This possibility intrigued Alice, and she turned to her father.

"Oh, Father, I think that I must be dreaming or in a story book. Am I really on Robinson Crusoe's island? Please pinch me, so I can find out if I am alive."

Grandfather Rowe gave her such a pinch that she never forgot it as long as she lived.

Later they walked over to the prison caves where convicts had been kept when Juan Fernandez belonged to Spain. Beautiful lacelike ferns grew in the crevices of the walls, covering up the crude sketches of the poor creatures who had lived and suffered there centuries before.†

My mother had brought Daniel Defoe's book *Robinson Crusoe* ashore with her, and she rubbed the soil of the island all over it to introduce the volume to the "land of its birth." The original of its hero, Alexander Selkirk, had lived on the island all alone for about four years. Defoe changed the island's location and the story itself, as well as Selkirk's name.‡ Thus was born one of the best sellers of all time.

For the next few days the Rowe family wandered around the island. The family met Mr. Meyers, the German who lived in the real Robinson

---

*The Spanish name is El Yunque. Convicts were given their freedom if they climbed it. Few succeeded, most falling to their death.

†Less than a mile offshore from the caves, the German warship *Dresden* was sunk. She was sent to the bottom by the British *Glasgow* and *Kent*, on March 14, 1915.

‡See my *True Tales of Pirates and Their Gold*, p. 241.

Crusoe cave where Selkirk dwelt from 1704 to 1709, and Alice called him "Robinson Crusoe, the Second." Mr. Meyers said that it was a good day to visit his home as the sea was calm. Harry Kidd, the former stowaway, and Charlie, one of the crew, got the boat ready, and Alice and her father and mother took their seats. Jess, the dog, scrambled up to the bow to serve in his usual position as lookout.

They had a wonderful trip, skirting the foot of the tall cliffs. The sheer walls of rock towered up over a thousand feet, so that when the members of the party attempted to see the top, they almost fell over backward. Soon they sighted a tiny beach. Captain Rowe guided the craft in on a big roller, the boat rushing up on the beach at a dizzy rate of speed. Following their leader along the shore and up a path which led through a natural tunnel in the cliff, the group finally reached the famous cave of Alexander Selkirk.

The room inside had been dug from solid earth. Natural earthen shelves were made all around the sides by scooping out some of the soil. A hammock was slung from side to side, making it look cozy and homelike; dishes and household articles were scattered around. Of course, when the time came to go they hated to leave the cave with its romantic attachments, but the surf was still pounding away and seemed to be getting dangerously higher. Nevertheless, Captain Rowe made a successful launching. After half an hour of good steady rowing, they sighted the *Russell* and within a short time reached their ship.

Several days later a trip was planned to the great lookout where a tablet has been erected to Selkirk's memory. The trail led over a wooded area where grew a strange type of burr which stuck all over their clothing, breaking into many tiny, sharp, needlelike pieces. After they had picked the burrs off, they ran into fresh trouble. This time they hit a section of land that contained jagged rocks five feet high. Grandfather Rowe, Harry, and Boatswain Charlie climbed them first, after which they pulled Alice and her mother up. Rock by rock they mounted until the poor women felt like saying they had to rest. But they went on, struggling higher and higher.

The next crisis came when they reached a narrow ridge three feet wide with a yawning gorge on each side. All five of them clung to each other and walked sideways, not daring even to lift their feet until they reached the other side. Half an hour later they had arrive at the lookout. By this time Alice was so exhausted that she flung herself down and rested, not even bothering to look at the view. Alexander Selkirk, of course, is said to have climbed up to the lookout every day, but once in a lifetime was enough for Alice.

While resting there she heard a voice shouting out, "I'm monarch of all I survey! My right there is none to dispute; from the center all around to the sea, I'm lord of the fowl and the brute!" It was Captain Rowe, who was standing on the topmost rock declaiming from memory in loud tones Cowper's poem, "Alexander Selkirk's Soliloquy."

They looked across far out to sea and down at the valleys of the island. The *Russell* appeared as small as a toy boat. Mother wrote that it looked as though you could upset it "with a pin." While up at the lookout she copied the words on the tablet erected to the memory of Selkirk:

IN MEMORY OF
ALEXANDER SELKIRK MARINER
A NATIVE OF LARGO IN THE COUNTY
OF FIFE SCOTLAND WHO LIVED ON
THIS ISLAND IN COMPLETE SOLITUDE
FOR FOUR YEARS AND FOUR MONTHS
HE WAS LANDED FROM THE
CINQUE PORTS GALLEY
96 GUNS A.D.
1704 AND WAS TAKEN OFF
IN THE DUKE PRIVATEER
FEB. 12, 1708
HE DIED LIEUT. OF H.M.S.
WEYMOUTH A. D. 1734 AGED 47 YEARS
THIS TABLET IS ERECTED
NEAR SELKIRK'S LOOKOUT BY
OFFICERS OF H.M.S. TOPAZ A. D. 1868

After reading the tablet Captain Rowe announced that the setting sun indicated an end to the visit, and the downward hike began. The captain decided that they might attempt a shorter route, so they plunged into a forest and reached a beautiful nook of ferns, after which they entered a dell covered with moss. To one place in particular they gave the name of Fern Paradise. Here hundreds of graceful maidenhair ferns festooned the rocks, while others covered the trunks of every tree, and lacelike moss carpeted the surrounding rocks and ground.

Following the brook they had discovered running toward the sea, they suddenly paused, for they were in trouble. Without warning it had plunged over a fifty-foot precipice. Realizing that they could not follow the stream itself, they also knew that they did not have time to return to the lookout. Captain Rowe led them to the right, after which they explored the area to the left, but there was no way out. They could not take any chances, because it was getting dark. They might cut down a tree and climb down it if they had an axe, but they had none. They could lower themselves by a rope, if they had one, but there was no rope.

Grandfather Rowe then thought of a plan that had merit, if everyone worked together. Perhaps, he suggested, they could bend a tree over. The first one they tried had wood that proved too tough. Another, considerably more pliable, was found, which they were able to bend.

Standing on a rocky ledge just above the trees, the five of them pushed with all their strength at a point about ten feet up on the trunk. Shoving, straining, and kicking, they rocked the tree back and forth. Finally, except for a few clinging roots, it was bent straight out from the top of the cliff. Harry and the sailor Charlie scrambled out to the branches, and their weight soon forced the tree top to the bottom of the cliff. There they held it until the rest of the party crawled down the trunk.

A major problem developed when the dog Jess would not come down the tree, and she barked and barked and nearly wagged her tail off. They were about to leave her at the top of the cliff, when suddenly she decided to take a chance, and started coming down the bare, steep cliff. Slewing and bumping, she slid around tail first after going a short distance. Then she dug her claws into the rock to slow herself, but it did not help much. Finally she arrived at the bottom. Her paws were torn and bleeding, but this was better than staying up on the cliff and becoming a permanent inhabitant of Robinson Crusoe's island.

The party emerged from the deep woods just as a group of men sent out by the governor were seen coming toward them. The governor had become worried and sent a rescue party. Soon all were back at the settlement. But the question in my mother's mind always was, did she climb up that tree, or down it?

Another journey, on which my grandmother did not go, I will always remember from my mother's graphic description of it. At one very low tide, they were rowing along at the foot of the cliffs when they noticed a black space with a deep opening. Captain Rowe decided to take them into explore. Years later Mother wrote of her experience that day:

"Now," Father said, "do just as I say. Pull hard at the oars and duck down your heads. I'll steer."

We did as he commanded, and in we shot, finding ourselves in a beautiful cavern! The flickering light was dancing over the interior with a blue tint, caused from the sunlight striking down through the azure depths of the water and reflecting up into the cave. It seemed like fairyland.

The roof was high inside, like a church, and hung down in pinnacles of rock. It extended in about a ship's length, and we could hear the waves breaking on a little beach. The water was the most brilliant blue I ever saw, and was filled with bright yellow fish.

Father said: "We must have your mother see this. I think we shall go back after her and bring some fish-lines and have fun."

The return to the ship was soon made, as Harry and I, each rowing with a pair of oars, made quick work of rushing the boat through the water.

Before long we were on our way back to the cave with mother and fish-lines. Of course we had not told her our secret, so when father said" "Down with your heads or you'll get them knocked off," she did look so surprised and a little afraid, as the boat headed right for the cliff. Harry and I gave a strong stroke and trailed our oars, and into the cavern we went!

How astonished mother was. Her eyes fairly popped out of her head! "I thought you had something up your sleeve by the way you acted, but I had no idea I was to see anything so marvelous as this! Oh, look at those pretty colored fish!"

"Here is your line so you can catch some of them," said father. Our boat was soon made fast, bow and stern, to some jagged rocks, then out with our lines, and what sport we had. The fish were not a bit afraid of us or the lines.

I became so excited catching them so rapidly that I made my line shorter and shorter, and still on they came, until finally I was just holding the baited hook in the water, and they bit as fast as they could!

Then I proudly said: "Watch me! I am catching fish by just holding the hook in the water, without any line!"

I had hardly finished saying this when the boatman shouted in a voice of terror: "Look out, Miss Alice!"

I jumped and snatched my hand out of the water, and as I did so a pair of jaws came together with a snap!

"Well, young lady," said father, "you just escaped having your hand bitten off. In the future never fish without a fish-line! That was a water snake or a young sea serpent about five feet long. I guess we had better get out of here as fast as we can if we have stirred up a nest of those creatures."

I was horribly frightened, and was trembling and looking at my hand to make sure it was still on my arm. I declared then and there that I would always use a fish-line when I went fishing and I always have.

We cast off our mooring lines and started for the mouth of the cave. There we found we were in a trap, as the tide had come in while we were fishing and the entrance was too small for the boat to go through.

But we had father who always found a way to do what seemed impossible. So if my reader gets caught in a cave in the South Pacific Ocean or any other ocean, remember what we did.

As the boat was higher than the overhanging rock, one side had to be tipped under the edge and pushed along while we all lay flat on the slimy fish. First one side of the boat, then the other, was tipped, and while we were tipping it we kept thinking, or I did, that if we upset we would be thrown in among all those water snakes with jaws full of big sharp teeth like a wolf's!

It was luck that we tried to get out of the cave before the tide was any higher, for we just managed it and that was all. We were a very happy set of folks to be once more out in the daylight, and soon got back to our nice little bark Russell.

What a supper the cook gave us that evening! Those yellow-tailed fish were delicious fried in salt pork and eaten with some island vegetables. I was pretty glad to be eating cave fish instead of cave fish eating me!

Another story which my mother often told became one of my favorites:

One day Harry was heard shouting: "Captain! Captain! There's something alive out on the water."

Father came striding up the companion steps from the cabin, gun in hand. His glance swept the surface of the bay, and quickly he aimed at a black object. Soon a loud report was heard!

"I've hit him," cried father, in his excitement. "It is a sea lion! Lower the boat; hurry now; get him before he sinks!"

The boat was in the water while he was yet speaking, and in a short time the creature was towed to the ship! In the next few minutes the sea lion was hoisted to the boat's davit and left to hang and bleed.

He certainly did bleed; why, the ocean was red all around the ship. We had a book with us telling of Lord Anson's visit to this island in 1741. He tells in his book of a sea lion that bled two hogsheads of blood! Of course we didn't measure how much blood there was in this sea animal as it was all in the water, but there must have been an awful lot of it. I felt terrible to see the poor thing suffer and wished father had not shot him.

After an hour or two father said to the sailors, "Get that dead sea lion on board."

They hauled him in, laying him flat on the deck and unhitching the ropes from his flippers. We all stood around looking at him, making remarks, something like the story of Red Riding Hood when the bad wolf ate up the grandmother and put on the old woman's clothing.

First someone said: "What a great big mouth he has!"

The someone else said: "What a queer nose he has—looks like an elephant's trunk!"

Then another said: "Look at those funny flippers."

I gave him a little poke with my toe and said, "He has even got whiskers, and what stiff ones they are."

Suddenly father yelled: "Run for your lives! He isn't dead at all!"

Did we run? Indeed we did because, to our horror, the sea lion actually came to life. Rising up on his tail, in marvelous fashion, he gave a hideous roar as much as to say, "I'm not dead at all. Just wait till I get hold of you!"

And then he started for us. *We not only ran, we rushed, we scooted, we scrambled just as fast as our legs would take us away from that horrible creature, who kept up such a frightful noise!*

I gave just one glance at his wide open mouth and fled screaming! All the others jumped up in the rigging or on the spanker boom. Harry hid out of reach, while I tumbled down the cabin steps.

If you ever saw an inch-worm walk, you will know how this sea lion walked, only instead of doubling up and taking one inch at a step, he took eight feet, and that was pretty bad when he was chasing a poor human being who could only take three feet at once.

In spite of our terrors, we realized that it was wonderful the way that creature went from end to end of the ship! In full charge, he was captain and crew! No one could do anything. Harry attempted to walk along the deck; the sea lion saw him and with a blood-freezing roar he started for the boy with terrific speed! Luckily Harry grabbed a rope and swung himself above the beast's head just in time to escape his horrible jaws.

Then how the animal raved! He jerked his body back and forth, trying to reach Harry, who was grimacing just a few inches beyond the beast's snorting nose. I gained courage enough to peek around the corner of the hatchway to see what the terrible bellowing was about, and when I saw what Harry was trying to do I was afraid he was going to be killed.

Just then someone shouted from forward, and the beast lumbered off toward the bow of the Russell. *The minute he was gone, down jumped Harry. Quick as a flash he dashed along the deck.*

Frantically I yelled: "Harry, come back or you'll be torn to pieces!"

As many of us were hiding in out-of-the-way places, Father could not shoot the sea lion for fear of hitting someone, but he seemed to know what Harry was after, and soon I saw the boy grab a sledge hammer and come racing back.

Yes, it indeed was a race! The sea lion had turned and was now after him, gaining fast! I shut my eyes, for I could stand it no longer! A moment later a great shout went up, and Father's voice came from across the deck.

"Good for you, boy! That jump was in the nick of time, but don't take any more chances. You know one of Lord Anson's men was killed by a sea lion right here on Robinson Crusoe's beach. The man had shot a baby sea lion and was skinning it when the mother came along. Of course she was furious. Sneaking up behind the man, she opened her huge mouth and took his head right in it and killed him."

Our own sea lion was madly going up and down the deck in an infuriated fashion, and every time he passed under Harry, the boy nagged at him and made him more and more enraged.

Finally, when the animal was exactly under the rigging where Harry waited, the boy said: "There, take that!" Reaching down with all his young strength, he struck the sea lion's head with a heavy blow, and the creature fell to the deck. All hands came from their hiding places, cautiously at first, and then, gaining courage, gathered around the sea lion. Nearly every one took a hit at the huge beast to make sure he was really dead. This time he did not come to life again, and we were glad of it.

I suppose the lonely man who lived so long ago on this island used to hunt sea lions as the oil was of so much use for many things, but that was not for me! We had the skin of the creature weighed and the scales read two hundred pounds!

On the final trip of the *Russell,* under the command of Captain Rowe, she carried a load of manganese ore for England. Four years had gone by since they had arrived at South America, and when they were just about ready to sail, it was discovered that the cargo was too heavy. Captain Rowe put in at Corral, Chile, and loaded some of the manganese onto another ship, a Danish brig.

During the unloading period Mother and Grandmother left the ship to gather ferns on the banks of several brooks which lead into the mountains, actually the foothills of the Andes. Grandfather and the boatman stayed behind to build a fire and make coffee. The two women, accompanied by Jess, the dog, followed a pretty stream for over a mile until it entered a beautiful valley.

Suddenly Jess began to whine. Crouching down at Mother's feet, the dog trembled, while looking intently at a large bush a short distance away.

"What is the matter, poor doggie?" Mother asked. Jess looked at Alice piteously and kept up her trembling, bobbing her head time and again at the bush up the stream a few yards.

Alice Rowe Snow's drawing of the bark Russell, commanded by Captain Joshua N. Rowe from 1883 to 1887

"There is something behind that bush," said Grandmother Rowe.

"Oh, I can see the bush moving," answered Alice. "What is it, I wonder?"

"I feel sure the dog can smell some wild beast," explained Grandmother. "We must go back to the shore just as quickly as we can. We do not dare to turn our backs, but let's walk away with our eyes on that bush. I've read somewhere that a wild animal will not jump at you if you glare at him and walk away backward."

So they slowly went down the brook, walking right in the water with the frightened dog cowering between them. As soon as the dreadful bush was out of sight they dropped ferns and flowers and ran for dear life way down to the shore where they were thankful to find Captain Rowe, talking to a native fisherman.

"Whatever is the matter? You look scared," said Grandfather.

Then they told him the whole story, and when the fisherman understood it, he threw up his hands and said: "Oh, ladies, it was a lion, and if you had not taken the dog along, you never would have come back."

Poor old dog Jess, Mother thought later, no wonder she was trembling and frightened. Soon after this, word came that some lions had carried off two children, and all that was ever found was one shoe.

Later on a big lion chase was organized, and the ranchmen for miles around joined in the hunt. Pits were dug and traps set. At a given signal the pursuit began with the beating of drums, blowing of horns, and banging on tin pans. As a result the beasts were driven toward the pits and caught. Twenty-two lions and cubs were killed.

Of this Alice wrote:

> *A week later father took me out to the farm of a German to see one of the lions that had been caught. When I stood and looked at him, he glared at me, and I wondered if he were the one who had seen me in the woods and that Jess had scared off. There was no way of finding out, so I didn't try.*
>
> *I was given a long stick as big around as my arm, to poke between the bars of the cage, and the lion, who was as large as a small cow, grabbed with a furious bite and crushed it in his jaws!*
>
> *Then father said: "Now suppose he was grabbing you, Alice!"*
>
> *I gazed at him in horror and made a vow never, never, NEVER to wander in the woods again.*

A voyage in the general direction of Brazil followed. After a calm spell a terrible storm crushed the deck of the ship, spoiling all the drinking water. Grandfather Rowe took a large tin can and filled it with salt water, after which he put it on a charcoal fire to boil. Over the boiling water in the can he placed a cover, and the steam collecting on the underside dribbled off as fresh water, allowing each person aboard a few tablespoons at a time. Then Grandfather made a condenser out of a piece of pipe and they were "just the happiest sort of folks," according to Grandmother Rowe, for they had enough water to drink.

After a two-month visit to Bahia, Brazil, the dreaded yellow fever broke out, and they left town at once. Luckily no one aboard caught the disease.

Weeks later they sighted the south of Ireland, finally entering Queenstown Harbor. The *Russell*'s next call was at Swansea, Wales. While entering the harbor in a dense fog they were almost run down by another vessel but eventually they reached the city.

With the voyage at an end, the moment of parting came. Mother and Grandmother were bound for New York and said good-by to the "dear bark," on which they had spent four and a half years of their life. The farewell was a sad one. Standing on the deck of the *Russell* for the last time, Alice said good-by to all the sailors she knew and dear Jess, the dog. "I just hugged her for fifteen minutes," Mother said later.

Of course, the hardest farewell the women had to make was with Captain Rowe, and it was a particularly sad one. He went with them aboard their steamer, *Llandaff City*. Attaching his boat to the stern, Captain Rowe remained even after the ship was under way. Finally, when they were several miles out to sea, he turned and gave his loved ones his final farewell. As he headed back for land, Mother's "eyes were just blinded with tears." She only saw him once again.*

Coming into New York Harbor, the Rowes passed the Statue of Liberty, and after twelve years Alice and her mother were back in their native land. Mother's own words will end the account of her last sea voyage:

> *We began to wonder if we had been forgotten by our relatives, for we had been gone such a long time. I knew Father had written to his*

---

*That was just before he started up the Yukon River in command of the steamer *Argonaut*. He caught pneumonia at Lake LeBarge, and died October 18, 1898. He was buried in Skagway, Alaska.

brother, Adelbert Rowe, who lived in New York, but we did not know if he had received the letter. Perhaps he had moved away. How could we tell?

As the steamer docked we looked pensively at the huge buildings, at the men rushing to and fro, the piles of boxes and luggage of all kinds cluttering up every place and wondered what we were to do and where we were to go. Suddenly a tall man appeared and a big voice said, "Well, well, here you are at last. Been watching a week for you." As he spoke he jumped on board the Llandaff City *and first gave mother a hug and kiss, then turned to me. "So this is Alice, I suppose. How she has grown!" Then I got a nice big hug and kiss.*

"My wife is waiting for us to come along." So speaking, Adelbert loaded himself with our bundles and headed up the wharf. Following him we turned our backs on our sailor life forever.

———————— ～ ————————

Alice Rowe Snow related her exciting young life at sea in two books, *Log of a Sea Captain's Daughter* (1944) and *More Stories from the Log of a Sea Captain's Daughter* (1949). Both books contained excerpts from Alice's journals and were illustrated with her own drawings. Alice even personally colored in the drawings in some copies. In the introduction to *Log of a Sea Captain's Daughter* she wrote:

"One day when I had a group of good listeners gathered around me as I told my stories, someone said: 'Why have you never written a book about your unusual adventures?'

"I answered, 'Do you really want me to tell you? Well it is because I have been chained to the kitchen sink.'"

"'If that is the reason,' was the reply, 'then we will all help to break the chain.'"

Alice went on to describe how she met her husband and Edward Rowe Snow's father, Edward Sumter Snow. Alice was at the home of her Aunt Luella Snow in Rockland, Maine, playing "Come, O Come with Me, the Moon is Beaming" on her zither. The music attracted the attention of Edward S. Snow, who came to the door and made Alice's acquaintance. The two were soon married and later moved to Winthrop, Massachusetts, where Alice said she could "go out in a boat whenever I got the chance, and dream that I was back again on the dear old Bark *Russell*."

Juan Fernandez Island, where Alexander Selkirk was marooned, was officially renamed Robinson Crusoe Island in an attempt to draw tourists. Nearby Santa Clara Island was renamed Alexander Selkirk Island. Robinson Crusoe Island, more than 400 miles off the coast of Chile, is about 40 square miles and rises to 3,000 feet above the sea. The island today is home to about 600 people.

This is the cover of Log of a Sea Captain's Daughter *by Alice Rowe Snow, published by Meador Publishing Company, Boston, in 1944.*

CHAPTER 15

Joanna Carver Colcord

One of the great names in New England sailing history is that of Colcord. An outstanding member of that family, Joanna Carver Colcord was a good friend of my mother, Alice Rowe Snow, and they once compared notes to find that they were off Cape Horn at the same time in the 1880s. Joanna was born at sea on March 18, 1882, while the ship on which she sailed was about sixty miles off the coast of the French penal colony of New Caledonia.

At the time it was not unusual for entire families from the region around Searsport, Maine, to go to sea. Many of Joanna's sea-born friends were christened with names of the area where they were born, as, for example, Fastnet, Iona, and Mindoro.

"I have always been glad that my parents did not see fit to name me Caledonia," said Joanna years later.

When she was born, her father, Captain Lincoln Alden Colcord, was sailing from New Castle, New South Wales, to Yokohama, Japan. Joanna's birth was presided over by a midwife from New Castle named Grandma Searle. Later this same midwife took other voyages in Searsport sailing vessels and brought at least three more children into the world, among them Joanna's cousin Rupert, who was born on the ship *Centennial*, the son of Captain B. F. Colcord.

Joanna's birth was not as sensational as that of her brother Lincoln, who came into this world in 1883 in a gale of wind just after the ship, which was leaking badly, had rounded Cape Horn. Not only did the distracted

Joanna and her brother Lincoln Colcord on the deck of the barkentine Clara E. McGillvery, *aboard which they accompanied their father on a voyage to Rio De La Plata*

father have to look after all the details of his craft, but he had to officiate at his son's birth as well. After that, Joanna reported, "My mother finally decided that she had enough of sea-going for a few years."

On arrival back in Searsport, the family stayed home for about five years while the father continued sailing around the world.

Then Joanna and Lincoln accompanied their father on a voyage to Rio De La Plata, in the *Clara E. McGillvery,** a barkentine built at Searsport.

"Next year when I was eight," Joanna said, "I took my turn at seafaring and Linc got his introduction to the halls of learning. We put out from Portland, lumber-laden, into a full gale of wind and I was seasick for the first and last time. On the fourth day out it faired away and Father took me, convalescent now, on D deck and set me inside a life ring that was lashed to the top of the afterhouse."

She vividly remembered the little barkentine which ran so bravely through the great seas which, she said, "heave up all around in sunlit walls of liquid sapphire." When the *Clara E. McGillvery* rose on one of the huge swells, the seas stretched to the horizon, a living blue, barred

---

*The *Clara E. McGillvery* was eventually lost on the Carolina coast.

with mile-long white-topped combers. "The sun warmed me," she recalled, "and its play on the snowy seas fascinated me."

When Joanna recovered her strength at sea, she would play house with her dolls and her kitten in the nooks and crannies which are always present in a deck load of lumber.

She reports, "I still remember sailing up the broad La Plata and then into the narrower Parana with the jungle standing up to its knees in water on either side, far into the interior of Argentina to the little port of Rosario."

Years afterward when she had made the acquaintance of C. Fox Smith* the voyage was recalled for her in four lines by Miss Smith's poetry:

> *Oh, wake her—oh, shake her!—and it's good-by to the shore,*
> *With the north wind in her topsails and the whole wide world*
> *before . . .*
> *Sou'west an' a half west and steady as you go. . . . .*
> *For we've a long road to travel to Rosario!*

Unfortunately, at Rosario Joanna contracted dysentery and nearly died. There were tense moments suffered by the parents.

"My keenest recollection of Rosario is waking to find my mother beside me sewing a blue plaid dress for my doll, seeing her tears fall upon it, and wondering why she was crying," wrote Joanna years later.

Captain Colcord was in command of the speedy Boston bark *Harvard* between 1891 and 1898.† Joanna records that, "In her we made many voyages, short ones to the River and long ones to China."

The voyage that Joanna and Lincoln recalled most clearly was a two-year journey when they were entering their teens. It took them first to South Africa, across to Australia, and then around to China. Portland, Oregon, was the next port of call, and from there the west coast of Mexico beckoned, after which a trip back to Puget Sound was made.

---

*Under the initials of C.F.S., Miss C. Fox Smith for many years delighted the readers of *Punch* and practically achieved the position of poet laureate and historian of the merchant service.

†The ship was 181 feet in length, with a breadth of 35 feet, and a depth of 21. Her gross tonnage was 1,033 and her signal letters were JSVR.

On reaching Puget Sound, Mrs. Colcord and the two children came home overland while Captain Colcord sailed to several Chilean ports before coming home around Cape Horn.

Recollections of Joanna's trips include the feather market in Port Elizabeth, where she saw tons of ostrich feathers in great bins, as well as a "southerly buster" in that open roadstead, with stoppers on the anchor chains and the ships showing half their keels in their deep plunges during a violent storm.

Joanna had fond memories of calla lillies growing wild in the roadside ditches at Port Natal, nor did she ever forget the "Bogey Hole," a rocky pool at New Castle where the American consul's children took her swimming. At Molendo ill-tempered llamas bothered the party, and she also vividly recalled the trip by rail up to Arequipa. Crescent-shaped sand dunes and breathtaking gorges and precipices were her memory of that particular occasion. She often mentioned the Cathedral Plaza in Arequipa with the gigantic mountain in the background, El Misty, majestic and snow crowned. She enjoyed eating the ripe figs from the trees and seeing the nasturtiums clambering wild over the rocks. Occasionally, after she returned to her Maine home, a breath of wind of unusual force would recall the land breezes she had experienced years before rounding Cape Plumo at the end of Lower California. Trees cut down near her home in Maine often made her think of the "tangy smell of fresh pine logs at lumber yards at Tacoma." The "big things pass and the little things remain," Joanna reminisced years later.

In 1898, on a voyage which Captain Colcord made without the other members of his family, his beloved *Harvard* was shipwrecked at Turk's Island in the West Indies. Returning to Maine, he then "bought into" the full-rigged ship *State of Maine*.*

When she sailed from Atlantic ports, the course was due east. Shipmasters proceeding south struggled to go as far in the direction of Europe as the winds would permit before turning toward the equator. This plan prevented the prevailing easterly trade winds from heading off in rounding Cape St. Roque. Out to sea from this Brazilian headland, north and southbound routes lay close together, and in this region of light winds fifteen or twenty vessels would often be in company for days together.

---

*Built in New Castle, Maine, she was registered at 1,535 tons. Her length was 216 feet, her breadth 40 feet, and her depth 244 feet. Her builder was Haggett and Company, and the *Maine*'s home port was Damariscotta.

Joanna Carver Colcord, who was born at sea off the coast of New Caledonia aboard a sailing vessel of which her father was captain (courtesy of Mrs. Lincoln Colcord)

Everyone who has sailed in this area should remember the tall steeple of naked black rock rising out of verdant forest which is the island of Fernando de Noronha, from which sailing vessels took a new departure for the South Atlantic. After this the road ahead lay around the Cape of Good Hope "running the easting down," before great roaring gales and then across the Indian Ocean for a sighting of Christmas Island for the purpose of checking chronometers.

Joanna often recalled the first stop in a three-month journey at Sunda Straits, the channel between Java and Sumatra. This was one of the world's most important crossroads in sailing-ship days.

> *We would drop anchor in Anjer Roads where the pumice stone ejected in the great 1883 eruption of Krakatao volcano still drifted up and down with the tide; and our good friend, old Sa-Lee, the Javanese compradore,* would come off aboard, his crew singing in strange cadences as they rowed. He would bring out mail in a tin canister, a boatload of fruit, coconuts, eggs, vegetables, poultry—and news of*

---

*Native servant employed as head of the servant staff for white families.

"the fleet." Sa-Lee carried a notebook in which each successive captain left a brief account of his passage, and messages and mocking condolences to friends whom he had outstripped on the voyage.

After working our way past the North Watcher and up the China Sea we reached our port of destination where we often lay at anchor for a couple of months gathering cargo. The round voyage took nearly a full year. Sometimes both my brother and I made the voyage, sometimes one of us remained at home in school. Between the ages of eight and eighteen I spent about half my life at sea.

Although sail was on the decline all through Joanna's childhood, it was still Searsport's chief industry. She and her brother Lincoln could always count on finding some of their Searsport playmates among children on ships of all nations they met in every port. Although her mother and father made Joanna work diligently on her lessons at sea, whenever they reached port both she and Lincoln were given holidays. They went ashore to see strange sights, visit the homes of the businessmen, and play with their children. Occasionally there would be a great picnic for all the captains and their families.

Several times a week one ship or another would be the rendezvous where officers' wives and families would get together.

"Many a night," writes Joanna, "under the awning on some ship's deck, with the shore lights sending down long deep roads of flame into the harbor water, and cigar tips glowing and facing, the child that was I listened to marvelous stories from the world's best raconteurs— seamen—and agonized in the vain effort to stay awake to hear the end of the last and most enthralling tale."

Many oriental sellers of lacquer, jewelry, and embroidery often visited the ships and were permitted to spread out their wares on deck. Best of all, Joanna remembered the old Ceylonese peddler of jewelry and semi-precious stones in Singapore with his knot of hair and tortoiseshell comb like a woman's. One day when he discovered that it was Joanna's birthday, he untied a knotted rag to display a handful of moonstones and invited the girl to take her pick.

"True to form I chose the biggest. Then I noticed a peculiar smile on Mother's face. She pointed out to me that a flaw went all the way across the jewel, dulling its beauty. I wanted to put it back and take another, but she said I must keep it, to remind me that quality is better than size. I have that stone to this day," Joanna wrote in 1936.

> *More exciting still were the occasional visits of wandering jugglers.*
> *They would squat upon their squares of cloth spread upon the deck,*
> *plant the mango seed in front of them and make it grow before our*
> *wondering eyes. They would plunge the sword through the basket in*
> *which we had seen the little boy tied up and packed away—but*
> *always, when the horror was getting too great to bear, he would come*
> *running unharmed from the shelter of the cabin.*

In the daytime when the ship's sampans (shore boats which each captain hired for the duration of the stay) were not otherwise in use, the children sometimes organized trips around the harbor. These craft were floating homes of the boatmen to whom the American parents did not hesitate to entrust their children.

"We played with the Chinese youngsters without a word of common language, swapped cake and candy for gaudy paper lanterns, fished, and had a generally gorgeous time."

Thus Joanna's life was a combination of unusually stimulating and exciting periods in port alternating with long days of either peaceful or rough sailing.

Joanna had her small duties like the others. When a ship was sighted and came near enough for communication by flag signals, that was Joanna's moment of glory. She and her brother would search out the code symbols, select the many colored flags for the hoist, and translate the stranger's replies.

The manner of conducting the lesson on board ship should interest present-day parents and pupils alike. Captain and Mrs. Colcord would go to the schools before sailing to talk with the teachers about the lessons. Joanna and Lincoln used aboard ship the same books as the pupils in Searsport.

"We were living geography, although we knew only the edges of the continents," said Joanna.

One of the favorite games in stormy weather was to spread a chart on the cabin floor and, using dominoes for ships, charter, load, and sail the craft from port to port, with an occasional shipwreck or fight against Chinese pirates to liven things up. Mathematics was a living subject aboard ship, for the Searsport craft went all the way around the world by mathematics. As Joanna grew older, she participated in finding the sun's positions day by day, casting the ship's reckoning, and laying off on the chart the previous day's run.

Joanna says that they were wide, if not selective readers, as it was the custom to exchange libraries between ships in port. Many strange books and magazines came her way as the result of the barter. Her parents tried to keep anything they thought positively harmful out of the children's hands, but much of what fell to them was peculiar reading for youngsters. For example, she had Volney's *Ruins of Empire* alongside of which might be a volume of religious tracts. She read the words of Paul de Kock, after which she would read Aurora Leigh. And she devoured with equal interest H. Rider Haggard's *She* and *King Solomon's Mines*. When everything else failed Joanna could fall back on fat volumes of sailing directions. When she studied languages and sciences, she was handicapped, but in spite of this she kept up with her contemporaries in school at home. She took her final examinations from Searsport high school in Hong Kong harbor. The questions had been sent out by mail and the test was proctored by her mother. Her diploma was waiting for her when she returned to Searsport six months later.

Letter writing was, according to Joanna, an educational feature of seafaring life. Separation between members of families for long periods created an eagerness to share every minor happening with those faraway. The children imitated the elders and kept long and detailed journals both at sea and at home, learning in this way to break through the reticence of the average New Englander and describe with some degree of vividness what they saw and experienced. Joanna always felt certain that this early training in self-expression had a profound influence in turning both her brother and herself to writing.

From the very beginning of her sea experience she had to learn to adjust herself to the strict routine of life at sea. She never could remember a time when it was not completely accepted by her and her brother that they should never bother people who had duties to perform. Except for two hours in the evening, some of the officers who shared with them the afterhouse were always off duty and trying to sleep, and so she learned to play quietly. Even the dog they had aboard seemed to understand. Of course, in bad weather Captain Colcord had to snatch an hour or two of sleep whenever he could, and Joanna and Linc invented a system of signals by which they could play Authors and other such games in utter silence. They were under complete discipline every moment of the day, but so were all others on board. All the adults had the same restrictions. It no more occurred to Joanna than to any other of the ship's company to resist any command from the fount of all authority, her father. This was the normal way of life on shipboard, and the children never questioned the necessity for it.

Nevertheless, in his off hours Captain Colcord was a delightful playmate, a grand storyteller, and a good singer. When he read aloud it was indeed a pleasure to listen.

"His remarkable skill as a letter writer kept us from losing touch with him during our periods on shore," wrote Joanna. "His humorous and stimulating mind and his uncompromising attitude toward duty and right conduct were equally educational forces in bringing up his children." To their mother they could always go when anything troubled them. "But when Father became the Captain, we knew from our cradles," Joanna said later, "that we must not bother him with our small problems."

Of course there were fixed times when the children might consort with the officers—at meals, during their watch below if they were not sleeping, or when they were mending sails and doing such small jobs as that. "They were uniformly kind to us, and suited their conversation to our young ears," said Joanna.

One of the chief mates was, by the way, Louis Dermot of Rockland, the brother of Maine's famous actresses, Maxine Elliot and Lady Gertrude Forbes-Robertson.

When they had a Chinese steward aboard he was a crony of the children's.

"We were also allowed to visit the carpenter in his shop and even the Chinese cook in his galley after the day's dinner was over and before he retired to smoke, with great decorum, his daily pipeful of opium. Father always carried an extra supply in the medicine chest in case the old fellow should run short in a long voyage," Joanna recalled.

Of course, the problem of the men before the mast, who usually changed on every passage, had to be handled carefully. The captain's family could not speak to them even when they were standing at the wheel in the area in which the children were permitted to move around. This applied more strictly to Joanna and her mother than to her brother Linc, although he was never allowed to visit the forecastle where the sailors lived.

In port most of the crew were paid off, and if one or two stayed aboard to make the return voyage, that particular rule was relaxed. The children were allowed to talk to the men who were signing over again, and on the way home they could exchange little signals of recognition.

On one occasion Linc fell overboard while the ship was in the shark-infested waters of a Mexican port, and "Obrion, who plunged over to his rescue along with Father and Louis Dermot, was a privileged character on the rest of the voyage, of course."

Joanna's brother was allowed to climb aloft early in his life, but Joanna never had the privilege, and as she grew older her range on deck was more restricted than his. She might not go forward of the main mast and she always had to behave quietly "like a little lady." Also, she had to learn to sew, which her brother Linc did not have to do. She was a real tomboy and these restrictions, particularly the art of sewing, irked her deeply, but as she says, "I toed the mark."

The ship's discipline conveyed to the family of the captain no feeling that the sailors were inferior beings. Joanna always knew that her father and the officers, as well as all the other captains whom she met, had lived in the forecastle in their young days. Neither did race nor color of skin have anything to do with a man's standing on board a ship.

She recalled one exciting evening just before she sailed away from the little Mexican port of Santa Rosalia. An American citizen was ashore at the port. He was so deeply in debt through the vicious "company store" system that he was in virtual peonage to the mine where he worked, and Captain Colcord found out about it. One night a red lantern was hung as a signal on the beach, and the moment that the light blinked out the ship's boat went in. With muffled oars they landed and kidnapped this willing American citizen whose name was Harry. He was a colored man, but to Joanna and her brother the mere fact that he had dark skin only made him more interesting. An expert mechanic, he was given the donkey engine to run, which put him in the petty officer class. The children were allowed to talk with Harry all they wanted, except when he was on duty or trying to sleep.

Joanna often watched the lascars when they were aboard. Being Muhammedans they carried their own cook who prepared all their food, and Joanna loved to see him grind the herbs for curry on a stone slab. Sometimes they would sample the fiery dish when it was ready, and for years it remained one of the family's favorite foods.

Joanna was taught to be especially polite to Chinese businessmen, for whom her father's liking and respect were great. She felt distinctly honored when Ah Man with his violet silk robe, long fingernails, and plaited hair would share her cabin meal.

When the Bath ship *Emma D. Crowell*, commanded by Captain Andrew Pendleton of Searsport, was overdue at Hong Kong after a typhoon in the China Sea, it was Ah Man who lent three anxious Searsport captains his steam launch. He himself went along to help in the search and towed the dismasted craft to port when she was found helplessly adrift. It was the greatest surprise to Joanna when she returned to America to know that the color of a person's skin alone might determine his social qualifications.

There were, of course, some disadvantages to sea life. Vitamins were unknown in those days, and although they had the freshest air and the most unobstructed sunlight in the world, their diet during three or four months at sea lacked the milk, fresh vegetables, and fruit which are important for growing children. But they made up for it when they got to port. "Eat your nice spinach, dear," was never a necessary admonition in the Colcord household. "We were only too happy to oblige," says Joanna.

Then too, when they got home after a year's absence their 'longshore playmates had invented new games and were using passwords of which they had never heard. They were outsiders for a while, and it was awkward for them.

Otherwise Joanna could never remember any drawbacks and she did recall many advantages to an upbringing at sea. Children whose home was on a ship became acquainted with the way men live and work together in many lands. Joanna's life was part of the world's greatest internationalizing movement, commerce. Although it was seldom that danger actually threatened them, she was aware that it was always a possibility. She knew why small boats were lashed to the top of the forward house and why they were always kept in readiness for use. She understood the law of circular storms and what a change of wind meant when a cyclone was somewhere in the neighborhood of the ship. The dread chances that lurked in a heavy fog when coming to the coast were not kept hidden from Joanna. In this sense, early in life she learned to face realities, and she was not as sheltered as were children on land.

She was not, however, particularly conscious of being different from her companions ashore. The surroundings seemed to her perfectly natural and commonplace. Only as she grew older* did she become aware

---

*Her first long skirt was blue serge with brush binding on the bottom made by a Chinese tailor in Hong Kong, where she put up her hair for the first time and was invited to her first ball.

that there was something strange in the eyes of the people ashore about her mode of living. This made her all the more determined to stand on her rights.

When she arrived in New York in 1900 after a voyage to Hong Kong on the *State of Maine*, she knew it was the last trip for her. The ship was about to be sold as a coal barge. "Father was going into steam, as the saying is, where we would not be allowed to travel with him, and I was headed off to college," Joanna recalled. "I remember thinking with the cherished sadness of youth, as I went down the gangplank and out into South Street, 'The happiest days of my life are forever behind me.'"

That was not to prove strictly the case,* but in the days that followed she drew heavily on the lessons learned at sea. Without realizing it, she had taken into her very being the majesty of the oceans and the beauty of the ships made by man to sail them; the loveliness of sunsets on the line, of strange harbors and island landfalls in a rosy dawn; and the fascination in sea songs and stories. She always recalled the thrill of hearing the crew of a British ship lying beside them in Shanghai singing the old chantey, "Good-by, fare ye well," as they heaved up anchor and of comprehending for the first time that this was beautiful and distinctive music.

"We learned sterner things," writes Joanna, "instant obedience, orderliness, a necessary quality in the close confines of a ship, contempt for sham and double dealing because you cannot fool the sea. We learned that a job must be well done for its own sake, with that little extra touch for good measure that is implied in the word shipshape. And we learned something of the inexorability of duty, stern taskmaster of all our days."

One of the truly great personalities of "downeast" shipping, Joanna Carver Colcord will always be remembered for her intense love of the sea and her ability to translate that love into language which we can all understand.

Let us say our farewell to Joanna by joining the sailors aboard the *State of Maine* as they heave up anchor on the last of the "long-vanished ships" in which her "young years were spent," as Joanna wrote fifteen years before her death.

> *Now fare ye well, and fare ye well*
> *Good-by, fare ye well.*

---

*She married Professor Frank John Bruno on November 24, 1950.

———————— ～ ————————

Joanna Carver Colcord earned an undergraduate degree in chemistry and a master's degree in biological chemistry from the University of Maine. She later became a social worker after studying at the New York School of Philanthropy.

In addition to many articles, Colcord's books that drew on her experiences at sea included *Roll and Go: Songs of American Sailormen* (1924), *Songs of American Sailormen* (1938), and *Sea Language Comes Ashore* (1945), a dictionary of nautical terms in American English. She also wrote several books in the social welfare field and advocated for social security and health insurance during the Depression. "Nan" Colcord, as she was known to many, died in 1960. Her papers reside at the Peabody Essex Museum in Salem, Massachusetts.

CHAPTER 16

105 La. 39

Most followers of the sea associate the year 1898 with the Portland Gale, which swept across the northeastern United States with great force and speed, leaving more than two hundred craft sunk or damaged and several hundred people dead. At the height of the storm the steamer *Portland*, then attempting to steam from Boston to Portland, Maine, sank with 190 persons on board.

Nevertheless, in spite of all that has been written about the Portland Gale, another steamer that same year sank off Sable Island with a loss of life more than twice as great as that of the *Portland*. Her name was *La Bourgogne*, and it is about one passenger in particular aboard her that this chapter is written—namely, Angele Marie Langles.

Sable Island, near where the steamer went down, is located 150 miles out to sea from Halifax, Nova Scotia. It is twenty-four miles long, about half a mile wide, and lies almost directly in the path of ocean travel, which accounts for the more than five hundred ships which have met their doom off its shores.

I have had the privilege of landing at Sable Island twice, and each time have been intrigued by this treacherous strip of sand. Its underground bars give the sandy spit a total length of more than fifty miles, and it is actually a part of a giant series of bars in the general area south of Newfoundland. Included in the group are Nantucket Shoals, Emerald Bank, Sable Island Bank, Middle Ground, Canso Bank, Misaine Bank, Banquereau, St. Pierre Bank, Green Bank, and the Grand Banks of Newfoundland. These banks extend from fifteen to three hundred miles and are made up of particles of pebbles, coal, shells, and sand, with the depth of water above them usually no more than seventy fathoms.

Of the fourteen banks, only one, Sable Island, is above the high-water mark. Running from east to west, it is in north latitude forty-four degrees and in west latitude sixty degrees. It moves just a little every year, washing away on the Halifax end and building up on the western end. Deceptive in its coloring, which always seems to match the water, it is comparatively low. The highest hill, which conceals a shipwrecked clipper of more than a hundred years ago, is barely one hundred feet in height.

Angele Marie Langles, aged thirty-five, was believed to be aboard *La Bourgogne* with her widowed mother, Pauline Costa Langles, aged fifty-two, when the ship sailed from New York in 1898 toward those treacherous shores. The two women had journeyed from New Orleans to New York just a few days previously. Both mother and daughter owned extensive property in New Orleans where they had lived for a number of years.

For some reason, possibly because they decided that sea travel was uncertain, both had recently executed reciprocal wills* at New Orleans a few days before leaving for New York, the mother on June 25, and the daughter two days later. In her testament, the mother declared that "I give and bequeath to my daughter, Angele M. Langles, all the property of which I may die possessed, hereby constituting her my universal legatee. In case of the death of my said daughter prior to my death, I give [various personal and charitable legacies]. Two thousand dollars to be expended for my tomb."

The daughter, in her will, declared that she "by this, my last olographic† will and testament, entirely written, dated, and signed by me, I give and bequeath to my mother, Mrs. J. Langles, all the property of which I may die possessed, hereby constituting her my universal legatee. In case of the death of my mother prior to my death, I give [various personal and charitable legacies]. After all my debts are paid, the remainder

---

*For the legal aspect of the story I draw, with permission, from the article "Angele Marie Langles" by Eberhard P. Deutsch of the Louisiana bar, published in the American Bar Association's *Journal* of March 1962.

†Olographic is an "erroneous" version of holographic, which means written entirely in the hand of the person from whom it proceeds.

of my fortune I give for the support of the memorial hospital built by my mother. Three thousand dollars to be appropriated for my tomb. . . ."

On July 1, 1898, Angele wrote her cousin Alex Costa in New Orleans that she and her mother were sailing in the morning on *La Bourgogne* from New York. That letter was the last word ever heard from either Pauline or Angele Langles.

Actually there is no definite knowledge that the two women went aboard *La Bourgogne*, as those who survived did not recall having seen them on the ship.

On Saturday, July 2, the proud French liner sailed from New York, under the command of Captain Deloncle, bound for Europe. The passengers planned a celebration of America's national Fourth of July holiday two days later aboard the 7,395-ton vessel while she was plowing through the waves toward her destination. Built in 1886 for the French Line, *La Bourgogne* was not quite five hundred feet long, but was usually acclaimed as a great French floating palace.

Including crew and passengers, the 820 persons aboard made their first night at sea a happy occasion. Before morning, however, spirits became somewhat dampened when fog surrounded the vessel. The captain should have reduced the liner's speed to a moderate rate, but, as in the case of the *Andrea Doria** over a half-century later, schedule seemed more important than the safety of human life.

July 3 passed without incident, except that the fog continued to drift in. By midnight on the night before the Fourth the huge steamer had reached a position some eighty miles south of Sable Island. Sailing 160 miles off her normal course, she was going at excessive speed, and steaming through the fog in sea lanes usually taken only by sailing vessels. The fog again shut in worse than ever after midnight. Shortly before five o'clock on July 4, a steel bark, the *Cromartyshire*, entered the same area off Sable Island and headed unknowingly directly toward *La Bourgogne*.

Then a few moments before five o'clock the quiet of morning was blasted by a mighty crash. The two vessels had collided! *La Bourgogne* was hit broadside just abaft the starboard bridge by the bow of the steel bark, and a great, gaping hole was torn in the French liner's side.

One of the most heartbreaking scenes in all the history of Atlantic crossing then was enacted. Several episodes which may have been

---

*Sunk in collision with the *Stockholm*, July 26, 1956.

witnessed by the two Langles ladies as the great liner struggled to stay afloat are included in this chapter.

Two factors contributed to the pandemonium of terror that broke loose. First, a large number of the steerage passengers had already suffered and survived one shipwreck and were finishing their journey aboard *La Bourgogne*. These people, finding themselves once again subjected to the dangers of the deep, were doubly terrified as a result of their previous experience and were exceedingly difficult to control.

The second reason for panic was the behavior of the black gang, as those who labor in the engine room of a great steamer were called. It was claimed afterward that they lost all discipline. Arriving on deck in a solid phalanx, they swept through the terrified passengers to take control of the lifeboat launching. Careless in their fright, the engine room force trod under their feet dozens of women and children and climbed over their bodies. One by one they crowded into the boats, forcing the women and children away, until several of the craft and scores of the men were safely away from the sinking liner. Husbands were separated from their families and never saw them again.

Only six minutes had elapsed since the crash when three priests and the second officer came along the deck. Not one of them was wearing a life jacket, as each had given his to someone else. Realizing the full danger of the situation—tons of water were pouring into the steamer every second—the four men did their best to comfort the frightened passengers. Suddenly, less than ten minutes after the collision, the steamer gave a sickening lurch to starboard, and there was a terrible slant to the deck.

There is no knowledge whatever, as I have already mentioned, of what actually happened to the two ladies from New Orleans, but as only one woman, a Mrs. Lacasse, of the 300 aboard was saved, they must have gone down with the rest of the women and children. In fact, only 43 passengers out of 550 aboard were rescued, and no passenger who sailed with first-class accommodations lived to tell the story.

La Bourgogne carried in the steerage a considerable number of foreigners, including some Italians as well as the homebound crew of an Austrian ship which had been wrecked. When the men from the steerage reached the deck and found that women were being placed in the stern boats they went mad. Screaming and fighting, the foreigners boarded the craft, pulling the women from their seats, threatening them with clubs and revolvers, until they went back aboard ship with their children. The foreigners then all clambered aboard and worked the davits until their lifeboats were in the sea and they saved themselves. An editorial in the *New York Times* of July 8, 1898, points out that the fact that officers "of the *Bourgogne* lost their lives does not prevent the horrible scene of savagery that followed the collision from being a national disgrace. . . . We say a national disgrace advisedly, because we do not believe that in the annals of the British or the American mercantile marine any parallel can be found to that spectacle of unchecked cruel and brutal selfishness that was shown when the *Bourgogne* went down."

Although the bow of the *Cromartyshire* was torn off, she remained afloat. When the fog began to clear, she lowered her boats and aided in the rescue work, taking aboard 163 persons [mostly crew—*Ed.*]. Later the British steamer *Grecian* towed the *Cromartyshire* into Halifax Harbor, where news of the disaster was sent around the world.

Each country had its own legal decisions in connection with suits resulting from the disaster. The French courts held *La Bourgogne* free from fault, and it was claimed that her speed was not excessive at the time of the collision. It was also made clear ultimately by France's highest court of appeal—the Court of Cassation—that "no inference is to be drawn from the fact that the number of mariners saved greatly exceeded that of the passengers who survived the disaster."

The United States Supreme Court held that "it is too clear" that the French steamer was at fault because she was "going at a rate of speed prohibited by the International Rule."

In England the courts announced their series of decisions. It was held that they had jurisdiction, and the Trinity Masters reached a conclusion of fact that "*La Bourgogne* was in fact going at too great a rate of speed." The British Court of Appeal concluded that there could not be a doubt "that *La Bourgogne* was going at an utterly unjustifiable speed considering the density of the fog."

The deaths of Angele Langles and her mother brought an opinion in connection with Louisiana's law of descent and distribution. It also turned on provisions of the Code Napoleon, which had been brought over verbatim from France and incorporated into the civil code of Louisiana.

Harry H. Hall, a prominent New Orleans lawyer, was named executor of the estates of both the Langles ladies. After waiting a reasonable length of time to ascertain whether or not the two women had possibly

The monument erected in New Orlean's Metairie Cemetery in memory of Angele Marie Langles to fulfill the provision of her will, following her disappearance in the wreck of La Bourgogne

survived, Hall filed the wills for probate. In a relatively short time there were persons presenting claims for recognition of hereditary rights to the property of the two women. Attorney Hall filed a petition seeking approval of a proposed "tableau of distribution in order to avoid a multiplicity of suits."

The important question was whether mother or daughter died first. The heirs of the mother sought to show that as she was the stronger of the two ladies, she probably lived longer. Nevertheless the heirs of the daughter stated that according to the civil code of Louisiana, Angele must be presumed to have survived after her mother. The City of New Orleans, claiming the residuary legacies under both testaments, based its contention on simultaneous death. The jury found that as it was impossible to determine whether mother or daughter died first, it had to act upon a legal presumption of survivorship.

Thus the court concluded that "in the interest of the natural order of succession, and agreeable to which, in your case, it will be held that the daughter survived the mother." Thus it became necessary to adjudicate the validity of the particular and universal legacies of Angele's will.

The court took occasion to castigate the principal claimants of Pauline Langles' estate, because they had opposed the effectiveness of the latter's will and also dealt severely with the heirs of Angele Langles because they had sought to increase their inheritance by attempting to invalidate her direction to spend $3,000 for her tomb.

"We are surprised that the heirs of the deceased, inheriting her property under the circumstances they have, should have opposed, as they have, the carrying out of Angele Langles' wishes on the subject. They should have been willing to perpetuate her memory even in this slight way.

"We do not think that the direction of the testatrix that $3,000 should be expended by her executor for a tomb, should fail from the fact that the body of the testatrix has not been recovered and cannot be deposited in it. The world 'tomb' has been defined, among other meanings, to signify 'a monument or tombstone erected in memory of the dead.' We think this is a proper occasion to give the word its broadest meaning—a monument in memory of the dead."

Thus the executor of the estate of Angele was required to erect a monument in her memory at a cost of $3,000. The imposing granite sepulcher erected in Metairie Cemetery of New Orleans has perhaps the most unusual inscription anywhere in Louisiana. Possibly fearing that all who passed would think Angele's body was under the ceno-taph, the only writing in the monument gives the name of the deceased person whose money paid for the monument and a reference to that particular part of the legal decisions of Louisiana which records the case:

Angele Marie Langles
105 La. 39

─────────── ⌁ ───────────

La Bourgogne, 494.4 feet long, was built in France in 1885. Captain Deloncle of *La Bourgogne* was inexperienced and was on one of his first Atlantic cross-ings when the disaster described in this chapter occurred. The incorrect course put the voyage to Le Havre, France, behind schedule, and the captain was reported to have told one passenger, "Fog or no fog, we have to make up the lost time."

Varying casualty figures have been reported for the wreck of *La Bourgogne*. Around 165 survived, but there is no doubt of the sad fact that no children and only one woman were among the survivors. Somewhere in the vicinity of 546 people died.

The *Cromartyshire*, built in Scotland in 1879, was repaired but was wrecked in 1906 on its way from Australia to Chile.

CHAPTER 17

Greta's Adventure

One of the more unusual shipwreck tales which I am including in this volume is that of the steamboat *Stella*, engaged in the Channel Islands service just before the turn of the century. She was a fine, new, twin-screw vessel of 1,000 tons making her first daylight trip of the year on March 20, 1899, from Southampton, England, to Guernsey in the Channel Isles. In a dense fog, going at full speed, she ran onto the ill-famed Black Rock, one of the fatal Casquets group, and disaster followed.

More than sixty years later I am able to give you the story of one of the women passengers, Greta Williams. It was a joyous group which left Waterloo Station that Thursday morning. The railway run seemed short, and at noon the passengers went on board the *Stella*. Soon they were steaming down Southampton Water under a brilliant sun, and a short time later reached the open sea. The fresh sea breeze was a tonic for many of them who were getting away from London to have a holiday rest at Guernsey. The *Stella* was an eighteen-knot boat and she moved along rapidly, for she was due in Guernsey before dark. Knowing that they were to spend about seven hours on board ship, most of the passengers settled down to relax or read. As Greta Williams stated later, they made themselves "as cozy as we could."

Greta's own words follow:

> *I and my sister Theresa, who was traveling with me, went early in the afternoon to lie down in our private cabin, as the air was cold. The*

sun was vanishing, and the outlook was very unpromising because of one of those dangerous fogs which infest the Channel.

The fog thickened, and our siren hooted dismally at intervals as we steamed rapidly ahead into the ghostly, clammy atmosphere.

Nearly five hours had passed since we sailed, and we were still going smoothly ahead. Suddenly, without the slightest warning, there came a strange, grinding sound and a shock, which even the merest landsman knew was not caused by the sea. The check to our easy running, the sudden cries we heard, the hurrying of feet, and many dismaying noises told us that something terrible had happened.

My sister and I hurried from our cabin to the deck, and instantly the blanched faces of the people we saw rushing about or staring wildly confirmed our fears. Yet even then I did not realize the peril we were in. Everything was in a state of commotion. The very ship seemed affected, for she trembled like a living thing, and there was a dreadful and unnerving noise from her engines, which were still working.

Before I could collect my thoughts there was another grinding crash. This was due, as I found out afterward, to the fact that the Stella, *after first striking, left the rocky ledge and struck again. She was injured amidships, in her most vital parts, and traveling as she was, the damage was so extensive that the sea poured into the hull in enormous quantities.*

The awesome truth soon was flashed about the *Stella* that the ship had struck the terrible Casquets, located eight miles west of Alderney Rocks, which for centuries have meant doom to the boldest sailors. Even in clear weather they are a great danger because of the strong swirls and eddies caused by the channel tides. Of course, in heavy fog that day they were an appalling danger. Whatever hopes those on the steamboat had that the *Stella* might be saved, vanished when she struck again, and all aboard heard the order for the lifeboats to be lowered at once. When those words were uttered by the captain and his officers, it meant, of course, that the ship was doomed.

Rushing with her sister to the side of the craft Miss Williams saw through the fog the hideous fangs of Black Rock and watched the waves as they rolled over it. It was all so swift and so unbelievable. Greta then heard the voices of the officers who, as they directed the lowering of the lifeboats, were cheering the passengers with the assurance that not a life would be lost and that every one would get clear of the ship. Miss Williams, however, did not believe they would all be saved as the ship was going down too fast. Even as she rushed from her cabin, she saw that life belts were being given out and that the crew were working furiously to get the boats lowered in time.

"There was nothing that you could call panic," she explained later. On the other hand, "there were many glorious examples of British pluck and unselfishness."

A Mr. Barnes helped save Greta and her sister, and aided several others. The life belts had been stowed in lockers, which were made with open spaces between the planking so that the air could circulate and prevent rot. Since there was not time to get the lockers open in the proper way, Mr. Barnes pulled the planks right from the beams. Getting out one life belt, he passed it across to Greta and then took another, which he gave to Theresa. Mr. Barnes' wife was very courageous at the time, and did much to calm the two sisters.

The four people stood together briefly, and then came a piercing cry rising above all the others, "Women and children first!"

The wreck of the Stella *on March 20, 1899, in the English Channel off Alderney Rocks, in which Greta Williams and her sister nearly lost their lives*

Greta and Theresa hurried to a small boat that was about to be lowered from the *Stella*, which even then was listing so badly that her deck was like a sloping roof. There were seven lifeboats in all, and the two girls were about to climb into the one nearest them when Greta noticed how overcrowded it was. She decided that they should not get into it and glancing across the deck, she saw another which was not so full.

"Let's get into that one," she called.

They ran across the deck and struggled into the other boat, which was lowered at once. The moment after it had reached the water and pulled clear, the survivors watched in horrified silence as the *Stella* disappeared before their eyes. Greta sat transfixed as the lifeboat she had almost taken was pulled down with the ship, capsizing as she went under to drown every person aboard.

"Such are the tragic chances of the sea," she observed to her sister, for both would have perished had they not made that last-minute decision.

She wrote subsequently:

> *Seven short minutes only had passed since we were lying in our cozy stateroom in a strong and beautiful steamer—and now she had vanished, and we were tossing wildly on the seething waters which had just engulfed her.*
>
> *When we had somewhat overcome our horror and recovered our steadiness a little, when we realized that we had, at any rate, escaped the greatest danger—the suction of the disappearing vessel, and that we were afloat and with a chance of ultimate salvation—we had time to look about us and get some idea of the terrible havoc which had been done in one brief moment.*
>
> *The air was burdened with the most dreadful sounds—the cries of the drowning and despairing, and the infinitely worse appeals of those who begged to be taken into boats that were already overladen.*
>
> *How can I tell you of the things I saw? Yet I will brace myself to do so, for I believe that in such recitals may be found an incentive to responsible authorities to do everything that lies within the power of human skill and worldly riches to accomplish. Surely it is possible for these agencies, with such inventions as submarine signaling and wireless telegraphy, to obviate these perils of the deep—if you can but assure the exercise at all times of prudence as well as courage.*

For some few minutes there was danger that we should be drawn into that seething vortex; then a greater fear that the people who were struggling in the sea would prove our own destruction while they themselves perished.

They fought despairingly to get into our little craft—clinging to the gunwale and clutching wildly at those of us whom they could reach. One of the men in our boat beat them off with his oar, and they fell back into the water and took their chance again. Thank God, in some cases, at any rate, they were saved.

It was terrible that a thing like this should be done—a thing which seems so selfish, and, I suppose, arises from the wish for life over-powering all humanity in certain people.

But there was a brighter side to that dark picture, and that was afforded by many instances of the most glorious courage and self-sacrifice even as the Stella disappeared.

Never was there put on record a nobler deed than that of Mrs. Rogers, the stewardess. She was urged to save herself in the only way available—by getting into one of the boats.

"No, she answered firmly, "they are too full already. There is no room for me."

They told her that it was her only chance, and that she must take it.

"No," she persisted, firmly still—she would not save her own life at the probable cost of a fellow creature's.

She waves us farewell as we drew off in the boat, bidding us be of good cheer; then she raised her clasped hands toward the heavens, and with her last prayer of "Lord, have me!" she went down with the Stella—surely one of the noblest women who ever gave their lives for others.

And I think, too, that death must have come quickly to those who even to the last were not expecting it. The Stella went so quickly, leaning over and over gradually until she vanished all at once, that there was no time for people to realize what was happening. How also can you explain that even when she had struck the rock, one lady was collecting her luggage, and a little boy was getting together the toys with which he had been playing? Both perished.

There was wild confusion in our little boat. Into a space that was meant for fifteen persons, twenty-three were crowded—eighteen men and five women, some of us thickly clothed and wearing cumbersome lifejackets. To add to our danger in that pitiless swirl, only two or thee *of the men could handle an oar, and many strange things were done because of this.*

There was one extraordinary spectacle which I noticed when we had just got away from the wreck. There were struggling people all about us, mostly in the water; but a few appeared to be standing on some kind of support, and some were clinging to the sides of it.

The support seemed something like a raft, but I knew it could not be that; nor did I imagine that it was a rock which was level with the water.

Not until afterward did I learn the truth. Then I found that the strange object was a great furniture van which was on board the Stella *being conveyed to Guernsey. When the ship foundered the van slid off into the sea, and remained floating for some time, but not long enough to enable the survivors to be rescued, even if they had been able to withstand the bitter coldness of the water and exposure to the weather.*

One or two other boats were near us, and during the fifteen torturing hours we were on the water, one, with thirty-three survivors in her, kept very close to us. We looked wildly about us in every direction for a sign of help, but the fog was so dense that we could only see a little way.

Then darkness came to add to our miseries, and we resigned ourselves as best we could to the long, dreary night and its solemn thoughts. The other boat's companionship was a mutual comfort and relief. We rowed and bailed as best we could, and the human ramparts round the gunwales served as barriers to the breaking seas.

Somebody suggested that we should anchor, and the anchors were thrown overboard—though how they expected to get holding-ground in such deep, swirling waters, with a rocky bottom, I do not understand.

The hours went by slowly. Five hours after the *Stella* had gone down in the pitch darkness of that foggy night, the survivors realized that there was no hope of being seen. They were hungry and thirsty, numb with cold, wet and terribly distracted because of the frightful scenes they had witnessed. Unnerved as they were by those last cries for help which they could still hear in their ears, there came a period when all were overwhelmed by despair.

Greta then heard a low voice in the darkness, a voice of a young man praying, seeking courage and comfort from that source from which at such a time consolation can come. Greta thought how beautiful it was of him to pray and encourage the other survivors, but she knew that his words could not be heard by all the people in the lifeboat, and she thought that as she was a good singer, she could help with singing. She turned to her sister, "Theresa," she said, "would you like me to sing?"

"Oh, yes, Greta," Theresa answered, "I would indeed, very much. But do you think you can out here in the lifeboat in the darkness and fog?"

"Yes," Greta answered, "I think so. At any rate I can try."

Even then Greta, taking little comfort from the thought that she had an audience that would not be too critical, wondered what she should sing. The utter discouragement of all aboard the lifeboat decided her. Not long before a dear relative on her dying bed had often asked her to sing a favorite song, "Oh, Rest in the Lord, Wait Patiently for Him," and these were the words she sang to the survivors in the lifeboat.

She related the incident later and admitted her voice was not a steady one that night in the darkness on the lonely sea. They were troubled and imploring tones which came from the very depths of her heart, and while, as she found out later, they did comfort her hearers, they expressed hope which also filled her with assurance of delivery when daylight arrived.

Many of the comments she could not hear. On the other hand, she did overhear one woman say, "I would have liked to have boxed her ears." But others told her that the beautiful words of consolation made them feel braver, and gave them strength to face the night.

They believed that they were anchored when dusk fell, but the anchor had been dragging all night long, and they had been drifting across toward several more ledges of the terrible rocks. There were jagged boulders all around them, and if the lifeboat had smashed into one, it would have capsized and all would have lost their lives.

Suddenly there came a warning that the lifeboat was approaching a particularly dangerous row of jagged ledges, and the shout went up, "Row for your lives!" Everyone rowed desperately, and the boat cleared the danger by just a few feet.

A short time after this a lady, sitting near Greta and Theresa, fainted. It was impossible to help her for some time, although they all did what they could to bring her back to consciousness. Greta's fingers were numb with cold, she was weak and exhausted, and the boat was rocking back and forth with violent commotion. In spite of all this she was able to reach the lady, unbutton her clothing, and make her breathing easier. Finally, she regained consciousness, and Greta could turn her attention elsewhere.

Shortly after daylight a great steamer came along. Although the survivors could all see her very clearly, at first it appeared that the people aboard the vessel were not able to see the little lifeboat. The steamer, the *Vera*, was the sister ship of the *Stella*, but when she bore down to pick up the survivors, no one realized that.

Sailors were sent down the side of the *Vera* to help the survivors aboard, but no attempt was made by the crew to give assistance afterward. They had saved them, and that was all. A passenger, however, came along and looked at Greta.

"May I relieve you of your life belt?" he asked calmly.

"Yes, oh, please do," she answered, and with that he took off the cumbersome belt which she had worn for fifteen hours. Greta instantly ran below to the ladies' cabin and found that everyone was lying down, too seasick to take any notice of either her or anyone else.

As soon as they had established themselves aboard the *Vera*, Greta saw a friend of hers, who made no sign of knowing her. She had changed so much because of her suffering during the hours in the lifeboat that she was unrecognizable.

Finally the *Vera* landed at the pier, and Greta was taken with her sister to a hotel where both were put to bed. So exhausted were they that they slept peacefully and for the time forgot all about the perilous horror through which they had passed. But the terror of it came back year after year, intensified indeed in some cases.

Greta was not afraid, as she said later, during the whole time she was on the water, nor was she seasick as most of the others were, for she was a good sailor. One curious change came about, however, because of that fatal night. Before the wreck she had always been a little nervous when she appeared in public to sing, but after her experience in the lifeboat, she felt that every person in every audience was her friend. Later, she was given a brooch made of five notes of music, each a diamond, in remembrance of that unrehearsed performance at sea. They are the notes of "Oh, Rest in the Lord."

Out of 140 passengers and crew of 40, 105 aboard the *Stella* drowned, and 75 were saved. Greta could never forget how close she and her sister came to losing their lives in this disaster.

The numbers usually given for the *Stella* tragedy are 77 lost out of 190 passengers and crew, but there was no passenger list and thus no definitive figures. It was just before the Easter holiday, and the steamer was more crowded then usual.

The wreck was discovered intact and upright by a pair of divers in 1973, south of the Casquets Reef, some distance from where many had believed it to be. A team of divers operating from a Trinity House vessel recovered the binnacle from the *Stella* in 1999.

A memorial to the *Stella*'s legendary stewardess Mary Ann Rogers was established in 1901 opposite Southampton's Royal Pier, and Rogers is also remembered in a stained glass window in Liverpool's Anglican Cathedral. Researcher and tour guide Jake Simpkin believes that Rogers and her fellow stewardess Ada Preston carried out their duties in exemplary fashion to the end. But Simpkin finds reason to doubt the oft-told story of Rogers's conspicuous heroism, feeling it may have been invented by the *London Times* in an attempt to distract the public from the investigation of the *Stella*'s owners and captain. Some accused Captain Reeks (who went down with his ship) of the *Stella* of racing with another steamer at the time of the wreck, and the investigation concluded that the ship was moving much too fast in thick fog when it struck Black Rock. The Mary Ann Rogers story may be debatable, but the truth can't be known, and Simpkin admits to being "still captivated by the enigmatic stewardess."

The story of Greta Williams's singing of "Oh, Rest in the Lord" in the lifeboat was corroborated by witnesses.

CHAPTER 18

Tugboat Annies

Tugboat Annie first came into literary prominence because of the able pen of Norman Reilly Raine. Mr. Raine wrote many stories of this grand lady who was so efficient in getting her company's share of the towboat business. Many readers may recall the motion pictures which feature Marie Dressler and Wallace Beery as rival towboat captains, with Marie playing the part of "Tugboat Annie."

How many real-life Tugboat Annie personalities have there been? Possibly the oldest member of this select group was Mrs. Kate Sutton of Providence, Rhode Island. Known as "Ma" Sutton, she was an active employee of the company and did dispatching work among other things. Ma was often seen aboard the Providence tugs as they made their way around Narragansett Bay, and although never a licensed pilot, she took the wheel on many occasions. She died several years ago at the age of ninety.

Another woman, known as the Widow Murtagh, was active as a barge captain in the area around New York. However, only a very few women in the United States have earned a tug pilot's license.

Daisy May Godfrey, who hailed from Rome, New York, became a second mate on the oceangoing *Eugenia M. Moran* before she retired, and was granted a pilot's license by the government. It was indeed a family tugboat, for her husband was the master, her son was the first mate, and she was the second mate.

When interviewed some years ago she said that she could not have escaped a mariner's life. Her father operated a great fleet of schooners on Lake Champlain, and during the summertime vacation from school she served aboard one of his boats, spending most of her time in the wheelhouse. Although she was always asking her father if she could steer the boat, it was only occasionally that her request was granted.

In the year 1911 Daisy May married Captain Frank Godfrey. They promptly set out on the New York State Barge Canal in their own boat, which was loaded with iron ore bound for the port of Wilmington, Delaware. At the time Daisy did not have a pilot's license, but she knew that she would soon get one. The important thing was that she was aboard a tug helping her husband.

Although the city of Rome, New York, was the hometown of the Godfreys, they did not see it very much, and home to them became the deck of a tugboat. Not only did Daisy keep house aboard the craft, but she saw in the activity on the tugboat a life work for herself, and she soon made plans to become an expert in the operation of a tug.

Her study of navigation was temporarily halted by the birth of her two children, first a boy and then a girl, after which she renewed her work and received her coveted license. Possibly bewildered at this turn of events, Captain Godfrey signed her on as his second mate.

But a navigational license was not enough, and Daisy now decided to become the possessor of a master's license. For two months of the next winter she stayed with her children at her Rome residence, preparing for the examination. The following spring her parents volunteered to take the children for a few months, and she rejoined her husband's boat. When school vacation came, the children went aboard with their mother and father, and because of the youngsters, it was five years before she was able to take her examination and earn her master's license. Indeed, Daisy May was a determined person.

Joining the Moran Fleet, Frank and Daisy Godfrey traveled to distant lands on a powerful oceangoing tug. Once during the wartime U-boat scare, they were in Boston Harbor between Brewster Island and Deer Island Light for several hours. The submarine nets were down, and they were not allowed to proceed until they finally received radio-telephone orders to steer through the opened net door. Daisy May Godfrey was awarded the North Atlantic Star and the Merchant Marine Bar.

Mrs. Harvey J. Deveau, known as "Tugboat Mary," became interested in towboats when her husband worked for the Ross Towboat Company of Boston. She came from the hills of West Virginia and first knew of the company in 1955. When her husband bought the controlling interest in the organization, she went to work in the office to help him. Mrs. Deveau is now the president and marine dispatcher of the group. At present there are four towboats, the *Mary De*, the *Glen Thomas*, the *Sadie Ross* and the *Betsy Ross*. On occasion Mrs. Deveau, now living in Holbrook, Massachusetts, goes down the harbor on the towboats through the Cape Cod Canal to board other craft off the Cleveland Ledge Light on the Buzzard's Bay side of the canal.

The most exciting experience this marine dispatcher has had was her trip on the *Betsy Ross* out beyond far-flung Graves Light in 1956. Although it was a very rough day, she was lulled into a false sense of security going down the harbor itself because the waves did not seem bad until they approached Long Island Head Light. Then as the tug plowed her way through the seas in the Boston Harbor region between Deer Island and Lovell's Island, great swells began to form, rolling in and smashing against the bow. Soon the billows were surging right up over the pilothouse.

"About this time I began to wonder why I was aboard," Mrs. Deveau told me during my interview with her in April 1962.

The towboat finally reached her objective, a beam trawler which had broken down off Graves Light, and the crew were able to get a hawser aboard and tow her into port.

"That was the occasion when we use our first nylon hawser," she recalled. "When they put it on, it seemed to stretch and stretch until it looked something like a clothesline, and we wondered if it would ever stop stretching, but it worked all right and the *Betsy Ross* brought the beam trawler safely into port.

"I will never forget that particular journey," Tugboat Mary concluded.

In May 1953, Baltimore's own "Tugboat Annie," Justine Brown, is believed to have become the first woman in American (and possibly in world) maritime circles to be honored for having put in forty years of service with a shipping company.

At that time her boss, Captain H.C. Jefferson, president of the Curtis Bay Towing Company, was host at a dinner at the Sheraton-Belvedere Hotel in Baltimore for the many shipping friends of "Brownie." Since the maritime world is really a man's world, there were only a handful of women to keep the guest of honor company. Some of them had known her since she started in 1913 as a combination dispatcher, secretary, and jack-of-all-trades in a "two-man" office.

Always ready with a good, hearty laugh, she is also just as ready with her fiery temper to jump on a tugboat or ship captain who tries to put something over on her or the company.

No one in the harbor is better acquainted with the towing business than this fiery, petite woman of the Curtis Bay Towing Company. To many of the skippers who became acquainted with her during the more than thirty years she dispatched tugs in the port of Baltimore, she is still known as "Captain Brown."

Today her work is chiefly confined to a desk. Now she is the assistant secretary of the Curtis Bay Towing Company, and her activity involves desk work for one of the largest towing companies in America. As such, she holds one of the top executive positions among women in the city of Baltimore.

However, she still relishes the idea of ordering boats around the harbor and thinks how much easier it would be as dispatcher to handle the emergencies of a fire or bad freeze today than in the pre-radiotelephone days when she was at the helm.

Captain Jefferson, who swears he does not know what he would do without Justine as his "right arm," points out that she started with Curtis Bay in 1913 as a very young girl and grew up right along with the company. She has served them for a longer time than anyone else.

"When I first started, Curtis Bay had one tug," the secretary related in her husky voice. "Its name was *Curtis Bay*, and it attended only ships moving in and out of the Curtis Bay coal pier. I imagine that is where the name of the boat and company first came from.

"I guess you might say I got into this by accident. The general manager was boarding with a friend of my mother's. When he told the friend he needed a secretary, she recommended me. For a long time we were the only two working in the office.

"I'll never forget one of the tugs around the harbor," Justine says.

> She was named Neptune *and had sails on her. I'd never seen sails on a tugboat before.*
>
> *It was nothing in the old days to go clear to Cape Henry and pick up a sailing vessel and tow her all the way up the bay to Baltimore. Of course, you were never quite sure you'd get the job when you did get there. We used to pick up a ship chandler—runner in those days—who spoke the captain's language and we'd usually get the work through him.*

> *Everything in those days was done through competition. The first tugboat to talk to the captain usually got the job. As dispatcher, I had to see that one of our tugs was the first to get to that boat. There was real competition to reach an incoming vessel first.*

The only sailing Justine Brown has done outside of the company was aboard a coal collier to Boston and at another time on a regular passenger vessel to Miami.

When interviewed in 1951 by Helen Delich for the *Baltimore Sun*, Miss Brown admitted that the trip she enjoyed the most was in 1943 when she sailed down from Wilmington, Delaware. She was aboard the tugboat *Justine*, named after her. The last tug Curtis Bay built, *Justine* is considered one of the most powerful in the harbor. Justine was very proud of her namesake and properly so. She was quick to take offense if anything derogatory was said about her own tug.

Justine Brown, short, with an attractive figure, has small features and sandy-colored, short, curly hair. Her moderate application of make-up and her selection of tailored suits or simple dresses for work simply spell out her efficient, friendly character. She would rather talk about some of the emergencies for which she dispatched tugs than any of her secretarial duties.

There was the time that the *Wellbeck Hull*, an English ship, was tied up to grain elevator No. 3 when the latter caught fire. The ship was so hot when the tugs pulled her away that the rubber soles of the deckhand's shoes melted off.

Another time it was difficult to decide whether or not to risk having tugs pull away the tanker *F. Q. Barstow*, which was filled with gasses remaining from a cargo of naphtha distillate, out of the danger of a raging fire. Although there might have been serious trouble, there was no time for debate, and so the tugs were ordered in and eventually saved the vessel.

When I talked with Justine Brown on April 19, 1962, she told me that her present activity as assistant secretary of the company brings her more frequently in contact with the higher echelon, but she still looks back to the old days when she actively participated in the towing business of the Curtis Bay Towing Company.

Thus the spirit of "Tugboat Annie" is still alive and forceful in the actions of real-life women of the American towboat fleets.

———————— ～ ————————

When asked if she was the model for the character of Tugboat Annie, Kate Sutton of Providence replied, "I hope not."

Daisy Godfrey is believed to be the first woman to hold a master and pilot's license in the United States. During World War II she was second mate on a vessel that brought supplies and food to American troops.

In 2001, The Coast Guard Academy's sail training program received a donation of $80,000 to buy new dinghies, the result of a bequest given to the Coast Guard Foundation by the late "Tugboat Mary" Deveau.

Baltimore's Justine Brown retired in 1966 after fifty-three years of service with the Curtis Bay Towing Company, and she died a year later at the age of seventy-two. The tug *Justine* was sold and ended its days as the *Esther K*. It's now part of Fish Reef off the coast of Florida.

CHAPTER 19

Commodore Ann White

Ann White, a petite, vivacious brunette of Squantum and Orleans, Massachusetts, owns the oldest sailing ship still in service in the United States, the *Alice S. Wentworth*, which she operates as a Cape Cod summer cruise vessel. Popularly known as Commodore White, Ann is probably the only woman in such an enterprise. She told me once that she did it because she was a "real romantic at heart." But there is another reason. When she was married during World War II, her husband left for the Pacific, following a two-day honeymoon, and was later lost on a submarine in that area.

When Ann White first learned that the *Wentworth* could be acquired, she investigated the unusual background of the craft built at Norwalk, Connecticut in the year 1863.*

Long a part of the waterfront scene at both Martha's Vineyard and Nantucket, the *Wentworth* carried bricks and building material from Hudson River ports to Long Island on many occasions.

Then, under the command of Captain Arthur Stevens, her holds were filled with oil, gas, coal, and other commodities for the island

---

*Originally known as the *Lizzie A. Tolles*, her official number was 14734, her length 73.2 feet, her breadth 23.7 feet, and her depth 6.1 feet. Her gross tonnage was 68.57, her net tonnage 65.12, and for many years her home port was Bridgeport, Connecticut. However, there are some who say the *Wentworth* is not the original *Tolles*.

communities off Cape Cod, and she sailed out of Falmouth and Woods Hole.

By the year 1903 her topsides had developed some soft spots and her owner, Captain Arthur Stevens, took her up to Wells, Maine, where she was rebuilt above the waterline and rechristened for the captain's niece, Alice Stevens Wentworth, who is still living.

In the early twenties the *Wentworth* was bought by the famous Captain Zebulon Tilton, who had sailed with Stevens on her for some time. Zeb could neither read nor write, and his business methods suffered because of this. Debts began to pile up, and the schooner's freight business fell off. Finally came the day when he was in real trouble, and his schooner was to be sold at auction at Vineyard Haven.

On the day of the auction Captain Ralph M. Packer of Vineyard Haven was in his office when he heard that the sale of his friend's craft had already started. Rushing over to his office safe, which luckily contained a substantial amount of money, he emptied the strong box of all available cash and hurried down to the steamboat wharf, where he heard the bidding was at $700. He held up a bill, indicating that he had the cash, and offered $701.

"Sold for $701," shouted the auctioneer, who realized that a conspiracy of kindness for old Captain Zeb was behind this bid, and Captain Packer became the owner of the *Alice S. Wentworth*.

Later, when the inhabitants of Martha's Vineyard learned about Captain Zeb's trouble, they formed a corporation and issued shares in the schooner. Their only stipulation was that they be allowed to go aboard the *Wentworth* once a year for a sail and a buffet lunch.

A typical annual meeting, sail, and lunch was held on August 11, 1939, with the roll of shareholders being read by the clerk and the election of directors taking place, after which a report from Captain Zeb Tilton was in order.

Zeb was an unusual personality, and on this occasion, wearing a silk hat and long coat, he reported extemporaneously by word and song. Outlining the history of the original construction of the vessel, he explained how she was rebuilt and told of a similar craft which hailed from Belfast, Maine.

Once, becalmed at sea, the captain had tossed a two-bit piece overboard, and asked that the Lord grant him a breeze. Tilton continued the story, "During the night a breeze sprang up and soon developed into proportions of a gale. It took both masts off, chock to the deck, and the vessel drifted helplessly in the storm. As the crew clung to various portions of the wreck he turned to one of them and said: 'Lord, if I had known wind was so cheap, I wouldn't have thrown over but a penny.'"

During his talk, the captain burst forth into song and gave verse after verse without apparent effort.

Zeb was known as a national personality because of his radio appearances on a coast-to-coast hookup some years before. He first went to sea in 1882 with the late Captain Josiah Cleveland. Once he told me the story of how he sailed into Boston Harbor on the *Wentworth*.* Required to have a crew, which he did not have, he fixed up a straw dummy in the bow to which he gave the appearance of activity by running lines from the wheel to the dummy's arms.

Zeb also related his encounter with a solicitor for the island's Wayside Army, who asked him for a small contribution. He explained that the donation would eventually reach the Lord. Captain Tilton looked the solicitor up and down and said, "How old are you, young man?"

"Fifty-six," came the answer.

"Well, Sir," said the captain, "I am a little over seventy and the chances are I will see the Lord long before you, so I will make my donation in person to Him myself."

In 1939 Captain Zeb attracted nationwide fame when he announced he was to be married for the third time. His fiancee was Mrs. Grace MacDonald, sixty-two, of Fairhaven, Massachusetts. The couple was married in the Vineyard Seaman's Bethel at the wheel of the *Wentworth*, which had been taken off the schooner for the purpose. Zeb and Grace each held a spoke of the wheel as the ceremony was performed.

Hundreds of relatives and friends attended the wedding, which had been postponed because of an east wind. Immediately afterwards, the couple spent part of their honeymoon as guests of "We, the People" in New York, and then they lived for months aboard the *Wentworth*.

Finally, Captain Zeb was too old to go to sea and became a scalloper and quahogger. The *Wentworth* was reconditioned and resumed coastal sailing under the command of Joseph Viera of Nantucket, who had served as a mate under Captain Zeb. Later the schooner was sold to a

---

*I asked Zeb once about rumors of a murder committed aboard, but neither he nor anyone else I talked with had ever heard the story. It is probable that a man died aboard on one occasion, but he was not murdered, according to all indications.

Maine resident by the stockholders. In 1944 Zeb acquired the two-masted freighter *Coral,* which had been battered and nearly sent to the bottom in the 1938 hurricane, but within a few months he himself had to go into drydock for repairs to his own rugged frame. He had never been sick or even visited a physician before this trip to Brighton Naval Hospital for an extended stay.

The legend of his lifting the 700-pound anchor with his bare hands has gone down though the years. Actually, although it was said that he saw the anchor on the beach, picked it up, and walked home with it, that is not quire the case. The commander of the Coast Guard cutter *Acushnet* stated that four seamen were testing their strength by attempting to lift the anchor between them. Standing nearby, Zeb finally walked over and raised it high enough so that daylight could be seen under it.

He never drank, smoked, or "helled around" in his youth. Often he carried railroad iron, which made his compass useless, but he always came through. When asked how he did it, he explained that he bailed up a little water in a draw bucket, tasted it, and could tell exactly where he was. Zeb Tilton died on February 28, 1952, in Middleboro, at the age of eighty-five. His wife died in July 1952, aged seventy-three, at Martha's Vineyard Hospital.

In 1943 the *Alice S. Wentworth* was sold to Captain Parker Hall, who sailed her back to Maine single-handed; no great task for him, as he had sailed alone most of his life. The largest of his charges was the 136-ton schooner *George R. Smith.*

Parker Hall sold the *Wentworth* into the tourist trade, where she has been for the past seventeen years. With age she has flattened out, losing her graceful sheer, as her oak keel has straightened under the burdens of the years. Her first master was Frederick Guild and her last master was Captain Havila Hawkins.

Then came the day when Ann White bought the *Wentworth.* She ran her in 1961 as a cruise schooner out of Camden, Maine, and then moved down to Woods Hole.

Power for getting the *Alice S. Wentworth* in and out of her berth is supplied by a yawl boat, which has a sixty-horsepower Chris-Craft engine inboard. The mate lashes the yawl boat to the stern with its bow out of water. He then turns on its engine and leaves it pushing against the *Wentworth's* stern. As soon as he can, the mate goes forward to start the donkey engine to hoist sail. At the wheel of the *Wentworth* the skipper sets the course. Chugging along absolutely unattended, the yawl boat pushes the schooner forward until the wind swells her sails. Then the mate and deckhand shut off the engine and haul the yawl boat up on the stern davits. This is exactly the way old timers operated when they were prosperous enough to own a yawl boat. When they were not, their crew towed their schooner in a rowboat manned by oarsmen.

Cape Codders call the yawl boat the "jolly boat" or "push boat," the latter phrase being an accurate description. In this case the word "yawl" may be a corruption of "haul," because this type of boat was made to be a workboat. The *Wentworth*'s crew calls it the "liberty boat" as Navy men term their smaller craft which take them ashore, because the yawl serves as a water taxi to ferry passengers when the schooner swings on her hook nightly in a harbor.

The donkey engine on the *Wentworth* is forward in the bow. An ancient "one-lunger," it turns the winch which hauls sails and anchors. There is a converted horizontal capstan in the bow which oldtimers used to haul anchor by hand. The equipment goes back to the eighties. It is antique certainly, yet the donkey engine, "bless it, never fails to start at the mate's second try!"

Ann has always loved to cook for herself and her family and friends. Nevertheless, she felt she lacked sufficient experience to turn out three meals a day for twenty-odd passengers and a crew of five (captain, mate, deckhand, cook, and dishwasher).

In addition to directing her craft's cruise, Ann spent much time in 1961 in the galley and served for part of the summer as dishwasher. By September of the first year she had learned a great deal about the unusually difficult art of cooking at sea.

"On days when the ship had been tacking a lot while I baked, I would take brownies out of the oven and find the whole pan slanted-high on one side, low on the other," she recalls.

Slanted brownies, together with pies and cakes, were only one among several unusual culinary problems she had to cope with. Buying a week's worth of groceries at a time for a seagoing kitchen becomes an exacting process. The purchasing list, explains Mrs. White, must be checked against a master menu with an inventory including ingredients for every recipe for every meal.

"If you are out of cinnamon while at sea," she pointed out, "you just can't run down to the store before finishing the pie."

Summer cruises begin Monday morning at ten o'clock and end the following Saturday at noon. The weekly food order, including 600 pounds of ice, is delivered aboard the *Wentworth* each Monday morning at her home port, Woods Hole. Groceries and ice are hoisted on a crane and dropped via a chute into the galley.

A venerable woodburning stove proved wonderful, according to Mrs. White, for dishes requiring quick, high heat—such as pies. Items like baked beans and Indian pudding, which require long, slow heating, must be avoided, and Ann has crossed these off the menu.

When interviewed by Vicki Fitzgerald of the *Patriot Ledger* in Quincy, Ann said that there was always a kitchen crisis if someone requested a cup of tea when the fire in the stove had been allowed to go down— and another when a sudden change in the wind blew back down the chimney and filled the galley with smoke.

Her duties aboard include starting the fire in the stove at six in the morning. Despite the fact that the stove is slow to heat, Ann White admits she loves "the old thing." It burns hard oak, mixed with an occasional piece of applewood, and produces a wonderful fragrance, giving food a special character which modern gas or electric stoves don't, she explains. For her, that fragrance brings back dream-memories of a childhood at Lancaster, New Hampshire, and probably many of her passengers have similar memories.

Does a personal sailing background or a long family tradition explain her sea fever? Actually not, says Ann White. She has been on several other cruises with Captain Frank Swift of Camden, Maine, but was always just a "wishful, wistful sailor." So are many other Americans, she thinks. They still dream about sails and ships—and the good, old simple life that sailing symbolizes—and that is why dude or "windjammer" cruises are becoming so popular, she concludes.

Commodore White tries to achieve that "romantic" ideal of the good, simple life for her passengers for the week that they are aboard the *Wentworth*.

There is nothing fancy about this vacation cruise. Dress is informal— shorts, slacks, blouses, a bathing suit, and a warm jacket or windbreaker are the essentials. There is no entertainment and the keynote of the voyage, Ann stresses, is relaxation. Passengers can swim, fish, sunbathe, read, knit, or sketch. They can occasionally help the crew handle the ship and they eat hearty, delicious food.

Generous helpings of basically simple, well-prepared Yankee fare is Ann White's idea of the ideal cuisine for a New England sailing cruise. Her dinner menus include such specialties as lobster, clams, roast beef, ham, and chicken. The principal departure from Yankee cookery is a weekly Italian dinner of spaghetti with meat sauce.

Bountiful breakfasts aboard the *Wentworth* feature bacon and eggs, hot oatmeal, pancakes, and French toast. Hearty lunches include such items as split pea soup, an authentic fish chowder, stew, and toasted cheese sandwiches.

Commodore Ann White, owner of the Alice S. Wentworth, *the oldest sailing ship still in service in the United States [at the time* Women of the Sea *was first published in 1962], which she operates as a Cape Cod summer cruise vessel, with Mate Thomas W. Flynn.*

Mrs. White found it most sensible to follow a weekly master menu. "I became quite excellent at my three times six equals eighteen meals per week." she notes. Occasional variations are provided by passenger guest-cooks, who beg to try out a favorite recipe. Here the main problem again is lack of access to a supermarket for the inevitably missing ingredients.

Cruise meals have to be hearty, explains Mrs. White, because that sea air really makes people hungry. In good weather all meals aboard the *Wentworth* are eaten topside after being served buffet style in the main cabin. In bad weather sit-down meals, in two sittings, are served in the main cabin.

Ann also learned to cut a few corners, dispensing with saucers for coffee cups and reducing the array of silver on the table. Passengers merely chuckled though, she recalls, when asked to "hang onto your fork for dessert."

Her passengers, whom she describes as a typical cross section of America, people from all walks of life bound together with the common denominator of a touch of sea fever, include a few who, she hopes, will become lifelong friends. Several shipboard romances of the first summer "are progressing nicely" she has been informed by correspondents. Mrs. White would like to see performed aboard the schooner by her captain a marriage which resulted from a romance begun on the *Alice S. Wentworth*. She is at present waiting to hear from an admiralty lawyer the circumstances under which a shipboard wedding can be conducted by a schooner's captain.

As ship's cook, Commodore White will be, in ship-talk, "Cookee." This would add another to an already impressive list of titles: she is owner of the oldest commercial sailing ship afloat, the only woman running cruises on the East Coast, and the first person to operate such cruises in Massachusetts waters. Right now, being Cookee apparently interests her more.

One day, while aboard the *Wentworth*, I mentioned Ann's husband, William Thomas White, for I knew that there was a story of sadness concerning her brief married life.

"We were married in West Roxbury, Massachusetts, on May 28, 1943," she explained. "We had a two-day honeymoon and then he had to leave for Mare Island, after which he was shipped across the Pacific to Midway.

"There he was placed in submarine services, and the first billet which came up had two men applying for it, my husband and another man.

They tossed a coin for the billet aboard the submarine, and my husband won the toss. Thus he became a yeoman, second class, aboard the *Wahoo*, which sank twenty enemy ships representing 60,038 tons of enemy shipping before sailing on her last mission, the trip from which she never returned.

"Some time later I had a visit from the man who lost the coin toss with my husband, and it was a peculiar story which he told me. He had planned to marry, but his intended wife entered a convent and he lost all desire to make something of his life. It was all because of the toss of a coin at Midway!

"I feel much closer to my husband out on the ocean!" concluded Commodore Ann White, truly a courageous woman of the sea.

———————— ～ ————————

In his 1970 book *Wake of the Coasters*, John F. Leavitt called the *Alice S. Wentworth* a "beautifully sheered and smart little coaster," and declared it his favorite vessel of all. Leavitt spent much time aboard the *Wentworth* when it was owned by Captain Arthur Stevens.

In 1974, the *Alice S. Wentworth* was about to be restored when it was destroyed by a storm.

CHAPTER 20

Girl on a Life Raft

In an earlier chapter I tell of a little girl, Susanna Haswell, who was aboard a small vessel caught in a terrible snowstorm off the coast of Massachusetts, and of the shipwreck which followed. In this story, another little girl, Terry Jo Duperrault, is the heroine of as strange a sea mystery as was ever enacted on the Atlantic Ocean.

The waters of the Spanish Main have often been the scene of horror during the days of piracy, but even the notorious Blackbeard or the infamous Low would be taxed to the limits of his diabolical mind to duplicate such scenes of madness-inspired terror as transpired on the usually romantic Caribbean in the month of November 1961.

It all began in Green Bay, Wisconsin, when Dr. Arthur Duperrault, a forty-nine-year-old* contact lens optometrist of that city, planned an ideal vacation for all the members of his family. He and his wife, Jean, who was thirty-eight, decided to take their three children—Brian, fourteen; Terry Jo, eleven; and Renee, seven—down to Florida from where they would sail to the enchanted Bahama Isles.

After reaching Fort Lauderdale with his family, Duperrault visited the waterfront. Going from craft to craft, he examined many of the beautiful yachts, schooners, and ketches ready for charter. One sixty-foot ketch in particular caught his fancy, and when he walked around for a

---

* In press accounts his age is given as forty-one or forty-four.—*Ed.*

view of the stern he found that she was named *Bluebelle*.* He learned that her skipper was Captain Julian Harvey, an adventurer who had been an Air Force pilot in both World War II and Korea. The Wisconsin physician chartered the *Bluebelle* for $100 a day on condition that Julian Harvey and his wife, Mary, would serve as the working crew, with the guests from Green Bay assisting in the running and steering of the craft whenever necessary.

Captain Harvey and his wife had been married only three months, and the groom had insured his bride for a substantial sum.

For a day or two all went well on the cruise. The days were sunny and bright while the tropical nights were clear and gentle. The first Sunday at sea, November 12, 1961, was delightful. Late in the afternoon the *Bluebelle* cleared Abaco, and set a course for another Bahama Isle, Great Stirrup Cay, fifty miles distant.

Then, according to Harvey's story told several days later, at eight-thirty that Sunday evening the beautiful weather changed abruptly when the *Bluebelle* ran into a line squall. The Air Force veteran explained that a sudden, terrible gust a short time later snapped the mainmast, which crashed down through the deck, piercing the *Bluebelle*'s hull. The loose rigging soon pulled down the mizzenmast, injuring those in its path, and the ketch began to sink. Harvey then started the auxiliary engine, after which he decided to get a wire cutter from the cabin to clear away the debris cluttering the deck space.

Coming up from below, he saw to his horror that the cockpit was ablaze. He returned once more to the cabin, sloshing through two feet of water to reach the fire extinguisher, and then fought his way through the rising water to the deck. There he discovered that the blaze had made so much headway that a wall of flame cut him off from everyone else aboard.

"I could hear them crying out," Harvey explained, "but I knew the *Bluebelle* was doomed. Using the wire cutter to slice through the guard rail, I freed a life raft and pushed a ten-foot dinghy into the sea."

The *Bluebelle* was now settling rapidly. Just before Harvey climbed into the dinghy, he encountered the body of little Renee. He pulled her in with him, not knowing if she were alive or dead, and attempted to bring her back to consciousness. Soon he gave up his efforts. After

---

*Formerly called the *Minell III* and also *Lady Jane*, she was built at Sturgeon Bay, Wisconsin, in 1928. Her dimensions were 60 by 125.6 by 5 feet.

pushing the dinghy away from the sinking ketch, he had a brief glimpse of the burning hull before the darkness of a tropical night obscured everything from his view. The *Bluebelle* must have gone down shortly afterwards, he later stated. The little girl, Renee, never recovered consciousness and was dead long before daybreak.

According to Harvey's story, when dawn came the sea in all directions was empty. Late that afternoon he saw a tanker, which proved to be the *Gulfline*, and waved a tarpaulin at the vessel until he was sighted. Half an hour later he was taken aboard to tell his incredible story, and when the tanker reached Nassau he went to the airport for a flight back to Miami. On Wednesday, November 15, he landed at the Florida city, where he reported to the Coast Guard headquarters and again told his story.

Unfortunately for his future plans, at about the same time he was giving his version of the disaster another event which was to have great significance was taking place out on the high seas. The freighter *Captain Theo*, crossing the broad Atlantic from Europe, was entering the area of the Caribbean Sea, and even then was approaching the general vicinity where the *Bluebelle* had gone to the bottom. Proceeding toward the Northwest Providence Channel near Nassau, she was alerted by the Coast Guard to be on watch for survivors of the sunken ketch.

A special lookout was placed aboard the *Captain Theo* for the express purpose of sighting any survivors. As the day wore on the seas began to freshen, and soon it was apparent on the freighter that the possible sighting of any relatively small object was becoming more and more improbable.

Suddenly a lookout detected a tiny white object, which soon was identified as a life raft. All on deck crowded to the rail. The freighter's course was altered, and as the ship drew closer, binoculars revealed that a little girl in a white cotton blouse and pink corduroy slacks was lying on the bobbing raft. It proved to be Terry Jo Duperrault, whose taffy-colored hair was bleached by exposure to the rays of the sun, which had burned her skin until her complexion was lobster red, but she was still alive!

Maneuvering in close to the balsa raft, the *Captain Theo* took Terry Jo aboard and radioed the Miami Coast Guard of the remarkable rescue.

A relatively short time later a Coast Guard helicopter, dispatched out of Miami, reached the *Captain Theo* and lowered a stretcher to the deck. Within twenty minutes little Terry Jo was aboard the craft on the way to Miami.

When the shoreline of Florida finally appeared, Pilot Robert Pope glanced back at his passenger. Terry Jo stirred uneasily, and her pretty brown eyes looked up at Pope.

"Then she went right back to sleep," explained the pilot later.

Landing at Miami, Terry Jo was rushed to Mercy Hospital, where she was given treatment for shock and exposure. Then, gradually, she regained her senses and uttered her own name.

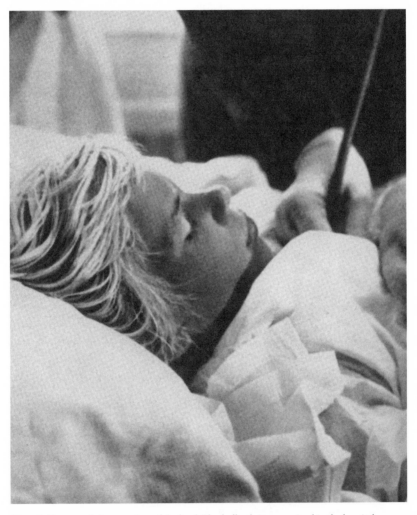

Terry Jo Dupperault, lone survivor of the ketch Bluebelle, *being examined in the hospital after her rescue*

The ordeal for Terry Jo had been a severe one, and at times it was thought that she might not recover, but by the end of the week the doctors decided that this little girl who had been alone on a raft for three and a half days without food or water out in the blazing sun was going to get well after all.

Meanwhile, having given his report to the Coast Guard, Julian Harvey checked in at a motel on Biscayne Boulevard, signing the register as John Monroe. He soon heard of the rescue of Terry Jo.

Harvey's career had involved a series of incredibly tragic accidents and unusual incidents. A veteran, he had won his share of decorations as a bomber pilot in World War II and a jet fighter pilot in Korea.

Then in 1949 while stationed at Eglin Air Force Base in Florida, Harvey crashed an automobile through a bridge, killing his wife and his mother-in-law. Six years later while cruising aboard his yacht *Torbatross* in Chesapeake Bay, he hit the underwater hull of the old American battleship *Texas* and sank a few minutes later. A helicopter flew over the five survivors, who had scrambled aboard a life raft, and all were rescued.

In 1959 Harvey's racer *Valiant,* while on a sea trip through the Panama Canal to California, sank off the coast of Texas.

Harvey also cracked up a plane at Eglin and bailed out of a jet trainer over Arizona after ejecting a passenger. The next few months were spent in a Pensacola hospital, and at the conclusion of his recuperation Harvey was given a medical discharge. He entered the yacht chartering business in which he finally met Dr. Duperrault at Fort Lauderdale, who engaged him for the cruise of the ill-fated *Bluebelle*.

Back at the motel, after hearing that Terry Jo had been rescued alive and was able to talk, Harvey realized that the girl's story would conflict with his account, and the true details of the Caribbean night of horror would be revealed to the world.

"I am tired, nervous and can't take it any longer," was part of the note he wrote to his friend, a Miami advertising man named James Boozer. He then killed himself with a razor.

When she had recovered enough to talk, Terry Jo told of hearing screams that Sunday night, and later of seeing her mother and brother lying in pools of blood on the deck of the cabin.

On April 25, 1962, after five months of research and investigation, the Coast Guard made an official announcement. Issuing a long statement, based on hundreds of pages of material weighing no less than five pounds, the Coast Guard concluded that Captain Harvey of the ketch *Bluebelle* murdered his heavily insured wife and three of his passengers with cold calculation, then scuttled his ship and saved himself.

Harvey needed money, the Coast Guard said, and was the sole beneficiary of his wife's insurance policy, which would pay $40,000 double indemnity if she died accidentally.

The Coast Guard stated that a few hours after Harvey heard the news of Terry Jo's rescue the former Air Force officer had killed himself with a razor blade in the Miami motel room. Had he lived, he would have been prosecuted for murder on the high seas, the Coast Guard said.

The Coast Guard concluded "that the ketch *Bluebelle* was intentionally scuttled in Northwest Providence Channel, Bahama Islands, on the night of November 12, 1961, in approximately 780 fathoms (4,600 feet) of water, by the master, Julian A. Harvey.

> *Arthur Duperrault, Jean Duperrault, Brian Duperrault, and Mary Jordan Harvey lost their lives at the hands of Julian A. Harvey prior to the sinking of the vessel. The exact nature of the circumstances whereby these lives were taken or the order in which they perished cannot be ascertained. The most probable cause of the casualty was the state of mind of Julian A. Harvey.*

The report did not elaborate on Harvey's "state of mind," but a Coast Guard spokesman in Washington stated when questioned that "any person who commits the acts this man committed must be of an abnormal state of mind."

In Green Bay, Wisconsin, where the orphaned Terry Jo now lives with relatives, a family attorney said shortly after the Coast Guard findings were released that Terry Jo was back in school and "getting along fine."

Harvey had not harmed Terry Jo or Renee, "probably in the assumption that they would drown when the vessel sank," the Coast Guard said, adding that Harvey probably recovered Renee's body later and kept it to lend credibility to his story.

The Coast Guard said Terry Jo was alive today because of five "fortuitous" circumstances.

1. Captain Harvey was prevented from assuring himself that she did not survive because a dinghy had gone adrift and he had to retrieve it.

2. Eleven-year-old Terry Jo was able to free a small balsa life float and climb onto it.
3. Madman Harvey was unable to find Terry Jo in the darkness.
4. Mild weather permitted Terry Jo to survive without food, water, shelter, or adequate clothing.
5. Her raft was almost directly in the path of the freighter which rescued her.

A member of the *New York Times* editorial staff wrote the following epilogue to the tragic story of the *Bluebelle*:

> *There will forever remain about the* Bluebelle *the haunting air of mystery. What happened aboard the ketch in those final hours? What horrors of a sickly mind stimulated such a ghastly deed? Indeed, were there other circumstances, other events, which Terry Jo's childish eyes never saw, or that her mind could not comprehend? Probably, like the mystery of the brigantine* Mary Celeste, *immortalized (and fictionalized) by Conan Doyle, the* Bluebelle *will go sailing down the years a half-told tale, its full truth a matter of "wild surmise" until the sea gives up its dead.*

"She was so close to the water and so awfully small," said one of the crewman of the *Captain Theo*, describing the rescue of Terry Jo Duperrault. According to a 2002 article in the *Miami Herald*, "As she was strapped into the basket of a Coast Guard rescue chopper, she opened her eyes and waved a feeble goodbye to her rescuers, lined up on deck. 'A lot of us prayed,' one said."

According to a UPI story, Julian Harvey's friend James Boozer said that Harvey had been "accident-prone." He had found his "dream girl" in his sixth wife, Mary, an airline stewardess, said Boozer. In their inquiry, the Coast Guard noted that Harvey had twice collected on insured boats, and in retrospect the accident that took the life of a previous wife and her mother was highly suspicious.

Press accounts also revealed that Harvey claimed to his friend Boozer that he had panicked and left the others aboard the *Bluebelle* to fend for themselves during the storm. Boozer said that Harvey was in "an extremely nervous state" when he related this version. "As he talked he was stuttering the worst I have ever seen or heard," said Boozer. "His right eye rolled in his head and his eyelid batted, but his voice was low and not hysterical." Shortly before his suicide, Harvey asked Boozer to swear that he would never reveal his story.

In a 1999 article in the *Green Bay Press Gazette*, Mike Blecha wrote that Terry Jo spent eighty-two hours on the five by two-and-one-half-foot raft before she was rescued. She still has the slacks and blouse she wore through the ordeal. "It's just part of me," she told Blecha.

When asked what message she'd ultimately like to impart about the tragedy that made news around the world, Terry Jo, now known as Tere, told Blecha, "I don't want them to say, 'Gee, that poor little girl.' I'd like them to say, 'She has gone on with her life.' That there is a happy ending."

Index

About the Author

Edward Rowe Snow (1902–1982) was descended from a long line of sea captains. He sailed the high seas, toiled aboard oil tankers, and worked as a Hollywood extra—all before attending college. Later he worked as a teacher and coach, and as a reconnaissance photographer during World War II. His education and work prepared him well for his legendary writing career—which was part maritime history, part show business.

The Islands of Boston Harbor, his first book, was published in 1935. In all, Snow wrote nearly one hundred books and pamphlets, illustrated with many of his own photographs. He also contributed newspaper columns to the *Quincy Patriot Ledger,* the *Boston Herald,* and the *Brockton Enterprise.* In the 1950s his radio show, *Six Bells,* was heard on dozens of stations, and he made many other appearances on radio as well as on television.

Snow is fondly remembered as the "Flying Santa." For forty years he flew in small planes and helicopters over the lighthouses of New

Edward Rowe Snow with his mother, Alice Rowe Snow, looking at the poison dagger taken from her father, Captain Joshua Nickerson Rowe, in the Philippines at Zamboanga.

England, dropping Christmas parcels for the keepers and their families. His efforts to preserve the islands of Boston Harbor as public lands are less well known. After his death in 1982, the *Boston Globe* lauded his support for conservation: "There are many political leaders and environmentalists who can justly share the credit for the preservation of the harbor islands, but among them Mr. Snow will hold a special place as a link to their past and a guide to their present."

Snow married Anna-Myrle Haegg in 1932. They had one daughter, Dorothy Caroline Snow (Bicknell), two granddaughters, and two great-grandsons. The young people who grew up "at his feet," reading and listening to his tales of New England maritime history, are countless.